Lessons i

Springer
London
Berlin
Heidelberg
New York
Barcelona
Hong Kong
Milan
Paris
Singapore
Tokyo

Related titles:

Towards System Safety
Proceedings of the Seventh Safety-critical Systems Symposium, Huntingdon, UK 1999
Redmill and Anderson (Eds)
1-85233-064-3

Felix Redmill and Tom Anderson (Eds)

Lessons in System Safety

Proceedings of the Eighth Safety-critical Systems Symposium, Southampton, UK 2000

Safety-Critical Systems Club

 Springer

Felix Redmill
Redmill Consultancy, 22 Onslow Gardens, London, N10 3JU

Tom Anderson
Centre for Software Reliability, University of Newcastle, Newcastle upon Tyne, NE1 7RU

ISBN 1-85233-249-2 Springer-Verlag London Berlin Heidelberg

British Library Cataloguing in Publication Data
Lessons in system safety : proceedings of the Eighth
  Safety-Critical Systems Symposium, Southampton, UK, 2000
  1.Industrial safety - Congresses 2.Automatic control -
  Reliability - Congresses 3.Computer software - Reliability
  - Congresses
  I.Redmill, Felix, 1944- II.Anderson, T. (Thomas), 1947-
  III.Safety-critical Systems Symposium (8th : 2000 :
  Southampton, England)
  620.8'6
ISBN 1852332429

Library of Congress Cataloging-in-Publication Data
Safety-Critical Systems Symposium (8th : 2000 : Southampton, England)
    Lessons in systems safety : proceedings of the eighth Safety-Criticial Systems
  Symposium, Southampton, UK, 2000 / Felix Redmill and Tom Anderson (eds.).
      p. cm.
    Includes bibliographical references and index.
    ISBN 1-85233-249-2 (acid-free paper)
      1. Industrial safety--Congresses. 2. Automatic control--Reliability--Congresses. 3.
  Computer software--Reliability--Congresses. I. Redmill, Felix. II. Anderson, Tom,
  1947- III. Title.
  T55.A1 S225 2000
  620.8'6--dc21   99-056289

Typesetting: Camera ready by contributors
Printed and bound by the Athenæum press Ltd., Gateshead, Tyne & Wear
34/3830-543210 Printed on acid-free paper SPIN 10742264

PREFACE

The papers in this book are the full set presented at the Safety-Critical Systems Club's eighth annual symposium — the Safety-critical Systems Symposium '00. The first two, on safety integrity levels and dependability assessment respectively, reflect a tutorial that was given on the first day. The subsequent fifteen were delivered in six sessions on the second and third days. The papers appear here in the order in which they were delivered.

The papers by Halvorsrud, Duggan, and Myhrman reflect the current interest in the principles and application of the safety case and of auditing safety. The next two, by Cockram and Jesty and others, report on new experiences in the essential function of safety assessment, and the following three, by Humphris and Dobbing, McDermid and Pumfrey, and Fox, offer lessons in the ever-difficult topic of software safety.

The papers by Jesty et al, and Harrison and Vickers demonstrate one of the purposes of the Safety-Critical Systems Club — technology transfer. Their lessons, derived from transport, are readily transferable to other industry sectors, as are so many experiences. The theme of experience is continued as both Boulton and Fowler report on the safety standard IEC 61508, and the exchange of lessons between the safety and security fields is encouraged in Brewer's paper. Finally, Ainsworth and Jackson write on safety-related networks and Dawkins and Riddle offer advice on a subject of much debate — commercial off-the-shelf (COTS) software.

Two thirds of the papers in this book are industrial and one third are from academic institutions. All offer Lessons in System Safety.

The safety-critical systems domain is rapidly expanding. Being the subject of a great deal of enquiry, its industrial problems are always candidates for academic research. It embraces almost all industry sectors, and lessons learned in one are commonly appropriate to others. We can improve the safety of our systems by reporting our problems and propagating our lessons — for which the Safety-critical Systems Symposium provides an annual forum.

On behalf of the Safety-Critical Systems Club, we thank the authors for their contributions. We acknowledge the continued support of our members, and thank the Department of Trade and Industry, the Engineering and Physical Sciences Research Council, the Health and Safety Executive, the British Computer Society, and the Institution of Electrical Engineers, all of which are active members of the Club's Steering Group. Finally, our reliance on Joan Atkinson cannot be exaggerated, and we thank her for her dedication, often under difficult conditions.

FR and TA
October 1999

The Safety-Critical Systems Club
sponsor and organiser
of the
Safety-critical Systems Symposium

What is the Club?
The Safety-Critical Systems Club exists to raise awareness and facilitate technology transfer in the field of safety-critical systems. It is a non-profit organisation which cooperates with all interested bodies.

History
The Club was inaugurated in 1991 under the sponsorship of the Department of Trade and Industry (DTI) and the Engineering and Physical Sciences Research Council (EPSRC), and is organised by the Centre for Software Reliability (CSR) at the University of Newcastle upon Tyne. Its Co-ordinator is Felix Redmill of Redmill Consultancy.

Since 1994 the Club has had to be self-sufficient, but it retains the active support of the DTI and EPSRC, as well as that of the Health and Safety Executive, the Institution of Electrical Engineers, and the British Computer Society. All of these bodies are represented on the Club's Steering Group.

What does the Club do?
The Club achieves its goals of technology transfer and awareness raising by focusing on current and emerging practices in safety engineering, software engineering, and standards which relate to safety in processes and products. Its activities include:
- Running the annual Safety-critical Systems Symposium each February (the first was in 1993), with Proceedings published by Springer-Verlag;
- Putting on a number of 1- or 2-day seminars each year;
- Providing tutorials on relevant subjects;
- Publishing a newsletter, *Safety Systems*, three times each year (since 1991), in January, May and September.

How does the Club help?
The Club brings together technical and managerial personnel within all sectors of the safety-critical systems community. It facilitates communication among researchers, the transfer of technology from researchers to users, feedback from users, and the communication of experience between users. It provides a meeting point for industry and academia, a forum for the presentation of the results of relevant projects, and a means of learning and keeping up-to-date in

the field.

The Club thus helps to achieve more effective research, a more rapid and effective transfer and use of technology, the identification of best practice, the definition of requirements for education and training, and the dissemination of information.

Membership

Members pay a reduced fee (well below a commercial level) for events and receive the newsletter and other mailed information. Without sponsorship, the Club depends on members' subscriptions, which can be paid at the first meeting attended.

To join, please contact Mrs Joan Atkinson at: CSR, Bedson Building, University of Newcastle upon Tyne, NE1 7RU; Telephone: 0191 221 2222; Fax: 0191 222 7995; Email: csr@newcastle.ac.uk

CONTENTS

Safety Integrity Levels — theory and problems

Felix Redmill
Redmill Consultancy
22 Onslow Gardens
London
N10 3JU

Abstract

Modern standards on system safety employ the concept of safety integrity levels (SILs). Increasing numbers of system purchasers are expecting their suppliers to demonstrate that they use the concept, so system developers are seeking to apply it. But the standards differ in their derivation of SILs and none explains the concept satisfactorily, with the result that it is often misunderstood and used inconsistently, incorrectly, and inappropriately.

The purposes of this paper are to explain the concept and its application, to show how SILs are derived, and to illustrate how they can be misleading.

1   Introduction

The concept of safety integrity levels (SILs) is now prevalent in the field of safety-critical systems, and a number of standards advocate its use in the design and development of such systems. However, not only do the various standards derive SILs differently, but none provides a clear and detailed explanation of how they are derived and applied. The result is that they are not well understood.

Further, although the derivation and application of SILs is complex and can be confusing, it is also conceptually simple and can be explained simply, with the result that the SIL concept is used inconsistently and often incorrectly and inappropriately.

One purpose of this paper is to explain the SIL concept. To do so, it offers not only a general description but also explanations of the ways in which SILs are derived and applied according to three recent standards.

A further purpose of the paper is to draw attention to the ways in which the SIL concept can be misleading and how it is being misunderstood and misused. The concept is a tool and, like any other tool, it can be useful if employed wisely but can cause problems if applied inappropriately.

2   What are Safety Integrity Levels?

The SIL concept has emerged from the considerable effort invested in the safety of systems during the last two decades. Two factors have stood out as principal influences.

The first is a move from the belief that a system can be either safe or unsafe, i.e. that safety is a binary attribute, to the acceptance that there is a continuum between absolute safety and certain catastrophe and that this continuum is a scale of risk. This has led to an emphasis on risk assessment as an essential feature in the development of safety-related systems.

The second is the huge increase in the use of software (and complex hardware, such as microprocessors) in the field of safety. This has led to a change in the balance between random and systematic faults. Previously, it was normal to assume (often implicitly) that safety could be achieved through reliability, and to deduce a value for the reliability of a system by aggregating, often through a fault tree, the random failure rates of its components. In some cases the failure rates were derived from historic use of the components and in others they were estimated, so the accuracy of the result was never beyond question. In fact, the greatest accuracy that could be achieved was that derivable from considering only random failures, for the method ignored systematic faults — those introduced, for example, through specification and design errors. With software, which does not wear out and in which all faults are systematic, there is no possibility of deducing system reliability by a method which is restricted to the consideration of random failures.

Another feature of software is its inherent complexity. Not only is it impossible to prove the absence of faults, but for even relatively small systems it is not possible to derive, in reasonable time (or in many cases in finite time), high confidence in reliability from testing.

So a number of problems arise for the developer, who needs not only to achieve but also to demonstrate safety. Some of the problems may be summarised by the following questions and brief discussions.

- How do we define the safety targets to be achieved by a system? As software failures result from systematic and not random faults, direct measurement of the probability of failure, or the probability of a dangerous failure, is not feasible, so qualitative risk assessment must be employed.

The results of the risk assessment are interpreted into SILs which, depending on the standard in use, may or may not be equated to numerical ranges of failure rates.

- Given that greater rigour in the development of software is correlated with increased cost, how do we define the level of rigour which is appropriate to be applied in any particular case? Once risk assessment has led to a SIL, this is used to define the rigour of the development process. The higher the SIL, the greater the rigour, and tables are used in the standards to identify the methods, techniques, and management processes appropriate to the various SILs.

- If we can measure reliability directly, but not safety, can we define safety targets in terms of reliability measurements? In two of the standards discussed below, SILs are defined as rates of failure, and in one as the rate of dangerous (or unsafe) failures — all of which are reliability-type measurements.

- How do we define criteria against which to make claims of achieved safety? When a SIL has been used to define the level of safety to be achieved, it follows that that SIL should be the criterion against which a claim for the achieved safety would be made (and judged). But if numerical values for the expected failure rate of software cannot be derived with confidence, it may not be possible to adduce proof of such a claim.

So, the use of SILs is an attempt to address the above questions. The derivation of a SIL may be summarised as the funnelling in of the risk assessment process to a result, the interpretation of that result into the SIL, and then the funnelling out into the development process which is defined by the SIL — as in the 'Bowtie Diagram' of Figure 1.

In essence, the SIL principle is this. If something is to do an important job, it needs to be reliable, and the more important the job, the more reliable it should

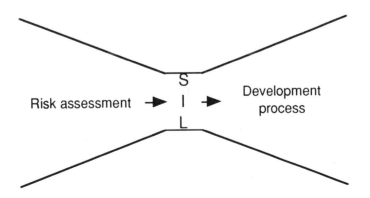

Figure 1: The 'Bowtie Diagram' showing the derivation and application of SILs

be. In the case of a safety-related system, the job is to achieve safety, and the greater the importance to safety of the system, the lower the rate of unsafe failures should be and the higher the SIL to indicate the need.

For those aspects of systems where random failures apply, a numeric value of a SIL (as in IEC 61508) is useful because it may be possible to demonstrate quantitatively that a certain architecture or design will satisfy it. With systematic failures, while it may not currently be possible to claim to have met the numeric value, the latter would be useful if it became possible to carry out more refined testing and measurement in a given time; then we could have confidence in higher direct measures. The numeric value also sets a reference such as to allow consistency of understanding of SILs across industry sectors.

There are different routes to the derivation of SILs depending on the standard in use, and three of these are examined in the next section.

3   SILs According to the Standards

3.1   SILs According to IEC 61508

The International Electrotechnical Commission's standard IEC 61508 [IEC 1999, Redmill 1998] is a generic international standard intended to provide guidance to all industry sectors. The model on which it is based (see Figure 2) assumes that we are starting out with some equipment, or plant — the 'equipment under control' (EUC) — which is to be used to provide some form of benefit or utility. Complimentary to this is a control system, and together the EUC and its control system may pose risks.

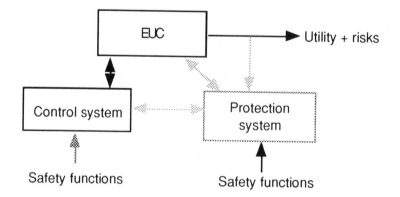

Figure 2: IEC 61508 system model

The standard recommends that the hazards posed by the EUC and its control system be identified and analysed and that a risk assessment be carried out. Each risk is then tested against tolerability criteria to determine whether it should be reduced. If risks are reduced by redesign of the EUC, we are back to the starting point and hazard identification and analysis and risk assessment should again be carried out.

When it is decided that risk-reduction facilities should be provided in addition to the EUC and its control system, and that these should take the form of one or more electrical, electronic, or programmable electronic systems, then the terms of the standard apply to it or them.

The risks posed by the EUC and its control system may be contributed to by many hazards, and each must be mitigated until its risk is considered tolerable. The reduction of the risk associated with each hazard is specified as a 'safety requirement' and, according to the standard, each safety requirement must have two components, the functional requirement and the safety integrity requirement. The latter takes the form of a SIL. The totality of the safety requirements for all hazards forms the safety requirements specification.

Safety requirements are satisfied by the provision of safety functions, and in design these are implemented in 'safety-related systems'. The SILs of the safety requirements become those of the safety functions which will provide them, and then of the safety-related systems on which the safety functions are to be implemented. The separation of safety-related systems from the EUC and its control system (as by the provision of a protection system — see Figure 2) is preferred, but safety functions may also be incorporated into the control system. Design is usually an iterative process in which the combination of safety functions in safety-related systems is decided on cost as well as on technical grounds.

The standard equates SILs with probabilities of unsafe failures in two tables, one for on-demand systems whose demand rate is low and one for systems with continuous operation or a high demand rate. These are shown here as Tables 1 and 2.

The SIL of a safety-related system reflects the risk reduction which the system must achieve. For example, if the tolerable risk is deemed to be 10^{-9} dangerous failures per hour and the EUC is found to have a probability of 10^{-2} dangerous failures per hour, it may be concluded that the required risk reduction would be achieved by a parallel safety function with a probability of dangerous failures of 10^{-7} per hour. From this, we can deduce from Table 1 that the safety-related system would need to be of SIL 2.

In Part 4 of IEC 61508, safety integrity is defined as 'the likelihood of a safety-related system satisfactorily performing the required safety functions under

Table 1: Safety integrity levels of low demand operation (from IEC 61508)

Safety Integrity Level	Low Demand Mode of Operation (Pr. of failure to perform its safety functions on demand)
4	$>= 10^{-5}$ to 10^{-4}
3	$>= 10^{-4}$ to 10^{-3}
2	$>= 10^{-3}$ to 10^{-2}
1	$>= 10^{-2}$ to 10^{-1}

Table 2: Safety integrity levels of high demand or continuous operation (from IEC 61508)

Safety Integrity Level	Continuous/High-demand Mode of Operation (Pr. of dangerous failure per hour)
4	$>= 10^{-9}$ to 10^{-8}
3	$>= 10^{-8}$ to 10^{-7}
2	$>= 10^{-7}$ to 10^{-6}
1	$>= 10^{-6}$ to 10^{-5}

all the stated conditions, within a stated period of time', and a safety integrity level (SIL) as 'a discrete level (one of 4) for specifying the safety integrity requirements of safety functions'. Thus, a SIL is a target probability of dangerous failure of a defined safety function.

3.2 SILs According to the MISRA Guideline

Whereas IEC 61508 is a generic standard, intended as the basis for preparing more detailed sector-specific standards, the Motor Industry Software Reliability Association's 'Development Guidelines for Vehicle Based Software' [MISRA 1994] is sector-specific. The document was tailored to the use of developers of software-based systems to be employed in motor vehicles.

In this guideline, SILs are based on the consequence of failure of the system in question. For motor vehicles, the ultimate consequence of a system failure (in terms of accidents and their possible outcomes) is speculative, so in the guideline the consequence of failure is defined in terms of something more predictable — the controllability of the vehicle by its occupants. So the

Table 3: Consequence-based SILs

Controllability Category	Integrity Level
Uncontrollable	4
Difficult to control	3
Debilitating	2
Distracting	1
Nuisance only	0

Table 4: SIL relationships

Controllability Category	Acceptable Failure Rate	Integrity Level
Uncontrollable	Extremely improbable	4
Difficult to control	Very remote	3
Debilitating	Remote	2
Distracting	Unlikely	1
Nuisance only	Reasonably possible	0

guideline advocates that system developers carry out a hazard identification and analysis and determine the worst possible result of the failure of their system — in terms of the controllability of the vehicle. Five levels of uncontrollability are defined (see Table 3) and SIL values are defined to accord with them. (The guidelines provide definitions of the controllability categories and readers are referred to the document itself if further explanation is required.)

The controllability category is directly related not only to an integrity level but also to an 'acceptable failure rate', as in Table 4. But the authors of the guideline, recognising that low failure rates of software cannot be measured with confidence, did not place numeric values on them — though the inclusion of qualitative values can be useful. For example, it might help a developer of a system whose failure could render the vehicle uncontrollable to know that failure of the system should be 'extremely improbable'.

Once a SIL has been derived, it is applied as in IEC 61508: to determine the rigour of the system development processes, with the implication that the processes appropriate to the SIL are estimated to be a cost-effective route to the desired system reliability.

In this guideline, SILs are referred to merely as 'integrity levels'. They are related to system reliability rather than to the rate of dangerous failures only, for in the context in which the guideline applies all failures of a given system are potentially dangerous.

3.3 SILs According to Defence Standard 00-56

'Def Stan 00-56' [MoD 1996] is a UK defence standard for system safety management. It states that 'it is widely accepted that the estimation of the probability of random events can be predicted to a reasonable degree of accuracy', but, recognising the difficulty of estimating systematic failure integrity, it defines the SIL concept as 'an indicator of the required level of protection against systematic failure'. It allocates a SIL to 'each abstract function' at the 'early design phases' and calls for this to be inherited by the components that implement the function.

The standard recommends a risk assessment process which, for a given risk, places the consequence in one of four categories and the probability of occurrence in one of six. It combines these two sets of criteria in a matrix which it refers to as a 'risk classification scheme' and populates this with four tolerability classes (see Table 5). Then the standard uses both consequence and probability of failure in determining SILs and defining what they should achieve. The SIL is determined according to the consequence to which the hazard could give rise, and the requirement of the SIL is defined in terms of the worst probability of failure of the function involved.

But the standard adds a complication, that of distinguishing between the first, or only, and subsequent functions on which safety depends (in the context of the risk in question). The SIL of the first or only function is based on the estimated accident severity, as defined in Table 6; that of the second function and any subsequent functions is based on the accident severity plus the failure probability of the first function (see Table 7).

The decision of whether to have a second function is not merely a design preference, for the standard adds a constraint which would in many cases

Table 5: An example risk classification scheme

	Catastrophic	Critical	Marginal	Negligible
Frequent	A	A	A	B
Probable	A	A	B	C
Occasional	A	B	C	C
Remote	B	C	C	D
Improbable	C	C	D	D
Incredible	C	D	D	D

Table 6: SIL for the only or first function

Catastrophic	Critical	Marginal	Negligible
SIL 4		SIL 3	SIL 2

Table 7: SIL for the second and subsequent functions

Failure probability of first function	Accident severity			
	Catastrophic	Critical	Marginal	Negligible
Frequent	SIL 4			
Probable		SIL 3		
Occasional		SIL 3		
Remote		SIL 2		
Improbable			SIL 1	

Table 8: Claim limits

Safety Integrity Level	Minimum failure rate that can be claimed
SIL 4	Remote
SIL 3	Occasional
SIL 2	Probable
SIL 1	Frequent

prescribe the need for one. It defines 'claim limits' (see Table 8) which limit the claim that can be made for the probability of failure of a function (however reliable it may be thought to be), depending on the SIL — by implication, on the possible consequence of failure. Thus, if it were considered necessary to reduce a 'catastrophic' risk (see Table 5) from 'probable' to 'improbable', a second function would be essential as a first function of SIL 4 could not be claimed to have reduced the probability any lower than 'remote'.

The standard also allows for a higher SIL to be achieved by the combination of components of lower SILs. For example, a SIL 4 function may be provided by two independent SIL 3 components with a SIL 4 'combinator'.

Whereas in IEC 61508 SILs are based on risk reduction, and in the MISRA Guideline on consequence severity, in Def Stan 00-56 they are based on both. As in the other standards, SILs are used to define development processes.

However, it is noticeable that here only 'design rules and techniques' are mentioned as being subject to SIL control rather than all safety management processes.

4 Some Integrity Level (SIL) Problems

4.1 Confusion between Standards

As will be seen from Section 3, various standards which use the SIL concept apply different interpretations to it and derive SILs in different ways. Thus, unless one states the standard which forms the context of a reference to SILs, misunderstanding and confusion could ensue.

4.2 Claim of Achievement against a SIL

In the first instance, SILs define what we expect of our safety functions and systems, so to start with they are targets. What confidence can we have that the systems which perform the defined safety functions really do satisfy the SIL requirements?

For simple systems with known fault histories in the application under consideration, a claim to have met a SIL may be deemed justifiable. Similarly, for systems composed of simple hardware components with known fault histories, in simple architectures, it may be credible to deduce worst-case failure rates by probabilistic means. But when a system is based on software or more complex hardware (e.g. microchips), so that systematic rather than random faults predominate and testing cannot in finite time offer reliable predictions of the rates of dangerous failure, a claim to have met a SIL cannot, in the present state of the art, be supported by measurement.

The value of the SIL is in providing a target failure rate for the safety function or safety-related system. It places constraints on the processes used in system development, such that the higher the SIL, the greater the rigour which must be applied. The processes defined as being appropriate to the various SILs are the result of value judgements regarding what needs to be done in support of a reasonable claim to have met a particular SIL.

However, the development processes used, however good, appropriate, and carefully adhered to, do not necessarily lead to the achievement of the defined SIL. And, even if in a particular case they did, the achievement could not be proved. So a SIL could not normally be said to define the actual rate of dangerous failures of the product.

Hamilton and Rees [Hamilton 1999] warn that relating SILs to process requirements can lure the practitioner into the following false safety argument: 'The requirement was for a SIL X system and I have adhered to the standard's process for a SIL X system, therefore I have developed a SIL X system.' They point out that the confusion stems from failing to recognise the twin goals of a safety engineering activity: to engineer a safe system and, while doing so, to build up evidence that the system is as safe as it is required to be. So, to be valid, the argument needs to be: 'The requirement was for a SIL X system, and good practice decreed that I adhered to the standard's processes for a SIL X system. In doing so, I have generated the evidence appropriate to a SIL X system, and assessment of the evidence has found that I have adhered to the defined processes.' Unfortunately, in practice the evidence is usually insufficient to show that the SIL requirement has been met, but it does increase confidence in the system and its software.

4.3   S is for Safety

The 'S' in 'SIL' refers to 'safety', so it is misguided to use the acronym 'SIL' outside the context of safety.

Yet, there is a move, in some industry sectors at least, to use it in all contexts (e.g., 'This is a SIL 3 pump'). This is misleading, and there is already confusion in the application of the term. An added problem, or at least a factor which compounds the problem, is that those who are misled are, in the main, not aware of the error.

Of course, the standards vary in their application of the SIL concept. In the MISRA Guideline, SIL does in fact refer to the overall reliability of a system — but the system has previously been identified as having an impact on safety, and the guideline is industry-specific and defines its use of the SIL concept clearly for its users.

In usage according to IEC 61508, it is not sufficient to relate the SIL to the failure rate of a safety-related system; it must be related to the dangerous failure rate. For this, we must distinguish between dangerous and non-dangerous failures. If SILs are used as indicators of reliability (the probability of a failure) rather than of the probability of a dangerous failure, systems will cost more to develop than they need to.

But how can we distinguish between dangerous and non-dangerous failures? Only by carrying out a safety analysis, identifying all the system's failure modes, and determining which are dangerous and which are not. Particularly for a control system, this is crucial. But too often the distinction is not observed.

The SIL concept appears to offer simple rules for the reliability requirements of safety-related systems. But the rules are not simple, and their apparent simplicity, combined with the perceived importance of SILs, seems to be encouraging some practitioners to neglect thorough safety analysis in favour of deducing SILs. But the proper deduction of SILs can only be based on thorough safety analysis.

4.4   Claims Based on Reliability Estimates rather than Process

When the term 'SIL' is used as a general statement of reliability, rather than in the strict context of safety, we hear such statements as, 'The system is SIL 2', when the truth is that the system in question has merely been calculated or estimated to have a particular rate of dangerous failures.

But claiming to have met SIL 2 implies that the processes appropriate to the development of a SIL 2 system have been employed and that independent assessment has confirmed that they have.

Thus, if SIL claims based on optimistic reliability estimates are taken at face value, they can be misleading and could lead to inappropriate equipment being used in safety-related applications.

4.5   Result of Loose Use of the Term 'SIL'

That the term 'SIL' is often used loosely has already been pointed out. So, can we be sure that we know what is meant when the term is used? Does it offer a guarantee that the system's probability of dangerous failure is appropriate to the SIL? Or does it say that the system's probability of dangerous failure is thought or assumed to be so? Or does it state that a process appropriate to the SIL has been used in the development of the system?

We need to be careful to enquire exactly what is meant when we are given SIL information about a system.

4.6   Hazards Introduced by a Safety-related System

A casual use of SILs often neglects the hazards posed by the safety-related system itself. In fact, most advice on SILs makes no mention of the possibility of such systems introducing new hazards and appears to carry the assumption that they do not do so. But let us consider the example of a fire control system intended to protect against fire by detecting heat or smoke and, perhaps, to act to control the fire by dumping a dousing or smothering agent onto it. Not only would there be a hazardous situation if the system did not detect the fire, but there would also be one if it incorrectly emitted an alarm and caused frenzied evacuation from premises such as a night club. Or if it deposited its dousing or smothering agent on a room-full of people when there was no fire.

Analysts may fail to recognise the hazards posed by safety-related systems, and the standards are not helpful in this respect. For example, IEC 61508 does not offer explicit advice on how to address safety functions which are incorporated into control systems.

4.7   Reference to a Component

Safety is application-dependent, and to attach SIL values to products outside the context of the systems in which they will function can be misleading. For instance, it would be incorrect to speak of 'a SIL X component'.

Yet, now that the term 'SIL' is in currency, and given that its implication is for certain processes to be used in a system's development, it is not unnatural for suppliers to want to apply the term to their products regardless of how or where they will be used. It would be possible to make clear and specific statements about an item's development processes, or about its estimated or historic failure rate, or about the intention or purpose behind its design, without reference to SILs. But it is becoming more common for the SIL concept to be used (often unspecifically) in support of products.

To avoid misunderstandings, misrepresentations, and the resulting unsafe systems, a convention is needed for the derivation and communication of confidence in safety-related products, both hardware and software. Issues to be covered should include:
*   Indications of the rigour that has been applied throughout development;
*   The nature and the independence of the assessment to which the development processes were subjected;
*   The testing and test results which provided confidence in the developed product;
*   The history of use which confirmed that confidence.

It would be stretching the use of the SIL concept to suggest that a product would be suitable for all SIL X applications because one, or even all, of these criteria met SIL X requirements. Further assessment of any new system of which the component became a part would always be necessary.

4.8   Beware of reuse

Beware of thinking that if you have achieved a system of a given SIL for one application it will be effective in another application which calls for a system of the same SIL. The safety of an item is application-specific and a single, seemingly trivial or even unrecognised, variation in the design or use between the new and old applications can have considerable safety implications. Reuse is dangerous. Yet, there is a move, even in the context of safety, to more extensive use of commercial off-the-shelf (COTS) systems and components, so there is an increasing need for care (and guidance) in this matter.

4.9   SILs Say Nothing about System Attributes

Reuse (of software or any component) in an new system of the same SIL is equivalent to applying SILs to components without reference to their safety application. There is a strong case against both. In reuse the critical characteristics required of a system are different between applications, and a SIL says nothing about which attributes of a system are of concern. It may not be obvious that those which were appropriate to its former application are not significant in its later context and those necessary in the latter were not emphasised in its development for the former.

However appropriate the development processes are to a particular SIL, they do not guarantee that the product is bestowed with the attributes necessary for its application. Only design and development in accordance with a good specification, with attention to the objectives of use, can approach this.

For example, in the case of an emergency communications link it may be availability rather than reliability that is the critical characteristic because satisfactory communication may be possible in spite of intermittent failures, as long as those failures are short-lived. Yet, the SIL concept is reliability-based and is intended to provide confidence in reliability rather than availability. In another case it may be crucial not only to have a highly reliable system but also one which can quickly and easily be reconfigured if it did fail. Consider, for example, a recently reported air traffic control (ATC) event. During routing testing, an ATC system crashed because of a momentary loss of power. But the system was incapable of rapid recovery and return to service required rebooting and recalibration which took about an hour, during which time all computer-based systems, including radar and back-up systems, were inoperative. Only an antiquated radio system allowed communication between AT controllers and pilots.

SILs do not provide clear indicators of the quality of any given attributes of the system, so it is not enough to develop a system to a given SIL, using appropriate processes. It is essential to identify the critical attributes and ensure that they are of the required integrity.

4.10   Combining SILs

Recently I was told that 'two SIL 2s make a SIL 3'. Combining SILs is catered for in Defence Standard 00-56, but the fact that the statement was made in the context of IEC 61508 demonstrates the confusion that is being caused by different standards using the same term or concept in different ways. In standards other than Defence Standard 00-56 there is no acceptance of creating a system of one SIL by means of a number of components of lower SILs. To make such a statement in a general sense is dangerous.

Another point worth noting is that Def Stan 00-56 does not allow indiscriminate combinations but lays down strict rules, for example concerning independence, for the conditions under which combination is acceptable. To ignore the rules is dangerous, as is the generalisation of combination formulae, even within the context of Def Stan 00-56.

4.11   The Need for Assessment Criteria

While it may not be possible to measure the rate of dangerous failures of a system, particularly in one in which systematic faults are likely to predominate, it is still worthwhile defining how we should derive confidence that the performance of the system approaches the demands placed on it by the SIL.

Lindsay and McDermid point out that a shortcoming of current approaches to SILs is that they offer little guidance on how to assess whether desired levels of safety integrity have actually been achieved [Lindsay 1997]. The emphasis is almost entirely on the process of development. So even if the belief of those claiming the SIL is that it has been achieved, the claim should be considered doubtful until their evidence has been examined.

Lindsay and McDermid point out that 'knowing what process was followed in developing a system is not assurance enough on its own: evaluation criteria should be defined, and related back to integrity requirements allocation, to assess how thoroughly the process was followed and how thoroughly the product was checked.'

4.12   Failure Modes of Software

Conducting a development process in accordance with a SIL provides some confidence in the product. However, it has already been pointed out that it is not normally possible to conclude that the rate of dangerous failures designated by the SIL has been achieved. Moreover, an overall level of confidence does not offer any guidance on how the software is most likely to fail or which types of failure would be most dangerous. It is therefore important to carry out studies, perhaps using techniques such as hazard and operability studies (HAZOP) and failure mode and effect analysis (FMEA) on the software to increase the knowledge of its likely failure modes and their effects. This could in some cases lead to additional safeguards to increase confidence that the worst types of failures were protected against.

4.13 Consideration of the ALARP Principle

In the standards, the SIL of a safety function or system is defined as part of its requirements. At the time of stating requirements, what is being identified is the specifiers' opinion of a tolerable level of risk, and the SIL is defined with respect to it. For example, see Figure 3 which shows the IEC 61508 means of deriving SILs. Here, R_a represents the assessed value (quantitative or qualitative) of a posed risk and R_t represents the 'tolerable' level to which it should be reduced; the difference between them (assuming R_a to be greater than R_t) gives rise to the SIL.

However, by the ALARP (as low as reasonably practicable) principle — a legal requirement in the UK — the risk must be reduced not merely to a tolerable level but beyond it to a level which is as low as reasonably practicable (represented by R_{alarp} in Figure 3). But R_{alarp} cannot be discovered until the design stage when it is decided how to implement the necessary risk reduction. At that time, trades-off involving technology, design options, and cost are proposed and considered, and often early decisions are overturned by later ones as an iterative process proceeds.

So, the risk level which is finally deemed tolerable under the ALARP principle may be different from that defined by the SIL — and it cannot be arrived at

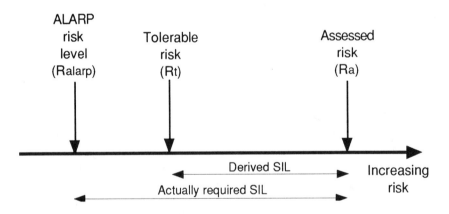

Figure 3: Relation between SIL and risk reduction as in IEC 61508

until after the SIL has been determined. Yet, system developers define essential safety-related system parameter targets (rate of dangerous failures in the case of IEC 61508, reliability in the case of the MISRA guideline, and so on) according to the SIL.

The SIL could therefore be misleading to developers. Should the SIL be defined as the difference between R_a and R_{alarp} rather than that between R_a and R_t as at present? A problem here is that the SIL could not then be defined until the design stage and it would not be available to place initial constraints on the design, as at present. But such a distinction may be a nicety, at least in the case of systematic faults, as in software, for then it is not possible to determine what risk reduction can in practice be achieved nor to demonstrate that it has been achieved (which is one of the reasons for the existence of SILs). So, the decision of what risk reduction is appropriate in a given case, whether it is defined (see Figure 3) with respect to R_t or R_{alarp}, is in effect a decision of what is ALARP. Thus, for systematic safety integrity, the process of deriving the SIL should be supported by the ALARP principle. Something to remember, though, is that the decision needs to be made independently for each risk.

There is a further point. ALARP requires that the level of accepted risk be constantly reviewed because if (for example because of changed or cheaper technology) it later becomes (or turns out to be) practicable to reduce the level of risk further, then that further reduction should be made. Should the SIL change to reflect this?

It seems that there is a need for a study of the relationship between SILs and ALARP.

5   The SIL Concept is a Tool

The previous section showed that the term 'SIL' can be misleading as well as helpful. The fact is that the SIL concept is just a tool. Every tool is designed and built for a certain purpose and to be used within certain constraints, and the SIL concept is no exception. Use outside its design constraints or out of context can lead to results that are incorrect or misleading. In the case of SILs, where safety is the central issue, the results could be dangerous.

No tool is indispensable, and here too the SIL concept is not an exception. Let us examine this. SIL has three main purposes: to define the safety integrity requirements for a safety-related system or function, to provide a guide to appropriate development processes, and to provide a basis for claiming achievement of safety requirements. In these respects it is useful and convenient. But let us consider the necessity of the SIL concept to each of these.

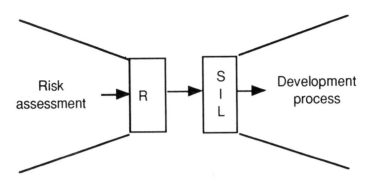

Figure 4: The SIL concept is not indispensable

With regard to defining safety integrity requirements, it may be simpler to say 'SIL 2' than 'A reliability of 10^{-6} dangerous failures per hour.' But it is quite possible to say, 'A reliability of 10^{-6} dangerous failures per hour'. Indeed, it is the required risk reduction (as in IEC 61508), the required reliability (as in the MISRA Guideline), or the accident consequence (as in Def Stan 00-56) which is first deduced, and from it is the SIL is determined. So, representing the required probability of dangerous failures by a SIL is convenient short-hand but not essential.

Regarding the provision of a guide to appropriate development processes, it is convenient to use a SIL as an intermediate point, as in the Bowtie Diagram (Figure 1). But, again, it is quite possible to use the reliability figures directly as a guide to the required process.

Similarly, with regard to the third purpose of SILs, it is quite possible to claim that the development processes appropriate to 'A reliability of 10^{-6} dangerous failures per hour' have been carried out rather than those appropriate to 'SIL 2'.

We may summarise these conclusions by reference to Figure 4, which is an extension of the Bowtie Diagram. Depending on which standard we use, our risk analysis process results in a value R from which a SIL is derived. The SIL is then used to inform the development process. But if no SIL were derived, the development process would have to be informed directly, rather than indirectly, by R. So the SIL concept is useful but not indispensable.

What is said here is not a proposal to dispense with the SIL concept, but a reminder and a warning to employ it within its intended scope and with professional judgement. To use it without understanding it is to use it dangerously. Likewise, to use it blindly, simply as a means of determining suitable development processes, is to use it inadequately and riskily. The term

'SIL' is now common currency so we need to understand it and use it correctly and usefully.

6   Conclusions

This paper has offered an introduction to safety integrity levels, explaining them and showing how three existing standards derive and use them.

The point was made that the SIL concept is only properly applicable in the context of safety, and that it is inappropriate to use it outside of this context. Moreover, there are many ways in which the use of the term 'SIL' can be misleading, and a number of examples were given. Some inadequacies of the SIL concept were also discussed. It was then emphasised that the SIL concept is a tool and that, like all tools, it can be useful when used within its valid scope but problematic when used outside it.

The SIL concept appears to offer simple rules for the development of safety-related systems. But to derive SILs correctly, we need to start from first principles and carry out thorough safety analyses. However, having done this, we find that we are also in possession of sufficient information to be able to carry out the development without SILs. So, although convenient, the SIL concept is not essential, and it can be replaced with the parameters which it represents. That is not to say that we should abandon its use. It is promoted by the standards, it is already employed, and we cannot ignore it. But we need to understand it and use it properly. Because it is not well understood, and there is already a tendency to use it incorrectly and inappropriately, it is all the more important that we understand it so as to avoid its misuse and recognise its misleading use by others. Indeed, it is as important to be aware of the dangers of misuse of the SIL concept as it is to understand its appropriate use.

So far, the recorded use of the SIL concept is small, and it appears that a lack of training has contributed to the fact that many of the problems (for example, of misunderstanding) have not been recognised by those employing it. There is an urgent need for documentation and open reporting of the use of the SIL concept, the difficulties experienced, and the benefits gained.

But the problems in the use of SILs are not all of the users' making. There is a need for harmonisation of the SIL concept across standards, and for improved guidance in the standards themselves. There is an urgent requirement for documented guidance, not only in the details of the use of SILs, but, importantly, for managers who need to understand the SIL concept so that they can effectively manage and make judgements about its use — and this documented guidance should be supported by high-quality training. If managers, through failure to understand or reluctance to take time to learn, abdicate their responsibilities and leave decisions on the derivation and use of SILs to their subordinates, the current misunderstanding and misuse will continue; improvement needs to be led, not only by the standards bodies but also by the management of organisations which seek to apply the SIL concept. There may also be a need, as suggested in the paper, for a more formal study of how the derivation and use of SILs interacts with other concepts of the tolerability and reduction of risk, such as the ALARP principle.

References

[Hamilton 1999]   Hamilton V and Rees C: *Safety Integrity Levels: An Industrial Viewpoint*. In Redmill F and Anderson T (eds), Towards System Safety — Proceedings of the Seventh Safety-critical Systems Symposium 1999. Springer Verlag, London, 1999

[IEC 1999]   IEC 61508 — *Functional Safety of Electrical/Electronic/ Programmable Electronic Safety Related Systems*. International Electrotechnical Commission, Geneva, 1999

[Lindsay 1997]   Lindsay P and McDermid J: *A Systematic Approach to Software Safety Integrity Levels*. In Daniel P (ed), Proceedings of the 16th International Conference on Computer Safety, Reliability and Security, York, 7-10 September 1997. Springer Verlag, London, 1997

[MISRA 1994]   The Motor Industry Software Reliability Association: *Development Guidelines for Vehicle Based Software*. The Motor Industry Research Association, UK, 1994

[MoD 1996]   Ministry of Defence: *Defence Standard 00-56, Safety Management Requirements for Defence Systems*. Ministry of Defence, UK, Issue 2, December 1996

[Redmill 1998]   Redmill F: *IEC 61508: Principles and Use in the Management of Safety*. Computing & Control Engineering Journal, Vol 9, No. 5, IEE, London, October 1998

The Problems of Assessing Software Reliability ....when you really need to depend on it

Bev Littlewood

Centre for Software Reliability, City University

London, UK

Abstract

This paper looks at the ways in which the reliability of software can be assessed and predicted. It shows that the levels of reliability that can be claimed with scientific justification are relatively modest

1 Introduction

The question of *how* safe a critical system needs to be is ultimately determined by what is regarded as an acceptable risk to society (usually as judged by its agents, such as regulators). It will involve an analysis of benefits and costs, particularly those associated with safety-related failures. See, for example, [HSE 1992] for an interesting and accessible discussion of this problem in the context of the safety of nuclear power stations.

Making a system acceptably safe, and *demonstrating* that this is so, is an engineering task. This paper addresses the last of these problems; more specifically it is concerned with the difficult job of assessing the contribution that software makes to the safety of a wider system.

Software is now ubiquitous in engineered systems, including safety-critical ones. Not only is it used to replace older, well-understood technologies, it is more and more frequently used to implement completely novel functionality. Some of these new applications (e.g. flight-critical control of unstable aircraft) pose very difficult problems to system designers, and result in considerable design complexity. Novelty, difficulty and complexity tend to militate against reliability of software, and of course this can become a threat to the safety of the overall system.

Reliability requirements for software will depend upon a safety analysis of the wider system of which the software is a part. Not only will the required levels vary from one application to another, but the nature of the reliability claims can differ. In a safety system, such as a nuclear reactor protection system, the requirement might be expressed as a probability of failure on demand (in the case of the software-based Sizewell B Primary Protection System, the requirement was 10^{-3} *pfd*). In a continuous control system, for example in aircraft flight control, the reliability requirement might be expressed as a failure rate (e.g. 10^{-9} probability of failure per flight hour). In some cases there may, in addition, be a requirement to meet an *availability* goal (e.g. the requirement for the US AAS air traffic control system was an expected downtime of no more than 3 seconds per annum).

Some of these reliability levels are extremely demanding - a figure of 10^{-12} probability of failure per hour has been mentioned in relation to some railway applications. Is it possible to assess reliabilities at these levels with sufficient scientific rigour to satisfy the needs of wider system safety cases? In the main part of the paper this question will be addressed in some detail, identifying the limits to the levels of reliability that can be claimed before a system has been exposed to extensive operational use.

Before coming to this, however, it may be useful to address briefly some misconceptions about the nature of software reliability, and in particular to show the inevitability of a probabilistic approach.

2 The nature of the software failure process

The distinction that is made in reliability engineering between *random failures* (meaning, usually, conventional hardware failures) and *systematic failures* (e.g. failures arising from design faults, usually - but not necessarily - from software) is very misleading. This terminology appears to suggest that in the former case a probabilistic approach is inevitable, because of the 'randomness', but that in the latter it is possible to get away with completely deterministic arguments. In fact this is not the case, and probabilistic arguments seem inevitable in both cases.

The use of the word *systematic* here refers to the *fault mechanism*, i.e. the mechanism whereby a fault reveals itself as a failure, and not to the failure *process*. Thus it is correct to say that if a fault of this class has shown itself in certain circumstances, then it can be guaranteed to show itself whenever these circumstances are exactly reproduced. In the terminology of software, which is usually considered the most important source of systematic failures, it is right say that if a program failed once on a particular input case it would always fail on that input case until the offending fault had been successfully removed. In this sense there is determinism, and it is from this determinism that we obtain the terminology[1].

In fact, of course, interest really centres upon the *failure process*: what is seen when the system under study is used in its operational environment. There is natural uncertainty in this process, arising from the nature of the operational environment. Specifically, there is uncertainty as to when a member of the set of input cases that trigger a particular fault will next occur. Thus there is uncertainty as to when the next failure of the program will occur. This forces the use of probabilistic measures of reliability even for 'systematic' failures.

The important point is that the failure *processes* are not deterministic for either 'systematic' faults or for random faults. The same probabilistic measures of reliability are appropriate in both cases (although the details of the probability models for evaluating software reliability generally differ from those used for hardware [Lyu 1996]).

---

[1] In practice, even design-caused failures may not occur in an obviously deterministic way. In software, it often happens that failures are difficult to reproduce because they depend on specific, difficult-to-observe conditions, like activities of other programs in the same computer. In hardware, some design faults will just make the system exceedingly vulnerable to some stressful condition (e.g., corrosion or electromagnetic interference). This fact only reinforces the need for a probabilistic approach to design faults.

3 Reliability evaluation based on operational testing

The only ways of directly *measuring* reliability require that we see the system running in an *operational environment*. The observed frequency of failures after a certain amount of exposure to this kind of testing (or the absence of failure) allows reliability estimates to be computed using statistical models.

Clearly, the difficulty of constructing a test regime that accurately captures all the relevant features of the actual operational environment will vary from one application domain to another. In some industries accurate simulation of operation has been possible for a long time: examples include the aircraft (flight-critical avionics) and nuclear industries (e.g. the extensive statistical testing used to evaluate the reliability of the Sizewell B PPS software after licensing [May, Hughes et al. 1995]).

The techniques for predicting future reliability from observed behaviour can be divided into two categories, dealing with two different forms of the prediction problem:

*   *steady-state* reliability estimation uses the results of testing the version of the software that is to be deployed for operational use ('as delivered'); the theory underlying this prediction is much the same as used in predicting the reliability of physical objects from sample testing;

*   *reliability growth*-based prediction uses the series of successive versions of the software that are created, tested, and corrected after tests discover faults, leading to the final version of the software that is to be evaluated. The data used in this case are the results (series of successful and of failed tests) of testing each successive version. Having observed a trend of (usually) increasing reliability, this trend can be extrapolated into the future.

Steady-state evaluation is the more straightforward procedure, and requires fewer assumptions. The behaviour of the system in the past is seen as a sample from the space of its possible behaviours. The aspect of interest of this behaviour, i.e., the occurrence of failures, is governed by parameters (typically, a failure rate or a probability of failure per demand) that can be estimated via standard inference techniques. Many projects, however, budget for little or no operational testing of a completed design before its deployment, or reliability requirements are set higher than their budgeted amount of testing can confirm with the required confidence. Reliability growth-based prediction is then an appealing alternative, because it allows the assessor to use the evidence accumulated while the product was 'debugged' rather than just evidence about its final version. However, any prediction depends on trusting that the trend will continue. In a macroscopic sense, this requires that no qualitative change in the debugging process interrupts the trend (e.g., a change of the debugging team, or the integration of new functionalities could bring about such a change). It also requires trust that the very last fix to the software was not an 'unlucky' one, which decreased reliability: this is particularly relevant in the case of safety-related systems.

In both cases, the success of such a procedure depends upon the observed failure process being similar to that which it is desired to predict: the techniques are essentially sophisticated forms of extrapolation. In particular, if we wish to predict the operational reliability of a program from failure data obtained during testing, it is necessary that the test case selection mechanism produces cases that are statistically representative of those that present themselves during operational use. This is not always easy, but there is a good understanding of appropriate techniques, as well as some experience of it being carried out in realistic industrial conditions, with the test-based predictions being validated by observation of later operational use [Dyer 1992; Musa 1993].

It is also worth emphasising that, although we often speak loosely of *the* reliability of a software product, in fact we really mean the reliability of the product *working in a particular environment,* since the perceived reliability might vary considerably from one user to another. It is a truism, for example, that operating system reliability can differ greatly from one site to another. It is not currently possible to test a program in one environment (i.e., with a given selection of test cases) and use the reliability modelling techniques to predict how reliable it will be in another.

3.1   Reliability growth assessment and prediction

Reliability growth models are statistical techniques that allow the direct evaluation of the reliability of a software product from observation of its actual failure process during operation. In their simplest form, it is assumed that when a failure occurs there is an attempt to identify and remove the design fault which caused the failure, whereupon the software is set running again, eventually to fail once again. The successive times of failure-free working are the input to statistical models, which use this data to estimate the current reliability of the program under study, and to predict how the reliability will change in the future.

There is an extensive literature on reliability growth modelling, with many detailed probability models purporting to represent the probabilistic failure process. Unfortunately, there is no single model that can be trusted to give accurate results in all circumstances, nor is there any way in which the most suitable model can be chosen *a priori* for a particular situation. In recent years, however, this difficulty has largely been overcome by the provision of methods for analysing the predictive accuracy of different models on a particular source of failure data [Abdel-Ghaly, Chan et al. 1986; Brocklehurst and Littlewood 1992; Lyu 1996]. The result is that we can now apply many of the available models to the failure data coming from a particular product, and gradually learn which (if any) of the different predictions can be trusted.

With the reservations stated above about the need for a statistically representative test regime, it is now possible to obtain accurate reliability predictions for software in many cases and, perhaps equally importantly, to know when particular predictions can be trusted. Unfortunately it seems clear that such methods are really only suitable for the assurance of relatively modest reliability goals. This can be seen by considering the following examples.

Table 1 shows a simple analysis of some failure data from the testing and debugging of a command and control system, using a particular software reliability growth model. The question 'how reliable is the program now?' is answered immediately following the 40th, 50th, . . , 130th failures, in the form, (in this case) of a *mean time to next failure.* Alongside the *mttf* in the table is the total execution time on test that was needed to achieve that estimated mttf. Clearly, the *mttf* of this system (and hence its reliability) improves as the testing progresses. However, the final column shows a clear *law of diminishing returns*: later improvements in the *mttf* require proportionally longer testing.

sample size, i	elapsed time, t_i	achieved mttf, m_i	t_i/m_i
40	6380	288.8	22.1
50	10089	375.0	26.9
60	12560	392.5	32.0
70	16186	437.5	37.0
80	20567	490.4	41.9
90	29361	617.3	47.7
100	42015	776.3	54.1
110	49416	841.6	58.7
120	56485	896.4	63.0
130	74364	1054.1	70.1

Table 1 An illustration of the law of diminishing returns in heroic debugging. Here the total execution time (seconds) required to reach a particular mean time to failure is compared with the mean itself.

Of course, this is only a single piece of evidence, involving a particular measure of reliability (*mttf*), and the use of a particular model to perform the calculations, and a particular program under study. However, similar results are observed consistently across different data sources and for different reliability growth models. Figure 2 shows an analysis of failure data from a system in operational use, for which software and *hardware design* changes were being introduced as a result of the failures. Here the current rate of occurrence of failures (ROCOF) is computed at various times, using a different reliability growth model from that used in Table 1. The dotted line is fitted manually to give a visual impression of what, again, seems to be a very clear law of diminishing returns. Once again, the level of reliability reached here is quite modest: about 10^{-2} failures per hour of operational use, which is several orders of magnitude short of what we could call 'ultra-high dependability' (compare it with the 10^{-9} per hour requirement of the civil aircraft flight control systems). More importantly, it is by no means obvious how the details of the future reliability growth of this system will look. For example, it is not clear to what the curve is asymptotic: could one expect that eventually the ROCOF will approach zero, or is there an irreducible level of residual unreliability reached when the effects of correct fault removal are balanced by those of new fault insertion?

This empirical evidence of a law of diminishing returns for debugging software, shown by these two examples, seems to be supported by most of the available evidence. Certainly it is a feature of all the data sets that have been analysed within the Centre for Software Reliability. There are convincing intuitive reasons for results of this kind.

A program starts life with a finite number of faults, and these are encountered randomly during operation. Different faults contribute differently to the overall unreliability of the program: some are 'larger' than others. 'Large' here means that the *rate* at which the fault would show itself (i.e. if we were not to remove it the first time we saw it) is large: different faults have different rates of occurrence. Table 2 shows a particularly dramatic example of this based on a large database of problem reports for some large IBM systems [Adams 1984].

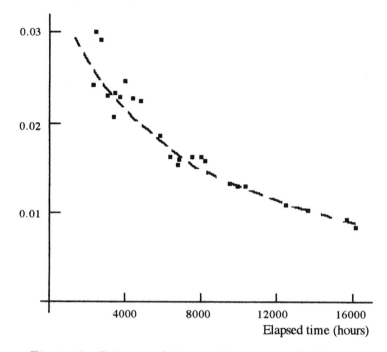

Figure 2 Estimates of the rate of occurrence of failures for a system experiencing failures due to software faults and hardware design faults. The broken line here is fitted by eye. Once again, the rate is not recomputed at each data point here: the plotted points represent only occasional recomputation of the rate during the observation of several hundred failures.

During reliability growth we assume that a fix is carried out at each failure. Let us assume for simplicity that each fix attempt is successful (this assumption, whilst thoroughly unrealistic, does not affect the general thrust of the present argument). As debugging progresses, there will be a tendency for a fault with a larger rate to show itself before a fault with a smaller rate: more precisely, for any time t, the probability that fault A reveals itself during time t will be smaller than the probability that B reveals itself during t, if the rate of A is smaller than the rate of B. Informally, large faults get removed earlier than small ones. It follows that the improvements in the reliability of the program due to earlier fixes, corresponding to faults which are likely to be larger, are greater than those due to later fixes.

Thus the law of diminishing returns shown in these examples is a result of two effects which reinforce one another. As debugging progresses and the program becomes more reliable, it becomes harder to find faults (because the rate at which the *program* is failing is becoming smaller), and the improvements to the reliability resulting from these fault-removals are also becoming smaller and smaller.

	Rate Class							
	1	2	3	4	5	6	7	8
	Mean time to occurrence in kmonths for rate class							
	60	19	6	1.9	.6	.19	.06	.019
Product	Estimated percentage of faults in rate class							
1	34.2	28.8	17.8	10.3	5.0	2.1	1.2	0.7
2	34.3	29.0	18.2	9.7	4.5	3.2	1.5	0.7
3	33.7	28.5	18.0	8.7	6.5	2.8	1.4	0.4
4	34.2	28.5	18.7	11.9	4.4	2.0	0.3	0.1
5	34.2	28.5	18.4	9.4	4.4	2.9	1.4	0.7
6	32.0	28.2	20.1	11.5	5.0	2.1	0.8	0.3
7	34.0	28.5	18.5	9.9	4.5	2.7	1.4	0.6
8	31.9	27.1	18.4	11.1	6.5	2.7	1.4	1.1
9	31.2	27.6	20.4	12.8	5.6	1.9	0.5	0.0

Table 2   Data from [Adams 1984], showing the very great disparity in 'sizes' of software faults. Here size is taken to be the mean time it would take to discover a fault (or alternatively its reciprocal, the rate of occurrence of the fault). Adams classified the faults into eight classes according to their sizes, and the most notable aspect of the above figures is the very large differences between the 'largest' and the 'smallest'. Perhaps most startling is that about one third of faults fall into the 60 kmonth class: i.e. a fault from this class would only be seen at the rate of about once every 5000 years!

3.2   Reliability estimation based on failure-free working

In the discussion above, there has been an important implicit assumption that it is possible to fix a fault when it has been revealed during the test, *and to know that the fix is successful*. In fact, there has been no serious attempt to model the fault-fixing operation and most reliability growth models simply assume that fixes are perfect, or they average out any short-term reversals to give the longer term trend. It is fairly easy to incorporate the possibility of a purely ineffectual fix (simply introduce an extra parameter representing the probability that an attempted fix leaves the reliability unchanged), but the more realistic situation in which an attempted fix introduces a *novel* fault seems much harder and has not been studied to any great extent. At the moderate reliability and criticality levels for which the reliability growth models are designed, this problem may not be too serious, but in safety-critical applications the issue must be addressed.

The difficulty here is that the potential increase in unreliability due to a bad fix is unbounded. The history prior to the last failure, at least as this is used in current models, does not tell us anything about the effect of this last fix. Of course, in principle we could learn about the efficacy of previous fixes (although this would not be easy), and attempt to estimate the proportion of previous bad fixes. Thus we might take this proportion to be a good estimate of the probability that the current fix is a bad one. But in order to have high confidence that the reliability was even as high as it was immediately prior to the last failure, it would be necessary to have high confidence that no new fault had been introduced. There seem to be no good grounds to have such high confidence associated with a *particular* fix other than to exercise the software for a long time and never see a failure arise from the fix.

This seems to be the most serious objection to the use of software reliability growth models for the assessment of the reliability of safety-critical software, and it applies whatever the required *level* of reliability. Thus for nuclear safety systems, it is probably more serious even than the practical objection discussed above concerning the law of diminishing returns - after all, these nuclear systems have fairly modest reliability requirements, and it may be possible to test them for long sequences of demands. But even if it were practicable to use a reliability growth model to obtain an estimate of reliability of the order of 10^{-4} *pfd*, say, there would remain this residual doubt that the last fix(es) had introduced new sources of unreliability, rendering untrustworthy any estimate based on an extrapolation of earlier growth.

The conservative way forward in this case would be to treat the program following a fix as if it were a *new* program, and thus take into account only the period of failure-free working that has been experienced since the last fix. This re-casts the problem in terms of steady-state reliability assessment. This problem has been studied in some detail in recent years [Littlewood and Strigini 1993; Littlewood and Wright 1997] but, not surprisingly, it turns out that the claims that can be made for the reliability of a system that has worked without failure are fairly modest for feasible periods of observation. Thus, in the case of a demand-based system such as a protection system, if we require to have 99% confidence that the *pfd* is no worse than 10^{-3}, we must see about 4600 failure-free demands; for 99% confidence in 10^{-4}, the number increases to 46000 failure-free demands: such a test was conducted for the Sizewell PPS [May, Hughes et al. 1995]. In the case of a continuously operating system, such as a control system, a 99% confidence in an MTTF of 10^4 hours (1.14 years) would require approximately 46,000 hours of failure-free testing; to raise the confidence bound on the MTTF to 10^5 hours, the testing duration must also increase to approximately 460,000 hours. In summary, high confidence in long failure-free operation in the future requires observing much longer failure-free operation under test. If this amount of test effort is not feasible, only much lower confidence can be obtained. For instance, it can be shown [Littlewood and Strigini 1993] via a simple Bayesian argument that, after seeing a system operating failure-free for t_0 hours, one can only claim that it has a 50:50 chance of surviving for a further t_0 hours before it fails.

4 Indirect ways of evaluating software reliability

There are clearly severe limitations to the levels of reliability that can be demonstrated using the direct evaluation approach, based on statistical analysis of operational testing data. Can this problem be overcome by using some other means of assessment? There seem to be three main candidates: claims based on quality of production, fault tolerance, and formal verification.

4.1 Reliability claims based on process quality

It seems to be assumed, in some industries, not only that the use of sufficiently good design and development practices can *achieve* very high reliability, but that the mere fact of their use *guarantees* that these levels will be met. For example, in [RTCA 1992] there is the statement:

' . . techniques for estimating the post-verification probabilities of software errors were examined. The objective was to develop numerical requirements for such probabilities for digital computer-based equipment and systems certification. The conclusion reached, however, was that currently available methods do not yield results in which confidence can be placed to the level required for this purpose. Accordingly, this document does not state post-verification software error requirements in these terms.'

The reader of these guidelines can only assume that the procedures and practices that are recommended in the document are somehow sufficient to justify reliability claims at the levels needed (10^{-9} probability of failure per hour for flight critical avionics!) without the need for direct measurement. Whilst no-one would deny that good practice is *necessary* for the development of extremely reliable safety-critical software, there is no evidence that it is *sufficient*.

The difficulty in claiming any reliability level for a program merely from evidence of the quality of its development process stem from two sources. In the first place, there is surprisingly little empirical evidence available of the operational reliability for software developed using particular development processes. Secondly, even if extensive evidence were available for a particular process, it would merely concern the reliability that might be expected on average. The actual achieved reliabilities would vary from one development to another, and thus there would be uncertainty involved in any reliability claim for a new product.

4.2 Fault tolerance based on design diversity

In hardware reliability engineering it is sometimes assumed that the stochastic failure processes of the different components in a parallel configuration are *independent*. It is then easy to show that a system of arbitrarily high reliability can be constructed by using sufficiently many unreliable components.

If software versions could be developed 'independently' of one another, so that the version failures were statistically independent, it would be possible to make claims for very high reliability based upon modest reliability claims for the individual versions (these could be based on the techniques for direct evaluation described above).

Unfortunately, experiments show that design-diverse versions do not fail independently of one another [Knight and Leveson 1986b]. One reason for this is simply that the designers of the different versions tend to make similar mistakes. Another reason is more subtle [Eckhardt and Lee 1985; Littlewood and Miller 1989]: even if the different versions really are independent objects (defined in a plausible, precise fashion), they will still fail dependently as a result of variation of the 'intrinsic hardness' of the problem from one input case to another. Put simply, the failure of version A on a particular input suggests that this is a 'difficult' input, and thus the probability that version B will also fail on the same input is greater than it otherwise would be. The greater this variation of 'difficulty' over the input space, the greater will be the dependence in the observed failure behaviour of versions, and consequently the smaller the benefit gained from the diversity.

On the other hand, the experiments [Anderson, Barrett et al. 1985; Knight and Leveson 1986a] agree that fault tolerance brings *some* increase in reliability compared with single versions - the problem is knowing how much in a particular case. If independence of failure behaviour cannot be assumed, reliability models for fault-tolerant software require that the degree of dependence must be estimated in each case. Trying to do this using the operational behaviour of the system simply leads to the same infeasible 'black-box' estimation problem encountered earlier. There do not appear to be any other convincing procedures.

4.3   Formal verification

It is tempting to try to move away from probability-based notions of software reliability towards deterministic, logical claims for complete perfection. Thus if a formal specification of the problem could be trusted, a proof that the program truly implemented that specification would be a guarantee that no failures could arise due to design faults in the implementation. It could be said that the product was 'perfectly reliable' with respect to such a class of failures. Whilst such an approach has its attractions, there are some problems.

In the first place, proofs are subject to error. This might be direct human error, in proofs by hand or with the aid of semiautomatic tools, and/or error by the proof-producing software in machine proof. In principle, one could assign a failure probability to proofs, and use this in a probabilistic analysis. However, such probabilities would be difficult to incorporate into a dependability evaluation: in the event that the proof were erroneous, we would not know anything about the true failure rate.

There are also practical difficulties. Although automated approaches to verification have advanced considerably, there are still stringent limits to the size and complexity of problems that can be addressed in this way.

Fianlly, it has to be said that it is often unreasonable to assume that the formal specification really captures the more informal engineering requirements. If the specification is wrong, a proof that the implementation conforms to the specification will not guarantee that failures cannot occur.

5 Evaluating reliability using several evidence sources

For real systems, claims for software reliability in safety cases are usually based upon many different kinds of evidence. For example, in the evaluation of the Sizewell PPS software the evidence came from the software production process, from extensive testing, from static analysis using MALPAS [Hunns and Wainwright 1991].

5.1 Expert judgement and BBNs

Combining such disparate evidence to make a judgement of the reliability of a program is difficult for two reasons. In the first place, it is often hard to know how much value to give to each strand of evidence. In the case of Sizewell, for example, whilst the MALPAS analysis was impressive in its scope (the largest exercise of its type ever attempted), it fell short of complete verification - indeed some of the more complex parts of the code defied analysis. Similarly, although the testing was intensive, the tests were not statistically representative of operational demands, so it was not possible to make direct reliability claims, in the ways discussed earlier.

Secondly, the very disparate nature of the different evidence strands makes their combination difficult. In particular, it is often hard to tell how dependent they are: if we have seen a large and successful test run, how much should our confidence increase when, in addition, we learn that extensive static analysis has revealed no problems?

Currently, answers to questions like this are provided quite informally by human experts. In the example of the Sizewell PPS, interestingly, the consensus was that the evidence did not support a claim for the originally required reliability of 10^{-4} *pfd*, but was sufficient to claim 10^{-3} (which turned out to be small enough, following a re-examination of the wider plant safety case).

There is considerable research going on to help the expert with these problems. One promising formalism for combining evidence in the face of uncertainty is Bayesian Belief Nets (BBNs) [Fenton, Littlewood et al. 1996]. These assist the expert by ensuring a kind of consistency in the handling of probabilities in complex situations. However, it has to be admitted that they provide little help in ensuring that the expert's combination of evidence is in accord with objective reality.

5.2 The use of both reliability assessment and proof for a safety system

One of the difficulties of using the types of evidence of the previous section is that most of them do not allow any *direct* evaluation of reliability in the sense discussed earlier. It could be argued that for safety-critical systems direct evaluation is more rigorous, and thus convincing, than assessment based on indirect evidence. This raises the interesting question: are there some system architectures that make it easier to justify reliability claims?

Some recent work suggests that this may be possible for special cases [Littlewood 1999 (to appear)]. It is based on the observation that a common architecture for safety systems is one in which a primary system providing high functionality (at the price of complexity) is backed up by a simpler (but less functionally capable) secondary system. An example is the Sizewell safety system that comprises a primary system based on 100,000 lines of software code, backed up by a very much simpler, hard-wired secondary system.

In such an architecture, any claim for reliability of the primary system must be probabilistic, since claims for perfection of a complex system will not be believable. The simple secondary, on the other hand, may be open to formal proof. If such a proof could be trusted, i.e. the secondary could never fail, then the overall safety system would have perfect reliability.

More realistically, it might be possible to assign a conservative *probability of perfection* to the secondary. It would be further conservative to say that, in the event that the SPS is *not* perfect, it will always fail precisely in those circumstances where the PPS fails - in other words, there is then 'complete' dependence. We then have the following:

P(safety system fails)

$$= P(\text{safety system fails|SPS perfect})P(\text{SPS perfect}) \hspace{2cm} (1)$$

$$+ P(\text{safety system fails|SPS not perfect})P(\text{SPS not perfect})$$

$$= P(\text{PPS fails|SPS not perfect})P(\text{SPS not perfect})$$

If we were prepared to assume that imperfection of the SPS and failure of the PPS were statistically independent, we have

$$P(\text{PPS fails|SPS not perfect}) = P(\text{PPS fails}) \hspace{2cm} (2)$$

and so

$$P(\text{safety system fails}) = P(\text{PPS fails})P(\text{SPS not perfect}) \hspace{2cm} (3)$$

The 'trick' here lies in (2). This independence assumption is very different from, and more plausible than, the assumption of *failure* independence between two versions (see 4.2), which is known to be unreasonable. Assuming independence would, for example, allow a claim for system reliability of 10^{-6} *pfd* based on a PPS reliability of 10^{-4} *pfd*, and a probability of 10^{-2} that the SPS is not perfect. The point here is that the system reliability claim clearly could not be demonstrated by direct evaluation, whereas the claims for the PPS and SPS may be sufficiently modest to be feasible.

6   Summary and conclusions

This paper has addressed the problem of assessing the reliability of software before it is deployed in a safety-critical system. The problem is a difficult one because claims for extremely high reliability appear to need extremely large amounts of evidence. Thus *direct* evaluation of reliability, using statistical methods based upon (real or simulated) operational data will generally only allow quite modest claims to be made - putting it another way, to make claims for ultra-high reliability this way would require infeasibly large amounts of operational exposure.

Indirect methods do not seem to be an answer to the problem. If anything they are weaker sources of evidence than observations of failure behaviour. Evidence of 'process quality', for example, is only weakly indicative of the reliability of a resulting software product.

Methods for evaluating reliability by combining evidence from disparate sources look promising, but much better understanding is needed of the complex interdependencies between different types of evidence before these approaches can be trusted for safety-critical systems.

It seems inevitable that judgements about the dependability of critical systems will continue to rely on human judgement, albeit aided by formalisms such as BBNs. There is after-the-event evidence that competent engineers *can* do this very well - examples include the in-service safety records of recent civil aircraft that vindicate the claims made for their safety before they went into service. On the other hand, no-less-competent engineers do get it wrong - examples include the recent Ariane V disaster. The question of *how much* it is reasonable to trust the judgement of experts is one that would repay further study.[2]

It should be emphasised that the results in this paper concern the limits to the levels of reliability that can be evaluated prior to the deployment of a system. This is different from the question of what levels of reliability can be *achieved*. It is evident that some systems have demonstrated very high reliability in operational use. Knowing this after-the-fact, however, is very different from making such a claim prior to deployment.

References

[Abdel-Ghaly, Chan et al. 1986] A.A. Abdel-Ghaly, P.Y. Chan and B. Littlewood, "Evaluation of Competing Software Reliability Predictions," *IEEE Trans. on Software Engineering*, vol. 12, no. 9, pp.950-967, 1986.

[Adams 1984] E.N. Adams, "Optimizing preventive maintenance of software products," *IBM J. of Research and Development*, vol. 28, no. 1, pp.2-14, 1984.

[Anderson, Barrett et al. 1985] T. Anderson, P.A. Barrett, D.N. Halliwell and M.R. Moulding. "An Evaluation of Software Fault Tolerance in a Practical System," in *Proc. 15th Int. Symp. on Fault-Tolerant Computing (FTCS-15)*, pp. 140-145, Ann Arbor, Mich., 1985.

[Brocklehurst and Littlewood 1992] S. Brocklehurst and B. Littlewood, "New Ways to get Accurate Reliability Measures," *IEEE Software*, vol. 9, no. 4, pp.34-42, 1992.

---

2   See [Henrion and Fischhoff 1986] for an interesting - and worrying - study showing the tendency for physicists, both individually and as a community, to be overconfident in their judgements.

[Dyer 1992] M. Dyer. *The Cleanroom Approach to Quality Software Development*, Software Engineering Practice. New York, John Wiley and Sons, 1992.

[Eckhardt and Lee 1985] D.E. Eckhardt and L.D. Lee, "A Theoretical Basis of Multiversion Software Subject to Coincident Errors," *IEEE Trans. on Software Engineering*, vol. 11, pp.1511-1517, 1985.

[Fenton, Littlewood et al. 1996] N. Fenton, B. Littlewood and M. Neil. "Applying Bayesian belief networks in systems dependability assessment," in *Proc. Safety Critical Systems Symposium*, pp. 71-94, Leeds, Springer-Verlag, 1996.

[Henrion and Fischhoff 1986] M. Henrion and B. Fischhoff, "Assessing uncertainty in physical constants," *Americal J. of Physics*, vol. 54, no. 9, pp.791-798, 1986.

[HSE 1992] HSE. *The Tolerability of Risk from Nuclear Power Stations*, London, HMSO, 1992.

[Hunns and Wainwright 1991] D.M. Hunns and N. Wainwright, "Software-based protection for Sizewell B: the regulator's perspective," *Nuclear Engineering International*, pp.38-40, September, 1991.

[Knight and Leveson 1986a] J.C. Knight and N.G. Leveson. "An Empirical Study of Failure Probabilities in Multi-version Software," in *Proc. 16th Int. Symp. on Fault-Tolerant Computing (FTCS-16)*, pp. 165-170, Vienna, Austria, 1986a.

[Knight and Leveson 1986b] J.C. Knight and N.G. Leveson, "Experimental evaluation of the assumption of independence in multiversion software," *IEEE Trans Software Engineering*, vol. 12, no. 1, pp.96-109, 1986b.

[Littlewood 1999 (to appear)] B. Littlewood, "The use of proofs in diversity arguments," *IEEE Trans Software Engineering*, 1999 (to appear).

[Littlewood and Miller 1989] B. Littlewood and D.R. Miller, "Conceptual Modelling of Coincident Failures in Multi-Version Software," *IEEE Trans on Software Engineering*, vol. 15, no. 12, pp.1596-1614, 1989.

[Littlewood and Strigini 1993] B. Littlewood and L. Strigini, "Assessment of ultra-high dependability for software-based systems," *CACM*, vol. 36, no. 11, pp.69-80, 1993.

[Littlewood and Wright 1997] B. Littlewood and D. Wright, "Some conservative stopping rules for the operational testing of safety-critical software," *IEEE Trans Software Engineering*, vol. 23, no. 11, pp.673-683, 1997.

[Lyu 1996] M. Lyu. *Handbook of Software Reliability Engineering*, New York, McGraw-Hill, 1996.

[May, Hughes et al. 1995] J. May, G. Hughes and A.D. Lunn, "Reliability estimation from appropriate testing of plant protection software," *Software Engineering Journal*, vol. 10, no. 6, pp.206-218, 1995.

[Musa 1993] J.D. Musa. *Operational profiles in software-reliability engineering.* IEEE Software. 14-32, 1993.

[RTCA 1992] RTCA. *Software considerations in airborne systems and equipment certification*, DO-178B, Requirements and Technical Concepts for Aeronautics, 1992.

AUDITS AND SAFETY CASES

The Traffic Controller's situation in Railway Control Centres – Lessons learned from Safety Audits

Gunhild Halvorsrud
Norwegian Railway Inspectorate
Oslo, Norway

Abstract

The aim of this paper is to highlight the work of the traffic controller in railway controls centres. In what ways can his or her job be safety critical, and what can be done to reduce the hazards that might arise from it? The basis for the paper is conversations the author has had with traffic controllers during safety audits.

1   Introduction

1.1   Norwegian Railway Inspectorate

The Norwegian Railway Inspectorate was established on 1 October 1996 and is an independent government department under the Ministry of Transport and Communications. The Inspectorate was established because Norway wishes to have an independent government agency with responsibility for supervising the various railway and tramway operators, regardless of whether the activities are public or private. The objectives of the Inspectorate are, as stated in our instruction:

- "To safeguard the government's interests in connection with safety issues etc. during the construction and operation of private and public railways – including tram, metro, underground and suburban railway lines – for the benefit of passengers, railway employees and the public in general."

- "To ensure that enterprises conducting railway operations comply with the requirement laid down in the Norwegian Railway Act (Act no. 100 of 11. June 1993) or regulations issued pursuant to this act."

The Inspectorate performs several different activities to safeguard the above-mentioned objectives, one of the most important is a system audit. In these audits we focus on the safety related activities the railway operators themselves have decided to perform, using the principle of internal control.

1.2   The background of this paper

During the last couple of years I have been taking part in a number of safety audits. The aim has been to survey the safety management structure in the infrastructure organisations. In these audits we have talked to people on every level of the organisation, from manager to traffic controllers and maintenance workers. I have taken a special interest in the work of traffic controllers and train dispatchers, and have been talking to a great number of them. I have gained a lot of insight from this, both about the traffic controllers' view of their work and about where we engineers fail to understand.

1.3   Railway control centres in Norway

In Norway there are several railway control centres located in different parts of the country. In addition there are control centres for tram and metro lines in the cities of Oslo and Trondheim. The technological facilities are very different, from the very latest in computer based technology, the control centre in Oslo, to relay based control systems, developed in the fifties. There are also some manually operated lines where the traffic controller uses telephone systems to communicate with train dispatchers at the different stations.

In the oldest systems, there are no automatic functions. Every train route is keyed in manually on a small keypad or keyboard using number codes for the station, and the movement planned. The movement authority and the actual train movement are indicated on a panel with lights symbolising the signals and train locations. These systems have no information about train identity. The traffic controller has to keep track of that manually. This puts a clear limit on how many trains the traffic controller can handle at one time, and is one of the main reasons for installing new systems.

In modern systems the trains are identified by their train numbers, and both the position and the train number are displayed in the control centre. There are also various automatic functions like route setting. More advanced systems, e.g. systems with conflict handling, are already available, but not implemented yet. This advanced functionality increases the number of train movements a traffic controller can handle.

The control centres are also very different in size. Norway is a sparsely populated country with about 25% of its inhabitants located in the south-eastern part. All major railway lines originate from Oslo, except the "Nordlandsbanen" that originates from Trondheim and the "Ofotbanen" that originates from Narvik. Consequently the traffic density and number of lines is much higher in the Oslo-area than in the rest of the country. This is reflected in the size of the control centres. In Oslo up to ten traffic controllers are on duty at the same time. The seven other centres (in Hamar, Drammen, Kristiansand, Stavanger, Bergen, Trondheim and Narvik) are much smaller. As an example: in Narvik there are never more than one person on duty.

1.4   Safety related work in railway control centres

The normal task for the traffic controller is to keep the traffic running smoothly. In railway signalling, most safety barriers are placed in the interlocking. The systems are designed to be fail-safe. If an error occurs, the interlocking is supposed to enter a more restricted state. In this situation the traffic controller will be the one to decide if the trains can be allowed to pass the stop signals. To do this he uses a dedicated telephone system or train radio, both with position control, to give orders / instructions to the driver. These conversations are recorded in order to be replayed later in case of an accident. If the traffic controller makes mistakes in this situation, there are no other safety-barriers. The traffic controller, who normally is focused on keeping the trains running on time, has to shift his attention to safety critical tasks. His aids in this work are the indications on his screen or panel that tell where the trains are. The indications are however not fail-safe. The communication with the driver is therefore crucial, and must be performed according to strict procedures.

2   The hazards of railway control centres

2.1   Failure modes

Few accidents or near misses related to the work of the traffic controller are reported today. There may be several reasons for this. One obvious reason might be that there are few such cases. Another reason could be that they are not reported. It is well known in the railway organisations in Norway today, that near misses are not adequately reported. Employees tend to avoid making reports on each other or themselves. As long as nothing happened, everything is OK. We also found that management did not expect them to make reports. Their systems for receiving and processing the data were inadequate, and very little feedback was given. When we talked to the traffic controllers under the anonymity of the safety audits, they admitted that near misses occur from time to time. It is not very often, but when it happens, they find it is mostly due to stress or trouble with technical systems. So when do accidents or near misses occur?

Dangerous situations arise when it is necessary for the traffic controller to give the driver orders to pass a stop signal. In this situation one can come up with the fault tree in fig 1 as a representation of the event. Mistakes made solely by the driver are excluded here.

The dominating causes are mistakes and misunderstandings made by the driver and traffic controller. The technical systems are more reliable by a factor of two or three decades. (Typical failure rate about 1×10^{-6} versus 1×10^{-3}). It is well known that factors like stress and personal problems have a significant influence on human error rates [Smith 1997]. What can be done to reduce these factors?

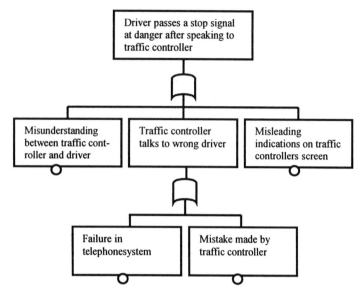

Figure 1. Fault tree

2.2 The traffic controllers' situation

The traffic controller needs technical tools he can rely on, and a satisfactory environment to work in. Satisfactory here includes both physically and mentally. Stress can be caused by many factors. We have identified a number of them and I'll discuss these in section 3. The technical tools are important, but maybe not as important as an engineer would think. The engineer is usually fascinated by the technological achievements that are made, and the possibilities which arise for automation and advanced functionality. The traffic controller has a different perspective. He wants technology that helps him doing his job; he doesn't want systems that make it less interesting, make him estranged from what he is doing and less fitted for handling an abnormal situation.

What usually happens when new technology is introduced is that the traffic controller becomes decreasingly a controller and increasingly a monitor. The designer might think this is a good idea. The traffic controller is relived from some of his / her routine tasks, and intervenes only when something is wrong. But humans are poor monitors. Even a highly motivated person is incapable of maintaining visual attention for more than about half an hour to a source of information on which very little happens. [Leveson 1995]. Luckily a lot happens on the railway traffic controllers' screen. The train moves from line section to line section, the signals change, and the train numbers move from place to place on the screen. But how interesting is it to supervise these movements, how can a traffic controller avoid having his thoughts drift away? And even if they manage to maintain attention to what happens on the screen, how do they make sure that they know what to do in an emergency? These very important questions have unfortunately easily been seen by engineers and managers as just expressions of the traffic controller's fear of losing influence or losing his / her job, and not as a genuine concern for safety. The trades unions may be given some blame here. They tend to use safety questions as a lever to get higher salary and more influence. But we have found that the traffic controllers concern is genuine, and they use different strategies to keep themselves alert. One of these can be to run the system manually from time to time. But as the number of lines and train movements increases, this will be impossible and inadvisable to do. Systematic training on simulators and courses and tests after absences will be necessary to maintain the skills of the traffic controllers.

The traffic controllers themselves, what do they think is important for them in the future? Again we find factors that are easy to forget. The answer I found sums up in:

- A management with a basic understanding of their situation.

- A satisfactory environment physically and mentally.

- Involvement in the acquisition of new technology.

3 The traffic controller's everyday life

3.1 Management and organisation

The traffic controller's position in the organisation does of course depend on the size of it. All the infrastructure administrations in Norway are relatively small, the largest being the Norwegian National Railway Administration with about 3700 employees. Still there are many levels in the hierarchy. We usually find the traffic controller at the bottom of it, but the distance from there to the management depends on the size of the organisation. We have visited organisations with only two levels, the manager and the employees, and organisations with six or more levels from top to bottom. The ability of the management to understand the traffic controller's working situation is clearly dependent on the number of levels the information has to go through. This affects the way questions about the control centre are handled.

The number of levels also affects the traffic controller's ability to see the whole picture of how the organisation works. In large organisations we often found the traffic controller did not have a clear picture of the line of command, and did not know about the goals and strategies of the management. They also had little understanding of the economical constraints. In the small organisations the traffic controller had a clearer picture and felt a more personal responsibility for the success of the organisation.

This feeling of personal responsibility had its drawbacks, too. We discovered that in some places the traffic controllers were so eager to keep all trains running on schedule, that safety was jeopardised.

The local management was very important to the traffic controllers. In one organisation we visited, the team leader of the control centre was located physically about a 15-min. walk away. When we asked the traffic controllers about their situation at work, their main problem seemed to be that the team leader was not situated in the same building as they were. This was for practical reasons. His managers wanted him close to them, so they could co-operate closer. Surely that was beneficial, but a very sore point for his subordinates.

3.2   The environment

We found that the environment in many cases is more important to traffic controllers than the technology. The facilities of the room in which the control centre is located has great importance for the way the traffic controllers perform their work. In the old control centre in Oslo, in operation until just a few years ago, the traffic controllers on different, but adjacent lines sat back to back. Thus, the traffic controllers had to shout when they wanted to say something to each other. The acoustics were bad as well and made them have to shout even louder. Then other traffic controllers also had to shout to be heard. When a person entered the control centre he/she would always get the impression of chaos, and you would think you faced an emergency situation every time you put your head through the door (if you even dared to…).

In the new centre all traffic controllers are placed side by side in three rows facing one large screen. If the traffic controllers need to talk, less frequently than before since all information is on the big screen, they can talk with normal voices. The acoustics of the room are very good.

When this centre were planned, some engineers considered the big screen a waste of money, since every traffic controller could see his stations on his own monitor. Today everyone agrees that a large screen is very useful at larger control centres like the one in Oslo. The quiet mumbling you hear when you enter the centre today tells you this is true.

3.3   The manpower

We also discovered the importance of having just a few more people at work than absolutely necessary. In one control centre they had just reduced the manpower by making the team leader work as a traffic controller most of the day, and doing management work when traffic was low. In theory this would work well, but in practical situations the other traffic controllers said he spent too much time with management issues and left them with all the work. The sentiments about this were running very high. The organisation saved a few thousand pounds each year this way, but what they got in return was a lot of discordance and hard feelings. I believe it was hardly worth the money saved. Does this influence safety? In an emergency I think it does!

3.4 The traffic controllers' attitude

According to our findings there is no reason to wonder why some traffic controllers with the very old-fashioned equipment are satisfied, while some other traffic controllers with modern equipment were equally dissatisfied. It sums up like this:

- In the old control centres the traffic controller has full control over his line. There are relatively few train movements so he can quite easily keep track of where the trains are. He is busy all day making decisions. If trouble occurs, he'll know what to do since he is updated on every aspect of the traffic. He knows his job well, and has a high responsibility for smooth and safe traffic.

- In the new control centres the traffic controller monitors the train movements. There are many of them, and the system issues the commands. To be updated on every aspect of the traffic the traffic controller has to keep very close attention to the screen. If something happens that requires him to take control, his task will be very complicated because of the high number of train movements. He might feel estranged from what he is doing.

- Still we found several traffic controllers being very satisfied with the new systems. We also got several hints as to the reason for this. Factors like management, environment and manpower were important, but the most important factor turned out to be the process used to develop and implement the system.

4 Acquisition of new systems

We found that the ways in which the traffic controllers were involved in the process of acquiring the new systems and man – machine interfaces were crucial to their attitude towards the systems later. The traffic controllers in the control centres in Oslo told us that in the beginning they were sceptical towards taking part in the acquisition process, largely in fear of becoming an alibi for user involvement, and not much more. The extent, to which they felt this to be the outcome of the process, depended on several factors. The most important ones are given here.

4.1 Involve the right person

It is usually not practical to involve all the traffic controllers. In most cases that would greatly increase the cost due to all the different wishes that would come up. So who should be involved? In many cases it is up to the trade union to choose. That might work depending on the trade union's ability to choose the right persons. Often the person is chosen according to his place in the trade union's organisational structure. Then it is only luck that decides if the choice will be a success or a failure. A lot of emphasis should be placed on convincing the trade union to chose someone suited for the job. If the management can pick the person themselves, it is very easy to pick a team leader, and only him. This too might work, but it is usually not a good idea. He might have a distance from his subordinates that could imply that he is not fully trusted. In any case, he has some distance from the everyday work that deprives him of the fingertip knowledge of how things are and how they should be. Last but not least, he doesn't have time to get fully involved. The person or persons selected must be relived from part of, or better still, all of their usual tasks to be able to get properly involved.

Who is the ideal traffic controller for this work? One manager we talked to had a very good rule. He said you could divide his people in three groups. Two of these groups are small, about 20 % of the traffic controllers in each. These groups are the ones that will always be negative to new technology, and those that would always welcome the new, no matter if it is an improvement or not. The remaining 60% are those that are a little sceptical, but want to see what they could get and looks for improvements. The system users to involve must clearly come from this last group. So the management or trade union must be convinced that this is right. That might involve some work!

4.2 The time from which they were involved

The user representative must be involved from the beginning. He should already be involved when the functional specification, on which tenders are to be based, is prepared. The functional specification puts a lot of restrictions on what can be altered later. The traffic controller will then also be given first hand information on what he can expect. This is very important. The traffic controller know something is coming, but he doesn't know what. When put in an uncertain situation people tends to think the worst. Information and participation is the best way of avoiding gossip. If possible, the traffic controller should also be involved in the decision process when the vendor is being chosen. It can be difficult to obtain a clear picture of how a system or interface will behave just by reading specifications. Let the traffic controller take a look at the different systems being offered.

4.3 Listen to what the traffic controller says

Don't use the traffic controller as an alibi. When you come to the man – machine interface, who knows best what it should be like? The traffic controller might have unrealistic expectations or demands about the system, but his views must be heard. If it is not feasible, he must be told why. It is also important to make it very clear, which issues the traffic controller is expected to have views about and which not. The man – machine interface and the list of alarms are such issues, the technical platform clearly isn't.

4.4 Avoid halfway solutions

Try to avoid halfway solutions or bad compromises. This is another important point that is often forgotten. If technology is to be changed it must give some advantage for the traffic controller, or else he won't see the point. Sometimes the systems are changed because the old ones are no longer maintainable. If the traffic controller gets no added functionality, but only more complicated ways of working, he is bound to be quite negative towards the system. An example: The old relay based controls were using keypads for entering data. In the new ones the traffic controller clicks with the mouse. If that is the only difference between the old and the new system, it is clearly not such a great step forward. The users have the codes in their heads and fingertips, and can enter them very quickly. Clicking down menus takes a lot more time. New and more advanced functionality must be implemented at about the same time as the new man – machine interface. Otherwise the traffic controller would perhaps be better off with a user interface resembling the old system for a few more years. In fact, this was done in a small control centre in Norway a few years ago when the relay system was changed for a PLC-system, but the principles of the man - machine interface were kept as they were.

4.5   Don't rush

Don't rush! Old-fashioned technology that works is far better than new technology that doesn't. I talked to a traffic controller who was very frustrated because the new control system often failed. The indications on the screen froze from time to time, and she had no way of telling where the train was, other than calling the driver. At the same time new interlocking was installed, and she had to give orders to the drivers by telephone. To be sure no that other train was in that section of the line, she had to call all other trains in the area and ask where they were. Quite a complex task during rush hour. And on top of this the engineers were planning to let the new system control even more stations. Closer co-operation between the traffic controllers and the engineers would have prevented this situation.

5   What have we learned?

From a safety perspective the work of the traffic controller is normally quite simple. The interlocking systems prevent them from making hazardous mistakes. But when the technical systems fail, the task of running trains safely can be quite complex. In these cases there are several factors that have to be taken into account to prevent human failure. It is important to bear in mind that the traffic controllers' perception of their own situation, both regarding to what extent they feel respected and their physical surroundings, has a great influence on their motivation and their ability to tolerate stress.

So first of all we have learned how important it is to talk to each other in order to understand each other. I understand a lot more these questions now than I did 5-6 years ago. At that time I was in fact planning control centres. I remember having very little understanding of traffic controllers being sceptical to new technology. We used to think they were afraid to loose their job, or that the trade union told them to be sceptical. Now I see that they might have had reasons to think like they did. We then found it strange that anyone would prefer entering numbers by keypads to clicking with the mouse. After talking to the traffic controller I no longer have a problem understanding their views.

We also learned that the work environment, the management and the manpower available were mostly more important to the traffic controller than the technology as long as the technology served its purposes. I think this has to do with the need to feel respected. I don't think the traffic controllers feel that their job is respected when their team leader is located in an office close to the top management instead of close to them. And I don't think they feel respected when manpower is cut down to a level they find unjustifiable. And I certainly don't think they feel respected when all their worries are put down as "trade union talk" or fear of new technology.

Last but not least, we learned that technology should be designed to fit the user, and not the other way around. User participation in the acquisition process from the very beginning is crucial for success. It can be hard to accept this; we engineers like to think we know best.

Acknowledgement

I would like to acknowledge all the traffic controllers who have spoken openly with me about their situation at work, and about what can be done to improve safety in their everyday tasks. I also acknowledge my friends and colleges who have commented on drafts of this paper and thus helped me get my thoughts and language straight!

References

[Smith 1997] Smith D J: Reliability, Maintainability and Risk, 5th ed, Butterworth-Heinemann Ltd, 1997

[Leveson 1995] Leveson N: SAFEWARE System Safety and Computers, Addison-Wesley Publishing Company, Inc, 1995.

SAFETY CASES in the RAILWAY SIGNALLING INDUSTRY

Author: Peter. R. Duggan
Westinghouse Signals

1   Are Safety Cases Needed?

With the entry of new operators into the railway signalling industry, and division of control between different companies, this poses potentially new and inadequately controlled risk onto the railway system.

The Railway Safety Case Regulations [HSE Guidance on Regulations 1994] is one of a set of regulations, others include Railway (Safety Critical Work) Regulations, Carriage of Dangerous Goods and Approval of Works, Plant and Equipment.

The safety critical work regulations entail placing a duty on employers, to ensure that employees carrying out work which is vital to the safe operation of the railway, are competent and fit to carry out that work. (This subject is outside the scope of this paper, but mentioned for completeness).

Likewise, carriage of dangerous goods is left to ones imagination and is outside the scope of this paper.

Approval of works, plant and equipment - details the process and mechanism for attaining approval for railway systems and type approval for equipment from the HMRI (Her Majesty's Railway Inspectorate). This includes rolling stock, locomotives, stations, signalling, level crossings etc. - This is also outside the scope of the paper.

Her Majesty's Railway Inspectorate were until a few years ago the approval body for railway systems. It is now invested in the Health and Safety Executive (HSE) to perform this task. HMRI are now part of the HSE.

2   Who Does the Railway Safety Case apply to?

There will be an Infrastructure Controller Safety Case covering operation of the railway, signalling etc.

In turn there will be Infrastructure Maintenance Railway Safety Cases maintained by the Infrastructure Maintenance Unit (IMU) covering maintenance activities.

There will be Train Operating Companies (TOC's) Safety Cases covering operation of their trains.

There will also be Station Operator Safety Cases covering station activities.

Each of the above have to be compliant with the Railway Safety Case Regulations.

Any new or modified rolling stock (all types not just electric traction) will require a Safety Case in line with current CENELEC/IEC regulations which links into the Infrastructure Controller Safety Case.

Finally, any new or modified signalling systems will require a Safety Case in line with current CENELEC/IEC regulations which links into the Infrastructure Controller Safety Case.

It is worthy of note that Westinghouse Signals has produced Safety Cases for some time before that for new and modified products in line with our own Safety Management Policy.

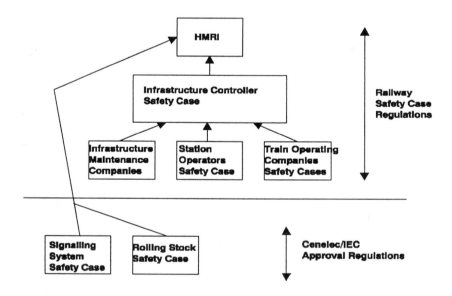

Figure 1 The Railway Safety Case

3 System/Product Safety Management (SMS)

In order to implement our Company safety policy, we have in place a Safety Management System comprising the strategy for how we achieve and demonstrate safety of a System/Product followed by processes and procedures necessary to meet our needs. As a company trading both within the UK and overseas, our Safety Management System is based upon International standards.

Creating your own in-house specific Safety Management System (SMS) is a pragmatic approach to the minimization of risk without stifling innovation and still achieving 'best practice'.

Whilst it may be argued that the major disadvantage of having your own SMS is cost, in the longer term, significant benefits can be gained, including:
- common approach to development;
- many customers stipulate a range of different standards to be followed. By having an SMS allows an expensive generic development to be re-used without the need for re-assessment and re-presentation of the safety case in a different format;
- safety in design is implemented at the start;
- learn from previous mistakes;
- less need for developers to determine 'best practice' and get on with the job;
- working practices (to which standards do not and should not cover).

However, even an SMS can suffer from the same problems as standards, out-of-date when issued, hence it is paramount that a brief is kept on what is happening out in the 'big wide world' and the SMS kept up-to-date.

By having an in-house SMS, based on the assumption that it is followed and complied with, customers world wide will receive the ubiquitous 'safety case' to the same format/approach using relevant analysis techniques allowing for cross acceptance.

4 The Safety Management System Content

The SMS should identify the 'why', the 'what' and the 'how'.
Why? - to demonstrate best practice.
- Strategy
  ⇒ how you organize resources to activities (independence issues);
  ⇒ requirements for competence/ roles and responsibilities;
  ⇒ standards, guidelines and practices to which the SMS is based;
  ⇒ methods for measurement/monitoring and audit.

What? - activities to be performed.
- Safety Plan
  - ⇒ layout, format, skeleton content
- Preliminary Hazard Identification
  - ⇒ techniques commonly performed and how
  - ⇒ examples, checklists
- Preliminary Hazard Analysis
  - ⇒ techniques commonly performed and how
- System Hazard Analysis
  - ⇒ techniques commonly performed and how
- Hazard Log
  - ⇒ layout, format, skeleton
  - ⇒ access rights, management control, procedure
- Safety Case
  - ⇒ layout, format, skeleton content

How? - to build safety into the product
- technical safety standards

5 SMS Based on 'Best Practice'?

There are a number of standards for safety-critical / safety-involved systems, to which many are industry sector specific. But are industry sector specific standards deemed to be 'best practice'?

It can take years to 'issue/mandate' a standard, which to all intense purposes, is out-of-date at time of issue. Technology is ever moving forward.

So what is 'best practice' and what does it mean when an unfortunate incident occurs and the legal system gets a hold of you!

The Consumer Protection Act 1987 (which is an implementation of the European directive on Product Liability) takes into account the time the product was supplied by the producer to another, 'best practice' at that time.

The controversial 'development risks' defense is (quoting the act) 'that the state of scientific and technical knowledge at the relevant time was not such that a producer of the same type of products might be expected to have discovered the defect in his products. (The relevant time is the time to supply).'

The onus is still on the defendant, and it is not enough to argue that it would have been expensive or impracticable to have discovered the defect, nor that the product was managed to accepted industry safety standards.

So, we have to define 'best practice'. The list below is a selection of standards which represent 'best practice' within the wider Safety Critical industry:

1. IEC 61508
2. DOD 178B
3. MIL 882C
4. DEF STAN 00-56
5. CENELEC 50126/50128/50129
6. IEC 61511
7. EN 50159-1/50159-2
8. MU8004
9. RIA-23
10. and there's more.

However, 'best practice' not only covers standards, but also guidelines (PES and SEMSPLC Guidelines for example), papers, emerging but not yet published standards, innovation.

The IEC61508 standard [IEC 61508 1998] is a foundation for many different safety related industries including for example:
- the process industry,
- the manufacturing industry,
- the transportation industry and
- the medical industry.

The CENELEC Standards that we apply are prEN50126 [CENELEC prEN50126 1995], prEN50128 [CENELEC prEN50128 1995] and ENV50129 [CENELEC ENV50129 1998]. These CENELEC standards are a derivation of the generic IEC61508 standard, and are the Railway Industry sector's interpretation. CENELEC members are the national committees of Austria, Belgium, Denmark, Finland, France, Germany, Iceland, Ireland, Italy, Luxembourg, Netherlands, Norway, Portugal, Spain, Sweden, Switzerland and the United Kingdom.

When issued, they will become a defacto standard across Europe, this can only be a good thing for creation of a 'level playing field' and dictate an acceptable standard approach for all within the Railway industry.

6 What is the Safety Case?

The Safety Case is the demonstration by analysis and test that the system/product does not, under defined conditions, lead to a state in which human life, economics or environment are endangered.

The Safety Case is summarized in what is known as the Safety Case Report. This report is the top level of the Safety Case, and references out to all quality, safety and technical documentation generated throughout the project.

Figure 2 Structure of the Safety Case

The following is the structure of the Safety Case prescribed by CENELEC EN50129.

- <u>Definition of the System</u>. Specifically detailing the system, scope of supply and what the Safety Case actually assures.
- <u>Evidence of Quality Management.</u> Description of the Quality Management system via the Quality Plan and compliance with the Quality Plan, an Internal quality audit and its findings/corrections , Configuration Management, how it was implemented and controlled.
- <u>Evidence of Safety Management</u>. Description of the Safety Management system, detailing the safety organization and responsibilities of all key personnel involved in safety, program monitoring (hazard log and its control, safety reviews were held and also progress reviews).
- <u>Evidence of Functional and Technical Safety.</u> Technical description of the system and justification of the design, including failure modes, a summary of all of the activities performed with summarized results (PHA examples: historical hazard identification, brainstorm, Functional Failure Analysis (FFA), HAZard and OPerability study (HAZOP), and outstanding hazards) (SHA examples: interface analysis, response times, power supply, power fail, EMC, electrical earthing/bonding human error and man machine interface) all as part of the safety analysis with detail of hazards remaining open. Additionally, evidence of correct operation verification activities field trials, validation testers on site, training req.'s and adequacy of manuals) and finally the adequacy of the data preparation process.
- <u>Related Safety Cases.</u> Reference to any related Product Safety Cases.
- <u>Conclusions and Recommendations</u>. Detailing the open hazards with mitigating features as appropriate, and recommendations concerning in this case that commissioning of the system/product application occur.

(Open hazards included Commissioning errors and Maintenance Errors). Note. This section could also include any restrictions or conditions placed upon the system.

It is also useful to provide an additional executive summary at the start of the Safety Case Report to give the reader an overview of the key safety aspects:

- Executive Summary. Project overview, safety activities performed and their relationship with the safety reports, and the functional and safety requirements.

7 Hierarchy of Safety Cases

There are three different types of Safety Case, specified in the CENELEC Standards:

1. Generic Product/Equipment Safety Case.
   example individual Electronic Module that is used as part of a railway signalling interlocking.
2. Generic Application Safety Case.
   example signalling interlocking as applied to a generic application.
3. Specific Application Safety Case.
   example site specific application of the generic case.

The approach to the creation of the Safety Case (whether 'generic product', 'specific application' or 'generic application') follows a clearly defined life cycle path with clearly defined deliverables (focusing on the scope of the safety case):

1. Safety Assurance Plan.
2. Preliminary Hazard Analysis (incorporating Preliminary Hazard Identification).
3. System Hazard Analysis.
4. Hazard Log.

and finally
5. the Safety Case.

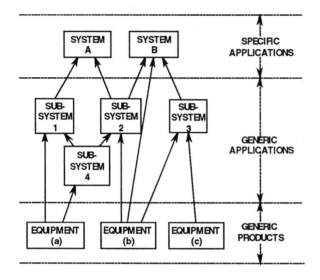

Figure 3 Hierarchy of Safety Cases

8   The Safety Assurance Plan

The Safety Assurance Plan contains.

1. The project safety organization and its relationships and lines of communication with the organization of the total programme, including major suppliers or sub-contractors;

2. The key safety personnel, their qualifications, responsibilities and authorities within the programme;

3. The objectives of the Safety programme and the perceived safety integrity requirements for the product;

4. The Safety programme milestones and activities, linked to the major milestones of the overall project life cycle (refer to figure 4);

5. The safety analysis and testing tasks required for verification and validation of the system safety, the procedures to be used and the responsibility for execution of each task;

6. Documentation requirements for each task;

7. The scope and depth of analysis to be performed concerning the application of analysis techniques to the system/product;

8. The Hazard Log and its mechanism of control;

9. The Failure Reporting and Corrective Action System (FRACAS) and its mechanism of control;

The Safety Assurance Plan will be monitored and updated as a project progresses.

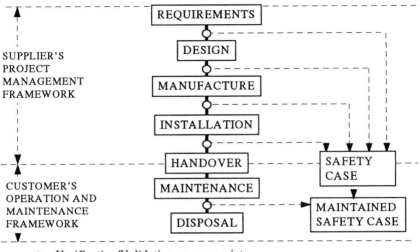

○ Verification/Validation as appropriate

Figure 4 Lifecycle Phases

9 Preliminary Hazard Analysis

The Preliminary Hazard Analysis Phase covers the initial system design and configuration stage. During this phase all credible potential system hazards are identified and logged in a Hazard log.

A variety of hazard identification techniques can be used, however there may be more, there may be less dependent upon the scope of the product analysis performed. Identification techniques include:

- Historical Data Hazards Identification (previous accident history)
- Functional Failure Analysis
- Brainstorm
- Hazop
- Previous developments

When performing the task of PHA, it is essential that the scope of the work to be undertaken is clearly defined and the boundaries of the system or product are clearly understood. Failure to provide this simple information can lead to significant time and effort being expended on issues outside the scope of the analysis.

When the preliminary hazard list has been created, it is then necessary to determine for each item in the list whether it is actually a hazard, a threat or a

Project Management issue. Failure to perform this task correctly can lead at worst to missing safety requirements or to significant and meaningless work.

The task is performed on the basis of the following definitions:

- A hazard is a physical situation, often following some initiating event, that can lead to an accident
- A threat is anything, which has the potential to adversely affect the reliability, maintainability or safety of the system or product.
- A project management issue includes activities yet to be performed and can include issues such as access to the railway to undertake testing, removal of recoverable equipment (ye olde and very collectable), changes to listed buildings (signalboxes and so on).

The PHA is used during the initial concept stage of the project to identify safety-critical areas and evaluate the major hazards associated with the system that must be controlled by engineering or eliminated by design. The safety considerations identified by the analysis form the basis of the system safety requirements, and are used in the evaluation of the various design options.

10 System Hazard Analysis

The System Hazard Analysis task forms the major part of the safety programme. It encompasses a number of different analysis techniques, which can be applied at different stages of the safety life cycle, to varying degrees of detail and depth dependent on the status of the product design and the requirements of the programme at any particular stage. The SHA is based on the results of the PHA and extends the work done in the PHA as the definition of the system increases.

The results of the analyses are used to improve the safety of the product design, and changes in the system design are reflected in the analyses as they occur.

10.1 The ALARP Principle

It is very difficult to provide tangible evidence to demonstrate that the ALARP principle (As Low As Reasonably Practicable), has been implemented where a system/product has already been developed or where modification to an existing system/product is concerned.

The process of applying risk reduction starts with the creation of a number of requirements on the development project. These include following specified and well-documented Procedures in the Quality and Safety Management System, which includes specific methodologies to be applied during the life cycle of the project. The process of control of ALARP in this case relies upon the product being designed in accordance with the procedures, design safety principles and strategies / philosophies, review and inspection of the design, and test and analysis being performed where applicable. During the above activities, iterations occur during the development life cycle. Hence to show 'concrete' black and white compliance is difficult.

Whilst acknowledging that ALARP can and should be demonstrated at the 'Requirements' level, the only way to demonstrate that ALARP is taken into consideration is by demonstration that no additional risk or introduction of additional risk has taken place, in essence meeting the system/product requirements.

10.2 Legacy Systems and Enhancements

The current format for Safety Cases and expectations of documented evidence was not prevalent in earlier years, and hence for some products, no specific Safety Case existed, though documentation concerning the equipment was produced and was considered sufficient in its day.

When it comes to modification of any equipment from an earlier generation, a Safety Case is now required to support it.

Remember that the Safety Case today has to satisfy relevant legal requirements, relevant standards and guidelines, regulatory authorities (e.g. HSE/HMRI), which I have already covered.

Concerning equipment which already exists on the railway, whereupon modification is necessary, (an example of a required modification could be to comply with latest EMC directives), in order to provide a 'Safety Case' for the changes, we have to distinguish between enhancements made, i.e. the changes (the added value to a system/product) on the one hand, and the rest of the design (the existing non changed part to which Grandfather Rights are claimed). We clearly state the changes made to the system/product, safety analysis and supporting documentation with a paragraph in effect, which states 'Grandfather Rights for the remaining design.

Grandfather Rights applies equally to systems as well as products.

11 The Hazard Log

The Hazard Log is initiated by the Preliminary Hazard Analysis at the outset of the project and is maintained throughout the system life cycle by the Project Safety Assurance Engineer.

The Hazard log provides the principle means of establishing traceability within the safety process, and progress on the resolution of unacceptable risks throughout the project. Hazards are closed by a safety review when the risk is considered acceptable.

The Hazard Log is a formal document with changes to the Hazard Log after the initial issue recorded by a revision record and subject to inspection where change is significant or closure of a hazard is proposed.

The Project Safety Assurance Engineer must be responsible for the creation and maintenance of the Hazard Log and not the designers or Project Managers, independence is a necessary part of the overall process to ensure safety of the system or product.

12 The Generic Product/Equipment Safety Case

To recap, the Safety Case Report has the purpose of providing the necessary evidence, arguments and information to demonstrate that the safety requirements for the system/product have been adequately captured and met

The Safety Case for the product completes with successful issue of:
- The Safety Case Report
- The Application Manual and Configuration System Manual.

As a result of the System Hazard Analysis, there were a significant set of rules and warnings and particular methods of application to be followed. The mechanism that we use to close these out (in essence the hazards) were to produce the manuals, which all Application Engineers who apply the product have to follow.

13 Specific Application Safety Case

The following is our approach to production of the Specific Application Safety Case, in particular it concerns the application of our WESTRACE product.

Our WESTRACE product was designed as an interlocking for railways controlling the safe operation of signals and points upon request from the signaler, however it can be applied to other application areas. In effect it is a 'safety-critical' controller, the example is its application as an automatic half barrier level crossing.

The safety life cycle and safety deliverables are the same for the specific application as for the generic product safety case so what is different?

Hazard Identification encompassed:
- Analyzing all aspects of the Level Crossing Controller as interfaced to WESTRACE physically and functionally. To provide examples:
  ⇒ Barrier Position Detection
  ⇒ Barrier angle
  ⇒ Barrier Valve Control
  ⇒ Boom Lights

      ⇒ Road Lights
      ⇒ Signalling Inputs
      ⇒ Track Circuits
      ⇒ Outputs
      ⇒ Power Supply
      ⇒ Battery
      ⇒ System Design
      ⇒ Traction Bonding
      ⇒ EMC
      ⇒ Functional Operation etc.

- A HAZOP utilising the results of a Functional Failure Analysis as input.
- Analysis specific to the Specific Location Automatic Half Barrier application

From this analysis the items in the hazard list are assessed and reduced to a lower total of manageable hazards. (Project Risks and threats are excluded). These included Occupational Health and Safety hazards and system safety hazards. All were passed to the System Hazard Analysis via the Hazard Log.

The System Hazard Analysis task forms the major part of the safety programme and encompassed:
- necessary analysis of each of the hazards,
- installation errors,
- testing errors,
- commissioning errors,
- operating errors,
- maintenance errors,
- common mode errors,
- design errors,
- WESTRACE incompatibility with its interfaces.
  (A major part of the analysis concerned the interfaces, whereupon each interface was analyzed with respect to response time)
- internal health testing effects,
- power supplies,
- power failure and recovery,
- EMC,
- Electrical Earthing and Bonding,
- compatibility with WESTRACE and human error.

Adequacy of manuals was also a significant task, demonstrating that all warnings, restrictions and particular methods of application from the Product Safety Case, had been implemented and or were passed to the user/operator/maintainer to be used.

The SHA Report culminated in the closure of most hazards, certain hazards for instance maintenance and commissioning errors were not closed, (how many people ask the maintainers how good the manual is six months down the line?), whereupon closure of the hazard should then occur.

14 The Generic Application Safety Case

The structure and content of the Generic Application Safety Case is very similar to the site specific Safety Case, however detail differences will occur as a result of a number of hazards being closed on the basis of warnings and application restrictions in the Generic Application Manual.

Additionally, there is the subject of maintenance, this can only be assessed on a site specific basis, as a result, a set of checklists is included in the Application Manual stating that a site specific maintenance manual must be produced, and include specific content in accordance with the checklist.

Obviously, by having a generic application safety case, the resultant analysis for site specific applications is significantly reduced, having already been performed, giving economies in scale. Needless to say, if the functionality of the AHB for a site-specific application differs from the functionality supported by the generic safety case and analysis, then further safety assessment is required for the changed/modified part of the system.

For the AHB applications, we have produced two specific application safety cases, followed by the generic application. Future Site-Specific Application safety cases should be 'very thin' relying on the analysis in the Generic Application Safety Case.

15 Independent Assessment

What is an independent assessor? What is their role? Why are they Necessary? and Who funds them?

Independent assessors play a pivotal role in the successful acceptance of a product by the customer. The degree of independence of the assessor is dependent upon the integrity level of the product under assessment and ranges from an independent department within the supplier organization to an external organization.

The role of the assessor can vary according to the scope of the project, but in general provide an assessment of the safety management/technical safety arguments, by peer review, audits etc. and assessing the adequacy that all system/safety requirements have been met.

Independent assessors are a necessary part of the overall safety management life cycle, and are 'highly recommended' to be used in many safety standards i.e. 'best practice'.

They are in almost all cases funded by the supplier.

By the very nature of international standards, they are a compromise of different interests and philosophies. This leads to:

- woolly non-prescriptive standards open to interpretation;
- many different interpretations between countries and within countries;
- interpretation as a result of translation into different languages;
  - $\Rightarrow$ i.e. safety box? or did it start life as 'safety net'?;
- different interpretations between independent groups on the same project;
- problems with cross acceptance;
- expectations from independent assessors from different industries i.e. nuclear sector processes/standards applied to the automobile sector;
- what standards should we actually use? - 'best practice'.

It is recommended that you involve an Independent Assessor from the start, identify the game plan up front. If you don't there is the risk of rework.

16 Conclusions

This paper has established the requirement for safety cases in the Railway Industry, by identifying relevant legislation. It has also identified a number of different safety cases within the railway fraternity, which together make up the 'railway' safety case.

Following on from this, the paper has described in further detail, the safety process followed for the safe implementation of systems and products on the railway from the point of view of the signalling manufacturing industry.

References

[CENELEC prEN50126 1995] - Railway Applications: The Specification and Demonstration of Dependability - Reliability, Availability, Maintainability and Safety (RAMS)
British Standards Institute

[CENELEC prEN50128 1995] - Railway Applications: Software for Railway Control and Protection Systems.
British Standards Institute

[CENELEC ENV50129 1998] - Railway Applications: Safety Related Electronic Systems for Signalling
British Standards Institute

[HSE Guidance on Regulations 1994] – Railway Safety Cases
The Stationary Office (formely HMSO)

[IEC 61508 1998] Functional Safety of Electrical/Electronic/Programmable Electronic Safety-Related Systems
British Standards Institute

A Retrospective Safety-Case in Retrospect

Gustaf Myhrman
Defence Materiel Administration
(Försvarets Materielverk; FMV)
Stockholm, Sweden

Abstract

Although safety has been a major concern in the Swedish Navy for a long time, its application has undergone essential changes during the nineties. This paper describes a case where the requirements did change during the project and how we handled that. It gives an outline of the system and its hazards. In the project the requirement of a safety-case for the complete system was introduced late and this paper illustrates the activities performed.

1 Introduction

The development of Torpedo 2000, or Torpedo 62 as it is known in the Swedish Navy, started in the late 1980s. In those days we already had rigorous safety requirements on munitions, but we did not have similar requirements on the complete system — System Safety Requirements.

During the development of the torpedo system, the new System Safety manual was adopted for the Swedish Armed Forces. The development was finalised last year and it was considered a Safety-Case was needed to comply with the new Safety Requirements.

2   Torpedo 62 (Torpedo 2000)

2.1   General

The Torpedo Weapon System 62 has been developed by Bofors Undewater Systems for the Swedish Navy and consists of the following main parts;

- Torpedo System 62 comprising torpedo, exercise head and auxiliary equipment

- Weapon platform including tubes and fire control

- Integrated Logistic Support, ILS.

Torpedo System 62 is a dual purpose torpedo system intended as the main armament for submarines, and as a supplement to missiles on surface attack vessels.

This is a heavy weight and long distance torpedo. It is about 6 meter long, has a 533 mm diameter, weights approx. 1400 kilos and it travels with a speed up to 50 knots.

2.2   Propulsion

The torpedo is designed around a new energy system based on High Test Peroxide (HTP) of 85% concentration, and paraffin as propellants.

The engine in the torpedo is an axial piston steam engine with seven cylinders which actuate a cam, shaped like a double sinusodial curve. The pistons are also connected to the pistons of a exhaust gas compressor. The exhaust gases are condensed into water which is led back into the steam building process. The residue from the combustion and condensation is a very small quantity of carbon dioxide which is pumped out into the surrounding water.

For safety reasons the HTP is not allowed to be used before the torpedo has left the ship. Thus the engine has to be started by propellant gas from a pyrotehnical gas generator (i.e. slow burning powder).

2.3   Guidance

After launching the torpedo communicates with the fire control by wire. The homing function is designed around a hydro-acoustic active/passive homing system.

Communication consists of information from the launching ship to the torpedo, as well as the other way. The operator can update the torpedo of target position or give other instructions to the torpedo. The information fed back could be about the position of the torpedo or homing information about the target. The torpedo has a high computer processing capacity, and if the link with the launching ship is broken, it can autonomously find its target, analyse the signals from the homing system and attack the target under difficult conditions.

The propulsor is a pumpjet, with a rotor connected via a flexible coupling to the engine shaft, and a stator. A pumpjet can be said to be very similar to a turbine. This gives the torpedo an extremely good manoeuverability and silent running. To enhance the manoeuvring characteristics, it has been designed to be basically unstable, and as such has to be controlled all the time. Otherwise the trajectory is totally unpredictable.

2.4   Warhead

The warhead has a main charge consisting of a low sensitive explosive, PBX, with high energy content. The charge is sufficiently large to kill or seriously damage all intend targets, e.g. large submarines or warships.

The proximity fuze function senses the underwater contour of a vessel and initiates the high explosive charge in the warhead when the torpedo is under the target.

For exercise purposes the warhead is replaced by an exercise head that uses the standard homing system. This exercise head contains a data logging system and an inflatable balloon, that gives the torpedo better buoyancy after a completed exercise run.

2.5   Hazards

As can be understood from the above there are some serious hazards involved in this system.

The HTP is a highly flammable fluid. Or, to be more precise, it is an oxygen carrier, that can turn a relatively safe material, as for example cloth, into something that will easily self-ignite.

The warhead and fuze doesn't need any comments about hazards and possible consequences.

The instability of the torpedo as mentioned above implies risks if the torpedo is launched with failing guidance system. Once ignited the gas generator in the starting system can not be stopped until the powder has burned out. That will give the engine power for about 15 seconds. One and a half ton running lose at high speed without control is not a nice scenario.

Other computer associated risks, like homing for your own ship, or other friendly vessels, can be listed.

3   Reasons for a Safety-Case

The early safety requirements concentrated on the ammunition properties of the system, or mainly the warhead and pyrotehnical gas generator.

During the course of the development, some new technical requirements had been introduced that would influence on our work.

Early in the programme it was decided that the torpedo should meet requirements on Insensitive Munitions (IM).

This means the that in a situation with abnormal environment, e.g. fire, the torpedo should not cause more damage than the situation as such.

These requirements request the munitions to be tested with fire of at least 900°C and to be shot at by small arms and shrapnel. During these tests the tested sample is allowed to burn but must not detonate.

As mentioned in the description of the system, above, there are other risks involved than the explosives. Although the supplier always has been known to deliver good systems with high standards regarding safety it was felt necessary to evaluate the whole system against requirements that would have been placed today.

The contract did not sufficiently require documentation of how the safety requirements are met or on traceability.

Consequently, with the System Safety approach in the Navy nowadays, we wanted to analyse and document the complete system to show that it fulfils all modern safety requirements. We decided to commence an activity that can be described as collecting a retrospective safety-case. This should result in a Safety Compliance Assessment with a Safety Assessment Report from the supplier and finally a Safety Statement delivered by FMV to the HQ of the Armed Forces.

4   How We Did It

To do the job described we needed the assistance from the supplier. This was not a problem as he was also interested in proving that the system should fulfil relevant safety requirements. We set up a team called System Safety Working Group (SSWG) in accordance with our System Safety manual.

We realised that that major part of the job was information gathering, so the key word must be "systematic". We had to seek lots of old data, records documents etc. An early disadvantage was that a key person, the safety officer at the supplier was new on his job and did not have the project history as a natural part in his mind. He overcame this by hard and good work and was found to be a good detective.

We set up the work along six lines:

$\Rightarrow$ risk assessment

$\Rightarrow$ old requirements

$\Rightarrow$ new requirements

$\Rightarrow$ software

$\Rightarrow$ additional tests

$\Rightarrow$ redesign

These lines were partly in parallel and partly consecutively.

4.1   Risk Assessment

In order to get a complete picture of the safety of the system we had to analyse it regarding potential hazardous events. All parts of the systems were analysed for all phases of predicted lifetime. To define the risk of each event, they were classified according to possible frequency and to the consequences of a mishap.

Whether the risk for a certain event could be accepted or not, was defined by a Risk Assessment Matrix.

If an event was found to have an intolerable risk, actions had to be taken to reduce the frequency and/or the consequence.

frequency:					
consequence:	Frequent	Probable	Occasional	Remote	Improbable
Catastrophic	Intolerable	Intolerable	Intolerable	Intolerable	Lim tolerable
Critical	Intolerable	Intolerable	Intolerable	Lim tolerable	Tolerable
Marginal	Intolerable	Lim tolerable	Lim tolerable	Tolerable	Tolerable
Remote	Lim tolerable	Tolerable	Tolerable	Tolerable	Tolerable

Lim tolerable = Limited tolerable, i.e. decision required separately for each case and for special circumstances.

Fig 1   Risk Assessment Matrix

4.2   Old Requirements

All safety requirements from the contract were listed. Documentation to show how the requirements were met, was searched for and traced. Sometimes we had to performed some extra analyses to evaluate if the requirements really were fulfilled.

It is not unusual to find that the documentation for a specific requirement had to be found in different documents. For example, the test report could refer to s test description, and then this could refer to an analyses that established that the test was relevant for that requirement.

4.3   New Requirements

The new requirements were of two sorts. The requirements that had been introduced as a change of the contract, and those which were not contractual but were regarded as necessary to establish satisfactory safety.

The former type were mainly the IM requirements. They were tested separately.

At a special test range, the torpedo was separated into warhead and the propulsion part. Each part was exposed to an oil fire that produced the required heat of 900°C.

The propulsion part, filled with the full quantity of HTP and propellant as well as a new gas generator with relevant amount of powder, had a smaller explosion, broke into two parts, fell into the oil and finally went up into small pieces with a big bang. Although this was a spectacular event, it happened well after the required time of endurance in the fire. The question was raised, whether this test had been a matter of over-testing as the parts fell into the oil. The question as such, was decided to be irrelevant, as the results had shown an acceptable system with good margins. Furthermore these tests are so expensive that you can't do them twice.

The warhead was a bit of disappointment. It did not explode, it just burnt or deflagrated as the technical term is. This is, of course, acceptable when you expose it to such heat.

At the shooting with small arms and specially designed shrapnel nothing happened. You could say it's a very dull way of to prove that you meet the requirements.

4.4   Software

Software has the disadvantage that it is not easy to prove by testing, that it cannot fail. Part of the assurance is in the methods and processes used to produce the product. To find out if the system for development had been satisfactory we relied on quality audits. Such were made by the supplier as internal audits and had also been performed by FMV as external audits.

Nevertheless, during the project the supplier's quality system had undergone changes. We had to make sure that during the different phases of the project an acceptable quality system had been in place and been applied for the development of the system.

The software in this project, although in total of a considerable size, consists of many smaller packages working in different parts of the system. It had been classified for different levels of criticality and an audit of this classification was made to assure that relevant methods were applied for any safety-critical software.

4.5   Additional Tests

For some parts of the system we were not certain that there were sufficient evidence of acceptable safety.

A special case is the arming and safety unit (SAFU). The decision was taken, even before the contract, that a device already in service with our previous torpedo, was to be used. This was designed to a set of ammunition safety requirements prior to those established in the contract.

Even when we started this work with the safety-case, we thought that the system would not meet the requirements. But thinking is not enough. We performed an analyses on the system and found that it didn't meet modern requirements. What to do? A new design was not conceivable, neither was a ban of the system or even restriction on the utilisation.

We had to look into design around the SAFU. We found that this arrangement around this unit was different form the previous application. For this new torpedo the SAFU was placed in a cylinder that might give us the acceptable solution.

The basic problem was that a single fault in the SAFU, might give a failure and an ignition. If this problem could be isolated in a way, that if an unwanted ignition occurred in the SAFU it would not ignite the whole war head, we should have acceptable safety. The normal path for the ignition energy is blocked until the system is armed, but with a non-intended ignition would the whole arming system explode and spark the main charge. We made some analyses, and finally we designed a test with a complete SAFU in the relevant container and emulated the system and the whole sequence. This test proved an acceptable level of safety, in other words nothing happened outside the container.

Some minor additional tests had to be done to other parts of the system.

4.6   Redesign

One basic problem we had to deal with, was the designed instability, as mentioned under 2.5 Hazards, above. Early during the functional tests we had the indication of the problem. This was not a situation we could live with, so we tried various remedies.

We looked in to ways to alter the design to make the trajectory predictable in case of a guidance fall out. This was found not feasible.

We looked for a possibility to stop the gas generator or divert the gases in case of guidance. This was possible, and the technical solution was proposed and accepted, but it still only solved part of the problem.

The final way to reduce this risk was to minimise the probability of occurrence. The reliability of the guidance system, despite being acceptable for availability, had to be improved. A new inertial navigation system, with higher reliability was introduced, redundancy was added in power supply etc.

As a result of the work in our SSWG, changes in the design were made in many other areas. These changes were, however, of minor character.

6   Conclusions

The best conclusion to draw is; **don't do it**, or to be more specific don't do it as a **retrospective** Safety-Case. Take the decision beforehand. Set up the safety requirements on product, methods and documentation in the contract or at least at the start of the project.

If you have to collect a retrospective safety-case be systematic, set up your safety targets or safety requirements as beginning of your work. Decide what information you need and find it. It is most probably there. If you can't find evidence of acceptable safety try to find other data that can support a judgement on the safety, and show it. If you find evidence of non-compliance with the safety requirements, tell the decision-makers and let them decide whether to alive with it or alter the design.

ASSESSING SAFETY

Where Inspections and Audits Fit Into the Safety Process and How Can We Have Confidence in their Effectiveness

Trevor Cockram

Rolls-Royce plc and The Open University

Abstract

Inspections, audits and reviews have long been part of quality assurance processes. With the introduction of Defence Standards 00-55 and 00-56 independent safety audits have been introduced to monitor the safety process. In this paper I discuss how safety audits are conducted, where we can learn from inspection techniques to improve the way in which safety audits are conducted. I also discuss how we can gain confidence from inspections and audits, given that their effectiveness depends on the people conducting them as well as the quality of the products being considered. I discuss a mathematical model, which can used to estimate the effectiveness of inspections and report some results of its application.

1 Introduction

Independent safety audits have been required for contracts which call up Defence Standards 00-56 and 00-55 to monitor the system developers safety process and to assess the safety case and supporting evidence. This is not to suggest that developers are not doing their job correctly. The requirement for an Independent Safety Auditor (ISA) is to bring a fresh pair of eyes to the system, for the benefit of the procurer or customer of the system and is only concerned with the safety of the system.

Many systems and software development standards including Defence Standard 00-55 [Ministry of Defence 1995] and 00-56 mandate the use of rigorous techniques for the development and verification of the systems. By requiring an independent audit there is a less rigorous human process being introduced as a parallel verification path for safety. We can ask the question why introduce an auditing process that is less rigorous than some of the mathematically formal methods used in the development of the system. By introducing the correct human interaction into the system safety verification process classes of errors or hazards which may not be found by these mathematical rigorous techniques. For example, a development team may be producing perfectly correct software, however, there is a potential system condition that would cause the software to produce a system malfunction which an auditor coming from a different perspective could find.

2 Safety Audits

2.1 The Independent Safety Audit process

The Independent Safety Audit process can be summarised as shown in figure 1

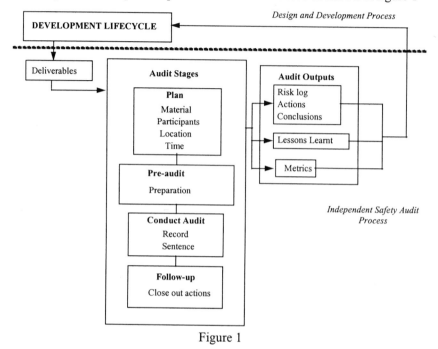

Figure 1

2.1.1 Independent Safety Audit Plan

The plan will contain:

1. Definition of the purpose and scope of the Independent Safety Audit activities, including the identification of systems and subsystems being covered by the plan.

2. A description of the management structure and control for the audit program and for interactions with each of the system/subsystem Design Authorities.

3. Definition of the audit and review programme for each system/subsystem and the planned production/update of Independent Safety Audit Reports. This will require links to the development programmes of each Design Authority, to support flexibility the audit programme may be a separate document referenced by the Independent Safety Audit Plan.

4.   A description of each of the activities in the programme, including its scope and depth.

5.   A description of how the Independent Safety Audit activities are to be integrated with the System Safety Programme Plans, the Software Development Plans, Software V&V Plans and Software Safety Plans for each system/subsystem.

6.   A specification of the contents of the Independent Safety Audit Report.

The audit activities operate in parallel with the development process and a typical audit timeline (figure 2) shows this. Two ISA activities are required, one being the formal safety audits and the second the continuing monitoring activity of the development process to identify potential safety issues early.

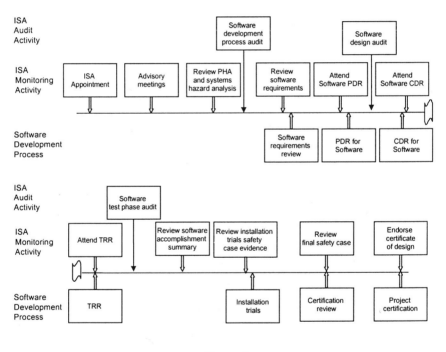

Figure 2

2.1.2 Pre-audit preparation

An effective audit relies on each party adequately preparing for the audit. The developers need to have the material prepared in advance and have marshalled the information they need to answer the questions that the auditors are likely to ask. The auditors in turn need to spend time so that they are familiar with the project being audited and have questions ready to test their understanding of the design and particularly the safety hazards and their mitigation. Whilst the individuals personal experience is important, use can be made from past mistakes and successes through the application of checklists.

2.1.3 Conduct

The detailed audits performed by an ISA will vary in depth in proportion to the safety risk associated with failure to identify a deficiency. The tasks conducted by the ISA can be considered as falling into one of seven categories.

1. Audit - Checking a representative sample of the results of an activity to confirm that they are consistent, factual and conform to expectations.

2. Review - Checking all the results of an activity to confirm that they are consistent, factual and conform to expectations.

3. Assessment - Checking the work that has been performed during an activity and the results of the activity to confirm that it has been conducted and documented in an acceptable manner.

4. Validation - Checking the results of an activity, or sequence of activities, to demonstrate that they are consistent with and partially or completely fulfilled the requirements on the software.

5. Testing - Checking the results of an activity by the observation of its response to specific test cases. Testing may be performed on an animation of a specification, a model of the proposed system, a prototype implementation or the produced software components.

6. Analysis - Checking the results of an activity to demonstrate the presence (or absence) of specific desirable (or undesirable) properties.

7. Verification - Checking the results of an activity to demonstrate that they fulfil the requirements generated by previous activities.

2.1.4 Records

Records generated during the audit will normally consist of reports, which include:

- issues raised during the audit,
- agreed actions with the developers,
- potential risks and hazards,
- close out of actions and conclusions

The results of the audits are released to procurers, customers and their technical representatives through safety audit reports, which indicate progress, outstanding issues and conclusions.

2.1.5 Follow-up

An audit cannot be considered complete until actions and issues raised during the audit have been closed out. The auditor should ensure that each action has been satisfactorily dealt with and agreed action plans to resolve the issues before confirming that the stage has been completed. Lesson learnt from the audit should also be recorded and checklists should be updated.

2.2 Independence

The degree of independence between personnel developing and system and software and personnel conducting the independent safety audit. The advantages and disadvantages of different degrees of independence are summarised in Table 1. The defence standards states that the necessary independence can best be achieved by using an independent company, but an independent part of the same organisation as the developer may be acceptable if adequate technical and managerial independence can be shown to director or board level.

Degree of independence	For	Against
Another person in the same group as the developer.	Familiarity with the project, and tools and methods used. Ability to discuss interpretation and issues with the developer, and to provide instant feedback. Lessons learnt can be used for process improvement.	Lack of objectivity due to similar mindset, common manager, common project constraints. Some errors may be corrected informally and therefore lost.
A separate department within the same organisation provides the ISA who has an independent reporting route to board level	Familiarity with the project, and tools and methods used. Ability to discuss interpretation and issues with the developer as the project progresses.	Less familiar with the details of the development. Still potential for project pressures to influence depth of audits and completeness of reports
Independent company provides the ISA under contract	Auditing is based solely on the documents provided and the interviews conducted. The formality of the interface requires a full recording of the audits.	Possible misinterpretation from supplied documents. Delays due to bureaucratic procedures. Little potential for lessons learnt to be fed back into the process. Still potential conflicts of interest, e.g. follow on contracts.

Table 1

2.3 Software Inspections and Safety Audits

Software inspections as described by Michael Fagan [Fagan M 1976] provide a systematic method to audit the quality of software code as a team activity. This method has been successfully extended to all parts of the software development process and I see no reason why these techniques used in software inspections cannot be extended into an independent safety audit.

Software inspection methods will improve the rigour of an audit, it will give it structure with clearly defined role for the participants. By adding formality to the process it then becomes possible to mathematically model the effectiveness of the inspection process as has been done for software inspections [Cockram TJ 2000].

3. Model of effectiveness

The model requirements therefore need to build from the attributes that affect (or cause) an effective inspection. Additionally the model should not require any information concerning the numbers of errors within the product being inspected. This is a new feature as all the published models of inspection effectiveness use the number of errors found during the inspection as an attribute. As a consequence, existing models can only be applied after the inspection. Further, if managers wish to predict the effectiveness of an inspection they would need to apply analogy between a past inspection and the planned inspection. The analogy approach has been used in estimating costs for projects, e.g. Boehms CoCoMo model [Boehm B 1981], but requires calibration of environment constants. By using a form of artificial intelligence within the model, once initialised the model can adapt to suit differing environments using a learning process. Again the use of artificial intelligence has not been previously reported in measuring software inspections.

A Bayesian Belief model for predicting the effectiveness of software inspections was selected. The process for developing a new Bayesian Belief network (based on the process use in [Spiegelhalter DJ, Dawid AP et al. 1993]) can be defined as:

1. Network definition
2. Initialisation - set up marginal distributions on individual nodes
3. Collect evidence
4. Propagate evidence
5. Observe the effects of the evidence on the network

As a starting point I could take a network diagram (Figure 3) of the causal influences for the quality of software inspections based on the fishbone diagram described by Fagan [Fagan M 1986].

This diagram however, describes the influences on the quality of inspection processes in general and not the effectiveness of a particular inspection. Fagan measures inspection effectiveness in terms of the ratio between the number of defects found during the inspection and the total number of defects found during the life of the product, which does not meet the requirements for an inspection effectiveness model given above. Fagan's diagram does give an indication of the type of attributes that influence the effectiveness of the information

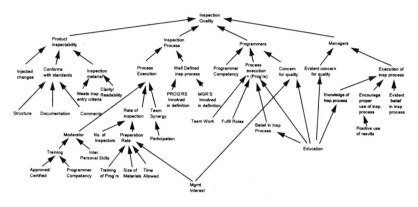

Figure 3

Tree diagrams present a means of modelling, however these suffer from the need to rationalise the level of information within a diagram, and although containing directional arrows does not indicate the meaning of the relationships and the nature of the dependencies. A modelling technique used in representing knowledge, which provided this information, is a semantic network [Hodgson JPE 1991], [McGraw KL and Harbison-Briggs K 1989].

Semantic networks where developed as a form of cognitive modelling that allows individual or collective knowledge to recorded in a systematic way. A semantic network is a graph whose nodes are defined by the objects of a network and whose links denote the relationship between the nodes. The links between nodes are labelled with the relation between the nodes. Two forms of relationship can be used: an "IS-A" relationship denoting a member of a set, or a "HAS" relationship denoting a property characteristic.

I developed a semantic network (Figure 4) that represents the attributes that influence good software inspection effectiveness. Working from the objective a good software inspection the network was built down to the measurable attributes that will be used in the Bayesian model.

3.1 Model Description

The semantic network described in Figure 4 below requires to be presented in a form, which can used by the Bayesian inference engine. A causal network is a specific form of the semantic network where the structure of the network remains as the knowledge representation, with the nodes of the network representing the network attributes, either as input variables (evidence) or calculated inferences (outputs). The arcs of the network represent the dependencies between the attributes, which are defined by the state tables for the network.

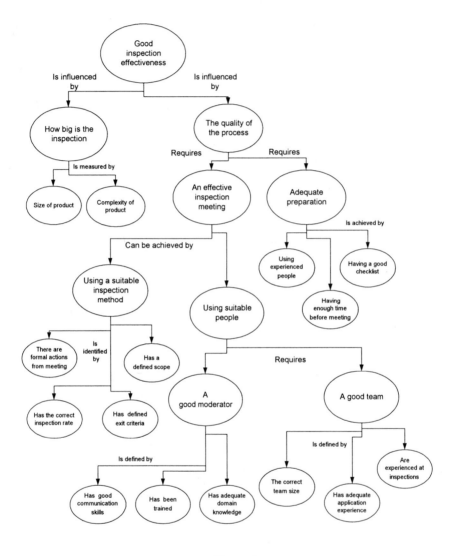

Figure 4

3.1.1 Network attributes

The evidence nodes in the model are populated by metrics that will be collected or estimated for each inspection under evaluation.

3.1.2 Network potentials

Given the structure of the network, the network evidence potential ψ for each clique of the network is defined below:

For the top node of the network – inspection effectiveness,
ψ = P (Inspection effectiveness | Quality of Inspection Process, Size of product, Complexity of product)

Fagan above (Figure 3) described the causal relationships for the quality of an organisation's inspection process. The causal attributes in his network diagram above are for an individual inspection. It has therefore assumed that the organisational influences described by Fagan will be common for all inspections within an organisation and therefore can be treated as a single calibration factor, which will be resolved by the Bayesian updating of the model during its calibration.

As discussed earlier the model predicts the ratio of errors found in a inspection compared with the total number of error in the product. To conduct the validation of the model we therefore need to know the total number of error. This would appear to make the validation of the model impossible, as the total number of errors will depend on the subsequent testing and use to which the software is put, which will vary between applications. Data from the Adams' experiment [Adams EN 1984] suggests that above a certain level of error finding effort, the number of errors found subsequently altered little. The empirical validation of the model can use the total number of error following testing to be sufficient to allow the law of diminishing returns suggested by the Adams' experiment to apply. It is assumed that the product being inspected has few findable[1] errors and hence the inspection effectiveness can be considered conditional independent of the quality of item being inspected.

In developing a model the key attributes for the effective inspection need to be rationalised. Taking the stages of an inspection, the major tasks are the quality of preparation for the inspection and the quality of the error logging.

ψ = P (Quality of Inspection Process | Quality of preparation, Quality of error logging)

For the quality of preparation, three attributes have been identified, these will be determined from simple Boolean metrics.

ψ = P (Quality of preparation | Experience at preparation, Adequate preparation time, Adequate inspection checklist)

---

[1] A findable error is an error that can be found as a result of inspection, analysis or test prior to the release of the software.

The quality of the error logging depends on the quality of the inspection method or procedure being used and the quality of the inspection team.

ψ = P (Quality of error logging | Quality of inspection method, Quality of inspection team)

The quality of the inspection team consists of the quality of the moderator and the quality of the team members.

ψ = P (Quality of inspection team | Quality of moderator, Quality of team members)

There can be variations on the basic inspection method. The detailed differences between these have not be included in this study, instead the attributes of the basic inspection method have been included. Four attributes have been identified, these will be determined from simple Boolean metrics.

ψ = P (Quality of inspection method | Formal actions, Adequate inspection rate, Defined exit criteria, Defined scope)

The quality of the inspection team depends on the quality of the moderator and the quality of the team members. The previous models of inspection effectiveness have failed to address the human factor issues of the team.

For the quality of inspection team members three attributes have been defined, these will be determined by simple Boolean metrics

ψ = P (Quality of inspection team members |Team size, Experience in inspection role, Experience in application)

The importance of the moderator in facilitating the inspection was described by Fagan [Fagan M 1986]. Three attributes have been defined, these will be determined by simple Boolean metrics or from the moderators subjective judgement.

ψ = P (Quality of moderator | Adequate domain knowledge, Training/Experience, Communication skills)

3.2 Input metrics

The following metrics are used to obtain the evidence to populate the network described above.

- Product size

An effective inspection will clearly depend on the product presented for inspection. Of the product attributes, the size of the product will have the greatest influence. There is there a limit on the size of product than can be inspected with the detailed consideration it deserves. For requirements and design inspection, the size of the product is usually considered to be the number of pages. The standard metric for code size is NCLOC[2]. This measure is consistent for a language however the inspection task includes the quality of the comments and the style of the source code presentation.

- Product complexity

The complexity of the product will also influence the performance of the inspection [O'Neill D 1997]. A complex product will take more time to inspect than a less complex product. The issue then becomes which metric should be used. For requirements and design, structural complexity measures as described by Fenton [Fenton NE 1991] are used. For code there has been much debate over complexity metrics, for example [Shepperd MJ 1988], but as a simple indicator of complexity, McCabe cyclomatic complexity measure [McCabe TJ 1976] is used.

- Preparation experience

Looking a product to identify concerns and gaps in understanding to be tested during the logging meeting requires the inspector to be experienced. Bisant and Lyle [Bisant DB and Lyle JR 1989] suggest that in-experienced inspectors should work with a more experienced inspector. The metric selected uses the subjective judgement of the inspector. "Does the inspector think they have sufficient experience at inspection preparation?"

- Adequate preparation time

Ackerman et al. [Ackerman AF, Buchwald LS et al. 1989] and others cite adequate preparation time as a metric for determining the effectiveness of the inspection preparation. The question "Was there adequate preparation time?" is used.

- Adequate inspection checklist,

Most authors agree that checklists are required to support the preparation process as these represent the collected experience and lessons learnt. Myers [Myers GJ 1979] notes that an important part of the inspection process is the use of checklists to identify common errors. Using a checklist, however, should not be considered as the definitive requirement for the areas of concern, but as guidance. The question "Was there an adequate inspection checklist available?" will be used. The subjective judgement of the inspector will be used to determine what is adequate.

---

[2] NCLOC Number of lines on non-comment code, i.e. lines of program text that is not a line only containing comments or a blank line

- Formal actions

Formal actions from an inspection are required to ensure that the errors identified are addressed and that a follow-up occurs. The question "Do formal actions result from the inspection?" will be used.

- Adequate inspection rate

Fagan [Fagan M 1976] cited adequate inspection rate as a required metric, as he noted where an excessive inspection rate was used this caused fewer defects to be found. Experimental work, e.g. Porter et al. [Porter AA, Siy H et al. 1988] shows a correlation between inspection rate and the effectiveness of the inspection. The actual rate will be recorded and then compared with the recommended rates [Strauss SH and Ebenau RG 1994] for code $50>x<150$ NCLOC per hour or $5>x<12$ pages per hour for documents.

- Defined exit criteria

The conditions for which an inspection can be said to successfully complete and meeting its requirements are need. It also provides measurable targets for the inspection. The question "Does the inspection have a defined exit criteria?" will be asked.

- Defined scope

Having a defined scope for the inspection concentrates the effort in the inspection process on the objective of the inspection and does not to waste time on addressing side issues. The question "Does the inspection have a defined scope?" will be asked.

- Inspection team size

The size of the inspection team influences its quality. Too small a team (say just one inspector) can lead to issues being missed with the potential for mind-set thinking. Conversely too large a team leads to reluctance for an inspector to raise an issue. It cam also lead to diversions from the scope of the inspections, with the inspection becoming an educational process rather than a error identification process. By consensus in the published material, 4 or 5 including the moderator is considered the optimum size. Using this criteria the actual team size will be tested, $3< x >6$.

- Experience in inspection role

Selecting an inspector within experience in the role he or she has been asked to do was identified by Knight and Meyers [Knight JC and Meyers EA 1991] as a major improvement to the inspection process. Three years within the role has been selected as the value for extensive experience.

- Experience in the application

Experience in the application is also required to identify issues that are important to the application. Two years has been selected as the value for adequate experience.

- Moderator domain knowledge

A moderator is not required to have specific experience in the application or the project being inspected, however, they do need adequate knowledge of the domain. The moderator is requested to judge subjectively if their domain knowledge is adequate.

- Moderator Training and or experience

Moderator training and or experience was considered by Fagan to be an important attribute in the quality of the inspection process. The criteria for this are either completion of formal moderator training or three years experience at carry out inspections.

- Moderator communication skills

To facilitate an inspection the moderator must be able to communicate and to actively listen and encourage team members to communicate. The moderator is requested to judge his or her own communication skills as poor, fair or good.

3.3 Model Initialisation

The Inspection Effectiveness model requires initialising by establishing the prior belief of the conditional probability distribution of intermediate variables. The initialisation of a Bayesian network requires that the a priori belief for the conditional probability for each state the variables in the parent nodes is specified. Experience is used to provide a priori conditional probability values for each node matrix. For the evidence nodes, which are at the bottom of the network, the initial distribution for each state of these variables is set to be flat over its range, i.e. the evidence has an equal probability for each state. This experience was elicited by conducting a survey from two independent groups of engineers with experience of inspection. The two groups operate a similar inspection process at two different sites of the same organisation. As an example the results for the quality of moderator were:

3.3.1 Survey results

The opinion survey for the attribute contributing to quality of moderator produced the following table of the importance of the attributes (see table 2)

	Most Important	Important	Neutral	Not Important	Irrelevant
Communication skills	13	26	6	0	0
Inspection experience/ training	7	20	15	2	0
Adequate domain knowledge	3	21	12	2	0

Table 2

The attributes were also ranked in order of importance in table 3.

	1	2	3
Communication skills	19	14	6
Inspection experience/ training	12	12	15
Adequate domain knowledge	9	11	19

Table 3

These results were then translated into the a-prori conditional probability tables that are required for the Bayesian Belief Network. These tables were completed using a brain storming activity with a sub-set of the inspectors surveyed, with the ranking determination being used as the guidance for completing the table. It would have been possible to request all the inspections to complete the tables, however, this idea was rejected as this would have been very time consuming and it would have resulted in a lower number of returns. There would also be a potential for personal agendas to unfairly weight the tables.

An alternative method would be to use the normalised values from the survey and then use a given distribution, e.g. a Beta distribution to populate the a priori conditional probability tables. For continuous distributions there is some support provided within Hugin version 5.2, although this is not provided for discrete distributions, which is being used here. Although this method is more mathematically based, it will provide prior probabilities based on the given distribution, rather than the expert opinion of inspectors.

As an example results of the activity for the quality of moderator are shown in table 4.

Poor	Fair	Good	Domain Experience	Inspection Experience/ Training	Communication Skills
0.85	0.1	0.05	Poor	Poor	Poor
0.5	0.3	0.2	Poor	Poor	Fair
0.2	0.3	0.5	Poor	Poor	Good
0.6	0.3	0.1	Poor	Good	Poor
0.2	0.6	0.2	Poor	Good	Fair
0.1	0.1	0.8	Poor	Good	Good
0.7	0.25	0.05	Good	Poor	Poor
0.25	0.5	0.25	Good	Poor	Fair
0.1	0.3	0.6	Good	Poor	Good
0.5	0.3	0.2	Good	Good	Poor
0.15	0.35	0.5	Good	Good	Fair
0.05	0.1	0.85	Good	Good	Good

Table 4

3.4 Model verification

At the time of writing limited verification of the model had been completed. The results as shown in Figure 5 show the results of inspections conducted on 100 items. The results show a reasonable correlation between the model prediction of inspection effectiveness with the actual distribution of inspection effectiveness measured by dividing the number of issues found during the inspection with the total number of issues found subsequently by later inspection test or installation.

Further verification and validation of the model is in progress. This includes sensitivity analysis of the network and the prior belief; the effect of network adaptation from calibration data, further sensitivity analysis and verification against actual sets of data for adapted networks and trials using data from other sources to determine the model's applicability to other inspection processes.

It is intended to report on the results of this further testing at the symposium.

4. Conclusions

The model described above provides a means of measuring inspection effectiveness objectively. If the effectiveness for a particular inspection was found to be low then changes to the inspection process or the amount of material being inspected at any one time can be adjusted to improve the inspection effectiveness. The model lends itself to allowing users to use it for asking "what if?" questions to see if a particular change will make the inspection more effective.

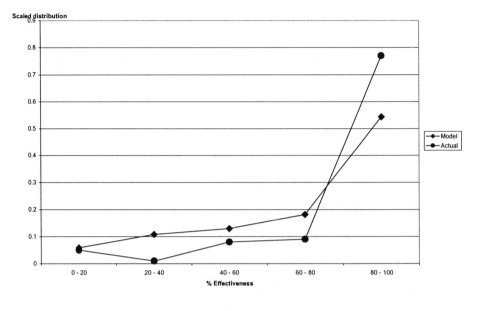

Figure 5

By using the software inspection technique for parts of a safety audit, the formality of those parts can be improved and the results measured in an objective way. The use of a measured technique as part of the safety audit process will give parties, such as the system developers, certification authorities and the safety audit team themselves, more confidence in that process.

Acknowledgements

I would like to thank my colleagues and my academic supervisor Prof. Darrel Ince for their support, helpful comments and suggestions.

References

[Ackerman AF, Buchwald LS, et al. 1989]. "Software inspections: an effective verification process." IEEE Software **May 1989**: 31-36.
[Adams EN 1984]. "Optimizing preventative service of software products." *IBM Journal* **28**(1): 2-14.
[Bisant DB and Lyle JR 1989]. "A two-person inspection method to improve programming productivity." *IEEE Trans Soft Eng* **SE-15**(10): 1294-1304.
[Boehm B 1981] Boehm B (1981). Software Engineering Economics. Englewood Cliffs, Prentice Hall.
[Cockram TJ 2000]. "The contribution of a measured process to software safety and productivity" (PhD thesis in preparation). Computer Science Department. Open University. Milton Keynes

[Fagan M 1976]. "Design and code inspections to reduce errors in program development." *IBM Systems Journal* **15**(3): 182-211.

[Fagan M 1986]. "Advances in software inspections." *IEEE Trans Soft Eng* **SE-12**(7): 744-751.

[Fenton NE 1991]. Software Metrics - A rigorous approach. London, Chapman and Hall.

[Hodgson JPE 1991], Knowledege Representation and Language in AI. Chichester, Ellis Horwood.

[Knight JC and Meyers EA 1991]. "Phased inspections and their implementation." *ACM Sigsoft Software Engineering Notes* **16**(3): 29-35.

[McCabe TJ 1976]. "A Complexity Measure." *IEEE Trans Soft Eng* **SE-2**(4): 308-320.

[McGraw KL and Harbison-Briggs K 1989]. Knowledge Acquisition: Principles and Guidelines. Englewood Cliffs, Prentice Hall.

[Ministry of Defence 1995] Ministry of Defence Directorate of Standardisation (1995). Defence Standard 00-55: The procurement of safety critical software in defence systems.

[Myers GJ 1979]. The art of software testing. New York, John Wiley.

[O'Neill D 1997] Software Inspections see:
http://www.sei.cmu.edu/str/descriptions/inspections

[Porter AA, Siy H, et al.1988]. "Understanding the source of variations in software inspections." *ACM Trans on Software Engineering and Methodology* **7**(1): 41-79.

[Shepperd MJ 1988]. "A critique of cyclomatic complexity as a software metric." *Systems Engineering Journal* **3**(2): 30-36.

[Spiegelhalter DJ, Dawid AP et al. 1993] Bayesian Analysis in Expert Systems BAIES Report BR-27

[Strauss SH and Ebenau RG 1994]. Software Inspection Process. New York, McGraw-Hill.

Safety Analysis of Vehicle-Based Systems

Peter H Jesty & Keith M Hobley
University of Leeds
Leeds, UK

Richard Evans
Rover Group Ltd
Coventry, UK

Ian Kendall
Jaguar Cars Ltd
Coventry, UK

Abstract

The Motor Industry Software Reliability Association Steering Group is producing guidance on the safety analysis of vehicle-based systems to support its original Development Guidelines for Vehicle Based Software. Using existing generic techniques, these new guidelines will explain how they may be used in the automotive context. Topics will include System Analysis, Hazard Identification, Hazard Analysis, the identification of Safety Integrity Levels, and the uses of Failure Mode and Effects Analysis and Fault Tree Analysis.

1 Introduction

In 1994 the Motor Industry Software Reliability Association (MISRA) published its guidelines for the development of software for vehicle-based systems [MISRA 1994]. A key aspect of these guidelines is that the hazards associated with a system must be both understood, and taken into consideration, from the beginning of its design cycle. It is therefore important to:

- assess the risks associated with the behaviour of a system;
- do this early enough in order to take design actions that can reduce those risks to an acceptable level;
- provide documentary evidence of the reasoning that lies behind the design decisions made.

Whilst the scope of the original MISRA Guidelines is software, system issues are covered to the extent that they influenced software development. Eight specific issues are addressed:

- Integrity
- Software in Control Systems
- Noise, EMC and Real-Time
- Diagnostics and Integrated Vehicle Systems
- Software Metrics
- Verification and Validation
- Sub-Contracting of Automotive Software
- Human Factors in Software Development

In the section on integrity the MISRA Guidelines call for Safety Analysis to be performed, which includes Hazard Analysis and Integrity Assessment. Whilst it does not mandate the use of specific techniques or methods for safety analysis it does refer to Preliminary Safety Analysis (PSA), which is part of the 'PASSPORT' methodology [Hobley 1995a]. MISRA has found that there are a number of approaches that can be used depending on the nature and scope of the system being analysed. A good example being a Preliminary Hazard Analysis (PHA) based on a Hazard and Operability (HAZOP) study [Redmill 1999]. The automotive industry has long been in favour of Failure Mode & Effects Analysis (FMEA) as a means to manage the system and hardware risks associated with its products. However, FMEA is not easy to apply before a design exists, and is therefore often under-utilised.

The MISRA Steering Group therefore decided to produce a document to show how these techniques are related, and to provide detailed and practical recommendations for bringing the techniques together. The document, due in 2000, will explain how to approach PSA for 'blue-sky' conceptual systems, and PHA for systems whose basic design can be already assumed. It will not only expand on the recommendations made in the original MISRA Guidelines on the issue of 'integrity' but will also augment the scope to include system and hardware as well as software considerations. The treatment of safety analysis will also be expanded to include Detailed Safety Analysis (DSA) as well as Preliminary Safety Analysis (PSA). The intention is to offer ideas which complement the automotive industry's quality system standards, which include specific requirements for FMEA [QS 9000 1995 and VDA 1996], in such a way as to bring the concepts covered by PASSPORT, and in standards such as [IEC 61508 1999] and [DEFSTAN 00-56 1996], into a single 'MISRA Safety Analysis' approach.

This paper describes the principal contents of the proposed MISRA approach to safety analysis. It is divided into three main sections as follows:

- A description of how PSA can be applied to vehicle system concepts, and of how PHA can be applied to top-level designs;
- A discussion of how Safety Integrity Levels (SIL) can be assigned to vehicle systems, both those that are related to the moving vehicle scenario and those which are not;
- A description of how FMEA and FTA may be applied to automotive systems as part of DSA.

The responsibility for the safety of a vehicle ultimately resides with the manufacturer, which must therefore be free to choose the most appropriate set of techniques for its circumstances. Thus, following the philosophy of the initial MISRA Guidelines [MISRA 1994], the safety analysis document will not mandate the methodology that should be used; instead the properties that should be demonstrated are given, together with some systematic techniques that may be used to obtain them.

2 Hazard Analysis of Vehicle Systems

Before one can perform a hazard analysis it is necessary to produce an abstraction, or model, of the system on which to base the analysis. By its very nature a model must be an approximation, since the only 'model' that can be identical to the system is the system itself [Carroll 1939]. It is therefore necessary to choose the approximation so that it highlights the features necessary for the particular task. Although some definitions of a hazard limit themselves to physical situations with a potential for human injury, in practice one should include all situations that can threaten people, property and the natural environment; thus any model that is used as a target for a PSA and/or PHA should highlight the boundary between the system under consideration and those 'things' that might suffer the hazard, and the interaction between them. The model must therefore show:
- Components, especially those close to the boundary, with their attributes;
- The interconnections between the components, with their attributes.
- The boundaries of various kinds;

2.1 Components

In its basic physical sense a system is built up with components. The level of detail at which one considers a component will depend on the nature of the work and the type of the system, but it is wise to choose a consistent level at each stage, e.g. all line replaceable units (LRU), or all electronic components.

The attributes of a component include not only its physical properties, but also the function(s) that it performs (for this reason it is sometimes called a *functional element*). Thus the failure modes associated with a component can be physical, e.g. short circuit, or functional, e.g. brakes do not act on the wheels.

The behaviour of a system, however, is usually more than just the sum of the behaviours of its components. A system may often exhibit *emergent properties* which can only be obtained when the components are working together. One consequence of this is that an analysis based on LRUs may not produce the same results as one based solely on the electrical and mechanical components of which it is comprised. This is particularly true when some of the components are programmable.

2.2 Inter-connections

Components work together through their inter-connections. Mechanical components use their connections to pass forces between each other, electrical components pass signals, and programmable components may pass signals and/or messages (information). The attributes associated with an interconnection are the 'thing' that is being passed, the rate at which it is doing so, and its value, accuracy, phase etc.

2.3 Boundaries

A knowledge of the boundary is essential in order to define the scope of any analysis. There are four different types of 'boundary', not necessarily distinct, which are relevant when performing a safety analysis on vehicle based systems:

- **System Boundary** - This defines the scope of the 'system of interest' to the development team. This is unlikely to be an entire vehicle, but the automotive industry does refer to its major vehicle units as 'systems' rather than 'sub-systems'.

- **Boundary of the Target of Evaluation (TOE)** - This term can be used to define the scope of the item being considered during a specific safety analysis. It will often be coincident with the system boundary, but may only take in a sub-set of the system of interest, e.g. the team developing the power train may wish to analysis the engine and gear box separately. A TOE is unlikely to cross the system boundary.

- **Zone of Responsibility** - This defines the scope of the authority held by the development team, and relates to the degree to which they can control, or influence, changes in both their own design, and in the design of other systems. This zone is likely to be defined according to the business and organisational requirements of the company, e.g. by office, building, department or country. Whilst it may be normal for the development team to have full responsibility for their own system of interest, it is essential that the company has a mechanism in place whereby, should the development team identify changes that are both necessary and outside their own zone of responsibility, then it is possible for this information to be acted upon in a proper manner.

  Figure 1 shows a possible relationship between the System Boundary, the Boundary of the TOE and the Zone of Responsibility, and an example is given in Section 2.6.

- **Moving Vehicle Boundary or Vehicle Hazard Boundary** - Whilst a few vehicle systems may be able to cause harm by themselves, most hazards will be related to the motion of the whole vehicle. In this situation it is necessary to consider the vehicle boundary and this is discussed below.

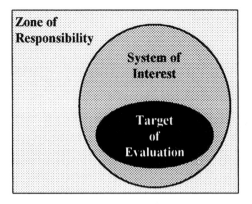

Figure 1 - Relationship between Three of the Boundaries

2.3.1 Vehicle hazard Boundary

This is the interface between the (emergent properties of all the) systems that make up the moving vehicle, and all the things with which the vehicle may interact, or influence, otherwise known as its environment. This environment includes the driver and passengers, the road, road-side furniture, other vehicles and the atmosphere. The mechanisms by which, and the interfaces through which, a vehicle may interact with its environment are varied and some of them are shown in Figure 2.

Figure 2 is not complete, deliberately, because new systems may introduce new interactions, and it is the responsibility of the team performing the hazard analysis to ensure that their version reflects the reality of their situation. The possible interactions with the environment are of three basic types:

- **Inputs** - These relate to all the devices that a driver can use to provide control signals to a system in the vehicle, e.g. throttle, brake pedal, switches;
- **Outputs** - These relate to all the displays and warning systems for the driver, e.g. speedometer, ABS failure lamp, vision enhancement systems;
- **Physical properties** - These relate to the nature of the physical materials used, e.g. flammability, sharpness, and the emissions that are expelled from the vehicle, e.g. exhaust, compressed air;

There are two main classes of emergent properties that are due to the combined effect of a number of individual systems:

- **Movement** - These relate to the basic longitudinal and lateral movements of the vehicle, e.g. acceleration, deceleration, and steering;
- **Stability** - These interactions relate to the ease with which a driver can control the Movement, e.g. yaw, pitch and roll;

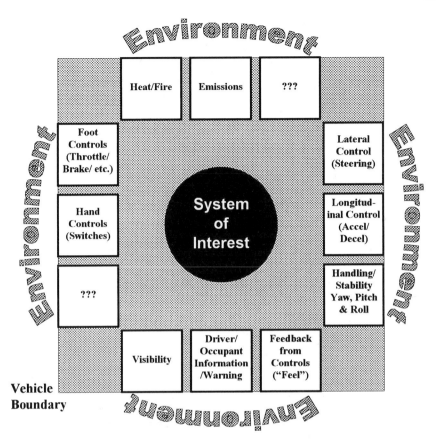

Figure 2 - Interactions and Emergent Properties at the Vehicle Hazard Boundary

2.4 Choice of Model

The choice as to which model should be used depends both on the type of system under investigation, and on how much is known at the concept stage of the design. There are two basic types of TOE associated with vehicles:

- A TOE with interfaces to people and/or other vehicles etc., e.g. autonomous cruise control with radar detection (see Figure 3a);
- A TOE with very well defined interfaces to other vehicle systems (see Figure 3b).

These different types of TOE tend to require different approaches to modelling at their respective boundaries. Figure 4 shows the situation at the boundary of any TOE. The TOE interacts with its environment through its Boundary Elements; these are situated immediately inside the boundary of the TOE. The 'thing'

96

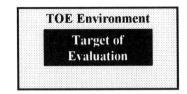

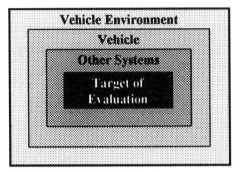

a) Open Target of Evaluation

b) Closed Target of Evaluation

Figure 3 - Different types of TOE

immediately outside the boundary of the TOE, and with which the Boundary Element interacts, is a Terminator.

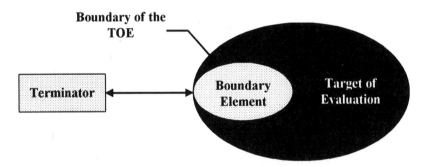

Figure 4 - The Boundary of the TOE

For systems of the form shown in Figure 3a the Boundary Element tends to be of three basic types:

- If the TOE is communicating with another system X, then the Boundary Element will normally be an 'Interface to X', or its name;
- If the Terminator is a person the Boundary Element will normally be the human machine interaction device;
- If the TOE is a control system then the Boundary Elements will normally include sensors and actuators.

Note that for systems of the form shown in Figure 3a the Terminators may not be well defined, however, for those shown in Figure 3b both the Terminators and the Boundary Elements are normally well defined and understood.

2.5 Preliminary Safety Analysis

For TOEs of the form shown in Figure 3a the PASSPORT methodology for PSA has been shown to be particularly effective as a systematic way of identifying hazards at the concept phase of the design [Hobley 1995b]. Hazard analysis is performed as part of PSA, along with system analysis and system decomposition, to the extent necessary to be able to allocate SILs. The recommended model is known as the PASSPORT Diagram, a very simplified version of which is shown in Figure 5. Note that the model only includes items that are situated within the boundary of the TOE, the description of the Terminators will be included in the textual description of each Boundary Element that must accompany the Diagram. Note also that the 'Data' is that which passes from the Boundary Element to/from the Kernel of the TOE, and not the data that passes from the Boundary Element to/from the Terminator, which may be different in nature due to some transformation that may take place inside the Boundary Element.

Figure 5 - Simplified Outline PASSPORT Diagram

2.5.1 Hazard Identification

Hazard identification is undertaken using an adapted version of FMEA that is sometimes called 'What If?' analysis. Each boundary element is considered in turn and the hazards to the environment are considered systematically (see Section 2.7), both for when the TOE is working normally, and when there is a failure in the operation of the Boundary Element, or there is an error in the data being transferred from/to it.

2.5.2 High-Level Safety Requirements

It is also possible to identify the top-level safety requirements for the TOE by analysing the information that does exist about the design using an adapted version of FTA called 'What Causes?' analysis. This will identify the (high level) faults that may result in a hazard, for which suitable safety requirements may then be formulated to mitigate their effect.

2.6 Preliminary Hazard Analysis

Whilst the PASSPORT methodology can be used for TOEs of the form shown in Figure 3b, especially if they are novel, the more normal situation is when an existing system is being replaced by more modern technology, or being enhanced in functionality. In this situation an outline design of the TOE and its Terminators can be drawn and the system analysis and system decomposition steps of PSA are not necessary.

At Rover Group Ltd, a Preliminary Hazard Analysis process has been defined in order to meet the MISRA requirements for Safety Analysis. It was strongly influenced by Defence Standard 00-56 [DEFSTAN 00-56 1996] but has been developed specifically for use with embedded automotive controllers. It has been applied during the development of engine management and transmission systems, and of chassis controllers.

The first phase of the Rover process involves hazard identification using Hazard and Operability (HAZOP) studies. The process used is very similar to that described in Defence Standard 00-58 [DEFSTAN 00-58 1996] but with specific deviations and enhancements where necessary.

The most important concepts defined in Defence Standard 00-58 are:
- **Entity** - A label associated with an interconnection between components;
- **Attribute** - A property of an entity.
- **Guide word** - A word that describes a deviation from the design intent.

The HAZOP study involves the construction of HAZOP cases through the combination of entities, attributes and guide words in order to describe some deviation from design intent. Each HAZOP case is then used to identify potential hazards e.g.

What if [Entity] [Attribute] is [Guide word]?

The process used by Rover can be characterised as follows:
- It is based on Defence Standard 00-58 [DEFSTAN 00-58 1996];
- The entities for the analysis are only associated with the outputs of the control unit;
- The choice of attributes is derived from behaviour at the electro-mechanical boundary;
- An application specific set of guide words has been defined;
- The causes of hazards are not investigated.

In the Rover PHA process entities are labels given to the outputs of embedded controllers. The restriction of the analysis to outputs is a pragmatic decision based on the assumption that an analysis of outputs will identify all those hazards that would have been identified during an analysis of the inputs. In addition, the behaviour that results due to deviations from design intent at the inputs depends on the functionality that has been/will be implemented. This may not be well defined at the earlier stages of the development, which is when the PHA should take place.

A common problem when performing a HAZOP study has been the choice of attributes. An output from a controller can be considered from many perspectives e.g. voltage/current levels, frequency, output state, position of an actuator, etc. Experience has shown that the best attributes to choose are those associated with the behaviour of components being controlled on the electro-mechanical interface.

Consider the example of the embedded controller depicted in Figure 6 which maintains the vehicle ride height by controlling an air suspension system. The output controls a valve that regulates the flow of compressed air into an air spring. The opening of this valve is managed by a solenoid, the current to which is regulated by varying the mark space ratio of a pulse width modulated signal at the output of the controller. Whilst the voltage at the output pin of the controller could be the focus of the HAZOP study, experience suggests that it is more meaningful and productive to consider the effects directly due to the behaviour of the actuator, rather than as a consequence of following the cause and effect sequence arising from some behaviour described at the output pin of the embedded controller. In other words, the HAZOP cases are mainly used to describe behaviour of an electro-mechanical actuator rather than that associated with the immediate boundary of the TOE.

The Rover PHA process defines its own set of guide words which have been chosen for relevance to the actuator technologies currently being used. If the nature of the system being controlled changed then the list of guide words may need to be revised.

Figure 6 depicts an embedded controller with one output signal that controls a pneumatic valve, and one input signal which is used to provide vehicle height feedback from a height sensor. The height sensor input will play no part in the HAZOP study because inputs are ignored. The interconnection between the controller and the valve becomes an entity for the HAZOP study. In this example, a good choice of attribute would be valve position, since it is associated with a component on the electro-mechanical boundary. It is then necessary to choose a set of guide words that are meaningful in the context of this system. One possible choice would be the guide word MAXIMUM so, for example, the HAZOP case would become:

What if [VALVE] [POSITION] is [MAXIMUM]?

This entity, attribute, guide word combination describes some deviation from the design intent, however, it does not have a defined meaning in the context of this

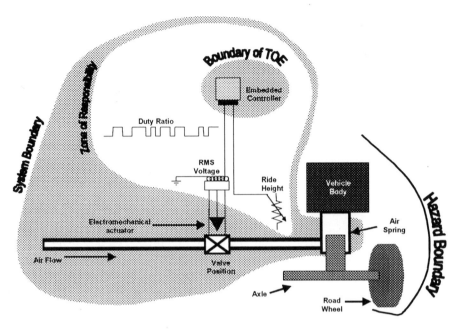

Figure 6 - Example air suspension system

system due to the generic nature of the guide words. It is therefore necessary to assign a meaning to this question. A possible interpretation of its meaning is that the valve is fully open. The effects of this behaviour would then be determined and traced to the relevant hazards. This would be achieved using the combined knowledge and experience of a carefully selected group of engineers.

Figure 6 also shows the relevant boundaries in the context of this example as follows:

- **System Boundary** - This denotes the vehicle system of interest. It includes all those components associated with the air suspension system - irrespective of technology.
- **Boundary of the TOE** - This only includes the controller because the purpose of the analysis in this example is to determine the SIL for the controller.
- **Zone of Responsibility** - This boundary exists by virtue of the company organisation. In this example this boundary encompasses the electrical/electronic and programmable electronic components within the air suspension system.
- **Vehicle Hazard Boundary** - This is primarily associated with the interface between the road wheels and the road, since an air suspension system may cause hazards related to the lateral control, handling and stability of the vehicle.

2.7 Vehicle Hazard Identification

The [IEC 61508 1999] definitions of Fault, Error and Failure highlight the fact that, in complex systems, there may be a chain of events between an initial fault and the final hazard. This is shown in Figure 7 for a vehicle, using the concepts introduced in Figure 1 and Figure 3b.

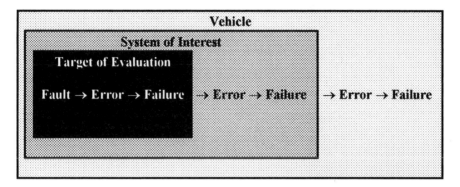

Figure 7 - Fault, Error, Failure Chain of Events within a Vehicle

Thus in order to identify most of the hazards associated with a vehicle, especially when the vehicle is moving, consideration must be given to the relationship of the TOE to Figure 2, noting in particular that the outputs of the TOE may be combined with those of other systems to produce an emergent property. Figure 2 may be used as a form of checklist whereby each interaction between the vehicle and its environment is considered in turn as to whether a property of, or a failure in, the TOE may produce a hazard at the boundary of the moving vehicle.

3 Safety Integrity Levels

In order to take advantage of being able to vary the degree of rigour with which a system may be specified and designed, as specified by [IEC 61508 1999] and followed by [MISRA 1994], it is first necessary to classify the hazards according to their severity, after which the system can be allocated a Safety Integrity Level (SIL). There are currently four discrete levels for specifying the safety integrity requirements to be allocated to the safety-related system, in order to reduce the risk (*probability of occurrence × degree of severity of harm*) of a hazard to an acceptable level. [IEC 61508 1999] suggests a number of different techniques for the identification of SILs but, because they are targeted at specific types of protection system, they are not universally applicable and each industry sector needs to produce its own interpretation [Redmill 1998].

Whilst there are a few protection systems within a vehicle, e.g. a system to stop an electric window trapping a limb, most moving vehicle systems exhibit different properties. Until now all the effort on this subject has been on providing a technique for categorising moving vehicle hazards (see Section 3.1.2), but MISRA felt that this should be enhanced to cover all vehicle system hazards.

3.1.1 Vehicle Protection Systems

It has been found possible to use a risk graph, similar to that shown in Figure 8, to allocate a SIL to a vehicle protection system. The exact meaning of each parameter and the final allocation of SILs must, however, gain consensus within the industry before the final version of the graph can be placed in the public domain.

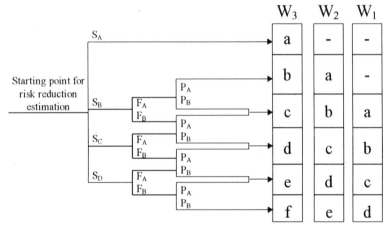

S = Severity of consequence risk parameter
F = Frequency and exposure time risk parameter
P = Possibility of avoiding hazard risk parameter
W = Probability of the unwanted occurrence
a-f = SIL or other safety integrity requirements

Figure 8 - Risk Graph based on [IEC 61508 1999]

There is an interesting issue with regard to certain vehicle protection systems whose objective is to reduce the risk of a hazard that is currently considered acceptable, e.g. a system to warn the driver of a high vehicle that it is about to pass under a low bridge. In this situation it should be noted that a SIL only defines the degree of risk reduction desired, whether or not the original hazard was considered acceptable. However, before one is tempted to reason that an anti-bridge-bashing system is not safety-related, because a driver should always check the signs, it must be born in mind that, once drivers are aware of the system's existence, they will be tempted to rely on it alone to indicate whether they can pass safely under a bridge.

It should be noted that it is not in the remit of MISRA to define SILs for any particular system, this is the responsibility of the designers and the manufacturers of that system. MISRA can only provide advice as to how the task may be done.

3.1.2 Controllability

There are, however, few vehicle protection systems and therefore few systems to which a risk graph can be applied; most of them are control systems. In addition vehicle based systems are obviously not static, and the road traffic environment within which they operate varies continuously. The consequence of this is that when analysing the "severity of harm", one usually ends up with "it depends on the situation at the time". Taking the worst case scenario is not much help either, because it is usually possible to dream up a situation where even what would normally be considered to be a 'mild' hazard could produce the worst possible conceivable event.

We therefore need a technique which is independent of the traffic conditions, and that can take into account the possible reactions of the road user to the occurrence of the hazard. It also needs to be independent of the number of units deployed so that, say, a high volume vehicle manufacturer would use the same SIL for the same system in the same application, as a low volume manufacturer.

A technique that satisfies all these conditions is known as *controllability* [Hobley 1995a & Jesty 1996]. This provides a qualitative assessment of the:

controllability of the safety of the situation (after a failure)

and is similar, though not identical, to the categorisation of aircraft hazards used in [DO-178B/ED-12B 1992]. The technique makes no attempt is made to classify the final effect of the hazard but uses the fact that during its occurrence, e.g. between a failure and a final event, there is a loss of control. The degree of loss of control is assessed by considering:

- The degree of control that the sub-system has on the safety of the system when it is working normally, and that therefore might be lost;
- The number, and type, of other sub-system(s) available to mitigate the loss of control (caused by the failure);
- The speed with which it is necessary for a user to react with the back-up sub-system(s) in order to mitigate the loss of control;

after which an assessment is made of the Controllability Category according to Table 1.

The distinction between the risk graph and the controllability approaches is that controllability does not consider the frequency of exposure to the hazard nor the probability of its occurrence. Travelling in a vehicle along a road is, by its very nature, a hazardous undertaking, and thus the 'frequency and exposure time' parameter is effectively a constant. The 'probability of the unwanted occurrence' parameter only applies to protection systems. Controllability therefore classifies the risk solely in terms of the immediate potential consequence to the vehicle occupants.

Controllability Categories	Definition	SIL
Uncontrollable	This relates to failures whose effects are not controllable by the vehicle occupants, and which are most likely to lead to extremely severe outcomes. The outcome cannot be influenced by a human response.	4
Difficult to Control	This relates to failures whose effects are not normally controllable by the vehicle occupants but could, under favourable circumstances, be influenced by a mature human response. They are likely to lead to very severe outcomes.	3
Debilitating	This relates to failures whose effects are usually controllable by a sensible human response and, whilst there is a reduction in the safety margin, can usually be expected to lead to outcomes which are at worst severe.	2
Distracting	This relates to failures which produce operational limitations, but a normal human response will limit the outcome to no worse than minor.	1
Nuisance Only	This relates to failures where safety is not normally considered to be affected, and where customer satisfaction is the main consideration.	0

Table 1 - Definition of Controllability Categories [MISRA 1994]

4 Detailed Safety Analysis

Once the design phase begins a detailed safety analysis (DSA) may be started. The objectives of the DSA are to:
- Confirm the findings of the PSA or PHA;
- Identify any additional hazards that may have been introduced as a result of the design used;
- Identify the possible causes of each hazard;
- Confirm the allocation of SILs;
- Predict the frequency with which a particular failure may occur;
- Identify the degree to which the system can accommodate any fault.

Whilst these processes should be undertaken for each iteration of the design, in practice they are usually only performed once, due to the time and resources required. This means that although issues may be identified, their solution may not be confirmed.

The two principal techniques that are used during DSA are FMEA and FTA. However, although they are in common use, MISRA discovered that the details of how they were done, and the objectives for performing them differed both between companies, and sometimes within companies. This is not surprising because, for example, the purpose of FMEA may include [IEC 812 1985]:

- Evaluation of the effects and the sequences of events caused by each identified item's failure mode, from whatever cause, at various levels of a system's functional hierarchy;
- Determination of the significance or criticality of each failure mode as to the system's correct function or performance and the impact on the reliability and/or safety of the related process;
- Classification of identified failure modes according to their detectability, diagnosability, testability, item replaceability, compensating and operating provisions (repair, maintenance and logistics, etc.) and other relevant characteristics;
- Estimation of measures of the significance and probability of failure, subject to the availability of data.

When FMEA is used to determine the criticality and probability of occurrence of the failure modes it is sometimes given the title Failure Mode Effects and Criticality Analysis (FMECA), but this is not applied universally.

The QS 9000 document set [QS 9000 1995], which includes a section detailing the unified approach to FMEA, was defined by the 'big 3' in the US (Ford, GM, Chrysler), and is now widely adopted by many of their subsidiaries and suppliers. Similarly the VDA (an association of German automotive manufacturers and suppliers) have published FMEA Guidelines as part of their Quality Assurance Guidelines [VDA 1996]. These publications include both 'Design FMEA', which is actually FME(C)A as defined above, and 'Process FMEA', which applies the same technique to the manufacturing process for a component.

FMEA is a bottom-up inductive technique that works up from a fault, or failure mode, to the resultant effect. A complementary technique is FTA which is a top-down deductive technique which starts from an event and seeks to determine its causes. The PASSPORT Methodology recommends the use of both FMEA and FTA as a means of providing an independent check, using FMEA to find the effect, and then using FTA to check whether the possible causes of those effects coincide with the original faults, or failure modes [Hobley 1995b]. The PASSPORT Methodology also recommends that, before either an FMEA or an FTA is begun there should be a check on the design for both its completeness and its consistency, since there is little point in analysing something that is inherently wrong.

4.1 Failure Mode and Effects Analysis

FMEA can be applied at many different levels in the hierarchy of a vehicle. Figure 9, which is one way of decomposing a vehicle, shows that there are a number of different levels at which it may be sensible to undertake an FMEA. However, as shown in Figure 3b, the only level at which the end effects produce hazards is at the vehicle boundary. It is therefore necessary to maintain traceability between the fault, or failure mode, and the final hazard through the 'intermediate effects' at each level.

4.1.1 Scoring

When performing an FMECA, the usual situation, the automotive industry tends to use three parameters for each failure, namely 'severity', 'occurrence' and 'detection', and to give each one a score between 1 and 10 (not critical - extremely critical). Whilst the generic definition of these scores are not tailored to the specific considerations relevant to programmable systems, both [QS9000 1995] and [VDA 1996] guidelines for FMEA allow for application specific scoring schemes to be defined. The MISRA Safety Analysis guidelines will therefore propose a scoring scheme that is tailored to programmable vehicle-based systems along the following lines:

- **Severity** - The hazards associated with each failure could be categorised by extending controllability (see Section 3.1.2) or the risk graph (see Section 3.1.1) into ten different levels;
- **Occurrence** - Whilst it is often possible to model the probability of random faults in hardware, this is not usually possible for systematic software faults. The occurrence of random faults should ideally be scored objectively using reliability data. The occurrence of systematic faults cannot be scored using probability, however, since FMECA is more of a management tool, rather than a pure engineering tool, a score could be based on the level of integrity associated with the SIL of its production process.
- **Detection** - A meaningful interpretation of this is a measure of the degree to which a programmable system can accommodate faults which manifest themselves during the operation of the system while in the hands of the customer. It could be made up of the probability of detecting the error, and the degree to which the risk associated with that error can be reduced by the system taking some beneficial action.

Historically the industry has multiplied these three scores to give a Risk Priority Number (RPN), and then concentrated on dealing with those faults, or failure modes, with a high RPN. In fact, however, the RPN should be used with great care, since it is a one dimensional assessment of three dimensions of information, i.e. information is lost during its creation. Of particular concern is the case where only one of the parameters has a high value; this may result in a low RPN but be highlighting a specific major problem. It is for this reason that some companies are now only using the 'severity' parameter.

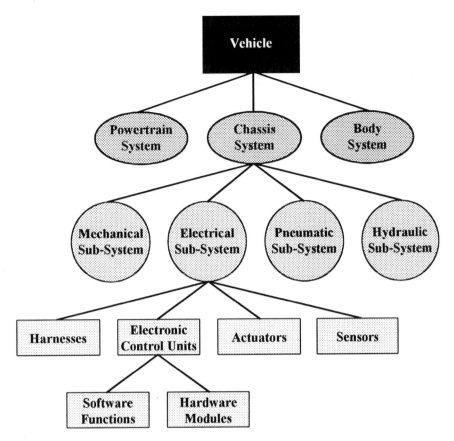

Figure 9 - Decomposition of a vehicle

4.2 Fault Tree Analysis

FTA is not as widely applied in the automotive industry as FMEA (e.g. there is no equivalent section of QS9000 covering FTA requirements). However there are two areas in which its use has been shown to be appropriate.

Firstly fault trees are often used by design engineers to communicate to those writing service repair documentation, or automated off-board diagnostic tools, the possible causes of typical vehicle faults which may be reported by a customer. In such cases the starting point will be, for example, "warning light is on" and the fault tree will be a means of identifying the possible causes, and therefore possible repair actions a technician may need to perform.

Secondly, and more relevant to this paper, they are beginning to become recognised as a valuable technique in the analysis of safety-related automotive systems. According to [IEC 1025 1990] FTA may be used to:

- Identify the causes, or combination of causes, that lead to the top event;
- Determine whether a particular system reliability measure meets a stated requirement;
- Demonstrate that the assumptions made in other analyses, regarding the independence of systems and non-relevance of failures, are not violated;
- Determine the factor(s) which most seriously affect a particular reliability measure, and the changes required to improve that measure;
- Identify common events, or common cause failures.

In the analysis of a safety-related system FTA is a complementary technique to FME(C)A and helps to give additional confidence that nothing has been missed. By starting with a hazard as the top event, it is possible to work down towards failures of LRUs, or basic events, which can give rise to the top event. This is done via a hierarchy which gradually refines the hazard through a series of intermediate (system and sub-system level failure modes) down to the failures of individual LRUs. It is possible to analyse the AND-OR logic of a fault tree to identify the combinations of basic events which can cause the top event. These are known as 'minimal cut-sets'. Where a minimal cut-set is shown to be a single basic event, this reveals a single point of failure which can give rise to a hazard. Depending on the severity of the hazard, and the known reliability of the LRU concerned, this may or may not be acceptable, depending on the level of risk. In addition, where there are multiple points of failure (i.e. more than one event in a minimal cut-set), it may be possible to make a subjective assessment as to how likely these events are to occur together, again in accordance with the acceptable level of risk.

Further analysis which can be performed on a fault-tree is the quantification of hazard occurrence rates based on the reliabilities of the LRU components of the system. Such quantification can range from a simple combination of probabilities (i.e. multiply for an AND gate, add for an OR gate), to complex time-dependent failure rate calculations ($R=1-e^{-\lambda t}$). Allowance can also be made for repairable systems, where planned maintenance and service replacements are involved, although this complicates the calculations still further. Of course, software packages are available which can assist this process.

Quantifying fault trees is standard practice in some industry sectors, but is not common in the automotive industry, and a number of notes of caution must be sounded. One key reason for this is the non-availability of valid figures for hardware component failures. Although failure rates can be measured or obtained from tables, e.g. [ROME Lab 1993], they tend to render any calculations excessively pessimistic. This is because a fault tree often works down towards very specific failure modes of an LRU, however the figures which are available tend to 'lump together' several failure modes. Therefore using these figures in an un-revised manner will lead to pessimistic calculations, which are of limited, if any, practical use for a vehicle development programme.

Where software is identified as a basic event, the question arises as to what figure should be used for the failure rate. The concept of software failure rate is not well defined, and there are a number of equally (in)valid approaches, e.g.:

- If available, use measured Mean Time Between Failure figures of software from a similar application, of similar complexity, developed to a similar process as the software for the system being analysed, by similar people in a similar organisation, using similar tools etc. etc.
- Assume that the software is 100% reliable (i.e. failure rate = 0). This approach is supported by the assertion that developing the software to a given integrity level seeks to provide sufficient confidence that this is the case.
- Apply the target failure rate figures from IEC 61508 for the appropriate integrity level.
- Estimate the software failure rate based on an algorithmic argument, for example based on the number of instructions executed, processor clock rates, and typical defect rates etc. [ROME Lab 1993]
- Guess, and attempt to justify its validity.

Despite these shortcomings, quantified fault trees can still be very useful in gaining an understanding of the failure mechanisms within a vehicle system. For example, even though the absolute validity of the calculated occurrence rates of the top event is questionable, the tree can be used to test assumptions and to perform sensitivity analysis on the effects of the uncertain component failure rates on system failure rates (sensitivity analysis). It may also be possible, accepting the pessimistic outcomes, to see how close a particular system design gets to the target figures in [IEC 61508 1999], for example when choosing between different vehicle system architectures.

5 Conclusion

The MISRA Steering Group has identified a need to provide advice on how to undertake safety analysis on automotive systems, and has decided to produce some guidelines based on the experience of its various members. Whilst many generic techniques exist, they do need interpreting for the specific sets of circumstances that are found in this industry sector. These guidelines will cover the various techniques that may be used to identify hazards, classify hazards and to analyse designs to ensure that the risk associated with each hazard has been reduced to an acceptable level.

References

[Carroll 1939]   Carroll L: Sylvie and Bruno Concluded, in The Complete Works of Lewis Carroll. The Nonesuch Press, 1939 (First Published 1893)

[DEFSTAN 00-56 1996]   DEFSTAN 00-56: Defence Standard 00-56 - Safety Management Requirements for Defence Systems, Issue 2. Ministry of Defence, 1996

[DEFSTAN 00-58 1996]   DEFSTAN 00-58: Interim Defence Standard 00-58 - HAZOP Studies on Systems Containing Programmable Electronics, Issue 1. Ministry of Defence, 1996

[DO-178B/ED-12B 1992]   DO-178B/ED-12B: Software Considerations in Airborne Systems and Equipment Certification. RTCA-EUROCAE, 1992

[Hobley 1995a]   Hobley K M, et al.: Framework for Prospective System Safety Analysis Volume 1 - Preliminary Safety Analysis. Deliverable N° 9a, V2058 PASSPORT project of the Advanced Transport Telematics (ATT/DRIVE II) sector of the TELEMATICS APPLICATIONS Programme, Third Framework Programme (1991-94), 1995

[Hobley 1995b]   Hobley K M and Jesty P H: Analysis and Assessment of Advanced road Transport Telematic Systems. Proceedings of the 14th International Conference on Computer Safety, Reliability and Security (SafeComp '95), Belgirate, Italy, G. Rabe, Ed., Springer-Verlag, 1995, ISBN 3-540-19962-4

[IEC 812 1985]   IEC 812: Analysis Techniques for System Reliability - Procedure for Failure Mode and Effects Analysis (FMEA). International Electrotechnical Commission, 1985

[IEC 1025 1990]   IEC 1025: Fault Tree Analysis (FTA). International Electrotechnical Commission, 1990

[IEC 61508 1999]   IEC 61508: Functional Safety of Electrical/Electronic/Programmable Electronic Safety-Related Systems. International Electrotechnical Commission, 1999

[Jesty 1996]   Jesty P H and Hobley K M: Integrity Levels and their Application to Road Transport Systems. Proceedings of the 15th International Conference on Computer Safety, Reliability and Security (SafeComp '96), Vienna, Austria, E. Schoitsch, Ed., Springer-Verlag, 1996, ISBN 3-540-76070-9

[MISRA 1994]   MISRA: Development Guidelines for Vehicle Based Software. MIRA, CV10 0TU, 1994 {http://www.misra.org.uk/}

[QS 9000 1995]   QS 9000: Quality System Requirements. Chrysler Corporation, Ford Motor Company and General Motors Corporation, 1995. Available from Carwin Continuous Ltd, Thurrock, Essex, UK

[Redmill 1998]   Redmill F, IEC 61508 - Principles and Use in the Management of Safety. Computing and Control Engineering, vol. 9, No. 5, Institute of Electrical Engineers, 1998.

[Redmill 1999]   Redmill F, Chudleigh M, and Catmur J: System Safety: HAZOP and Software HAZOP. John Wiley & Sons Ltd, 1999, ISBN 0 471 98280 6

[ROME Lab 1993] ROME Lab: Reliability Engineer's Toolkit. The ROME Laboratory, US Airforce Material Command, Griffiss Air Base, NY, 1993

[VDA 1996]   VDA: Quality Management in the Automotive Industry, Quality Assurance before Series Production: Volume 4 Part 2: System FMEA, Failure Mode and Effects Analysis. Verband der Automobilindustrie e.V., 1996

SOFTWARE SAFETY

ADA TASKING FOR HIGH-INTEGRITY SYSTEMS

David Humphris and Brian Dobbing

Aonix Europe Ltd,
Partridge House,
Newtown Road,
Henley-on-Thames,
Oxon RG9 1HG
United Kingdom
Tel: +44 (0)1491 415000

dhumphris@aonix.co.uk and bdobbing@aonix.co.uk

1. INTRODUCTION

As computer control becomes more extensive in all aspects of everyday life, the guarantee of reliability of software systems takes on increasing importance. The number of high integrity application sectors is rapidly growing. Financial systems depend on software for accounting services and money transfer. Human transportation systems are becoming fully automated. Hospitals depend on software for managing patient records and for controlling life-support systems. And most industrial plants, including those with absolute fail-safe requirements such as nuclear power stations, are controlled and monitored by software systems. It is clear that the safety of human life and the integrity of our material infrastructure now depend directly or indirectly on safe, reliable software.

Software production has regrettably been tarnished over the years by a lack of quality inherent in the use of unsafe programming languages and lack of control of the whole software lifecycle. The "Year-2K" problem is a major example of this, and could result in a chaotic situation of simultaneously failing computer systems. The US DoD addressed the issue of unreliable languages in the late 1970's leading to the birth of the Ada programming language [AJPO 1987], which was mandated for use in all DoD applications. However Ada is a general-purpose language and as such, retains elements within its definition that make static analysis of the code for verification infeasible. Nevertheless, the framework at the heart of Ada provides by far the most well defined and secure definition of program semantics, making it an excellent choice for high integrity systems.

Recent legislation has produced a number of directives designed to ensure safety. Companies are now obliged to guarantee that systems that they produce do not violate safety requirements. Company directors can now be held personally liable for loss of life or property resulting directly or indirectly from unsafe software installed, sold or included as part of a product sold by their company.

Most high integrity industries are in the process of setting, or have already set, specific standards for the development, testing and certification of safety-critical software. The combined efforts of government and avionics industry representatives resulted in the RTCA DO-178B standard [RTCA 1992] that provides strict guidelines for the certification of software used in airborne systems.

2. ADA – THE IDEAL FOUNDATION

Ada has numerous properties that make it an excellent choice for the development of high integrity systems:

2.1. ANSI and ISO Standard

The first definition of Ada became an ANSI standard in 1983 and an ISO standard in 1987 [AJPO 1987]. This was extended in 1995 to form a new ANSI and ISO standard "Ada95" [Intermetrics 1995]. The language is thus well defined and stable, and provides a portable foundation for the development of supporting tools and libraries. A mature validation mechanism, the "Ada Compiler Validation Capability" (ACVC) ensures trust in the quality of Ada compilers and in the correct execution of applications developed using them.

2.2. Object-Oriented Design and Programming

The Ada95 revision of the language includes comprehensive support for OOD and OOP models, such as extension, inheritance and abstraction.

2.3. Legible Style

Ada facilitates the achievement of the steps needed for formal certification, including peer review and walkthroughs, and also simplifies long-term maintenance.

2.4. Modular Structure

Separate compilation facilities enable the application to be written as a set of units consisting of well-defined specifications, supplying the visible interface, and bodies, supplying the hidden implementation. In addition, the interface and the implementation can each be decomposed into a hierarchical structure of dependent units. Correct use of the interfaces, and enforcement of changes to interface definitions, are rigorously policed by the compilation system. This allows verified construction of a program from individually trusted components.

2.5 Early Detection of Errors

Strong typing and precise interface checking ensure that most errors are detected statically by the compiler, and most remaining errors are trapped during execution.

2.6 Encapsulation of Target Dependencies

The use of target-dependent information by the program, such as the internal representation of data and the placement of objects at particular addresses is encapsulated into well-defined features of the language. This produces high portability of the code from one machine to another and simple adjustments of the machine-dependent parts.

3. ADA IN HIGH INTEGRITY SYSTEMS

Most of the high integrity software standards or guidelines make some reference to the software language to be used in safety-related systems.

3.1 What the Standards Say

Below are some example standards or guidelines that refer to software implementation language recommendations that point to Ada being the implementation language of choice for high integrity systems.

3.1.1   RTCA DO-178B [RTCA 1992] (Commercial avionics guidelines):

An area of key importance in the standard is the software language used as the basis for the final installed system. This must be well defined, have validated tools, enable modular structure, have strong checking properties, and be clearly readable. Of all the programming languages widely available today, only Ada provides an appropriate baseline for safety-critical and high integrity software.

3.1.2   IEC-61508 [IEC 1999] (Generic industry):

IEC-61508 contains a table that identifies the suitability of various implementation languages for use in systems developed to each of its Safety Integrity Levels (SILs). This table defines Ada as recommended, or highly recommended for all integrity levels and Ada subsets highly recommended for all integrity levels.

3.1.3   IEC-60880 [IEC 1986] (Nuclear industrial):

Appendix D describes the recommended features of Translators and Linkers to be used for systems to be certified to IEC-60880. This table highlights that:

• Tools should be thoroughly tested

- Reliability Data should be available

- Language syntax should be completely and unambiguously defined

- Semantics should be well and completely specified and understandable

- High level languages should be used rather than machine oriented ones

These recommended features fit well onto Ada with its non-ambiguous syntax and well-defined semantics with all Compilers required to pass a standard validation suite.

3.1.4   MISRA (European motor industry):

The MISRA guidelines [MISRA 1994] recommend the use of a restricted subset of a high-level language for programming safety-related systems.

MISRA subsequently produced the document "Guidelines For The Use Of The C Language in Vehicle Based Software" [MISRA 1998] which contains the following statement:

"… it should be recognized that there are other languages which are in general better suited to safety-related systems … languages generally recognized to be more suitable than C are Ada and Modula 2. If such languages could be available for a proposed system then their use should be seriously considered in preference to C"

3.1.5   Other documents:

When textbooks refer to programming language choice for safety-related systems then Ada (and Ada subsets) is invariably identified as one of the most suitable implementation languages.

For example from Safety-Critical Computer Systems [Storey 1996]:

"In projects that are assigned a high level of integrity … the most suitable languages are probably a safe subset of Ada or a safe subset of Pascal.

… In recent years more and more companies are turning to Ada for all their critical applications."

3.2   Ada subsets

Ada is a general-purpose language that contains a number of features that should not be used in high integrity or safety critical applications. Most general Ada solutions do not restrict operations that potentially cause problematic conditions such as memory fragmentation, unpredictable execution timing, and other non-deterministic events that are inappropriate for systems with high criticality requirements.

Experiences with the concurrency feature ("tasking") of original Ada83 precluded its use in high integrity systems due to the non-deterministic nature of some parts of its semantics. This was regrettable since such systems were often inherently concurrent, and the original set of requirements on the Ada language included support for highly reliable concurrent embedded systems. This problem was addressed in the recent revision to the language, Ada95, which introduced new deterministic features in the tasking area, and a more open interface to allow direct user control of parts of the runtime system that had previously been a black box, for example dynamic storage management. This opened up the way for Ada tasking to be used safely and predictably in high integrity systems.

Nevertheless, due to the requirement for Ada95 to be upward compatible with Ada83, the inherited problematic operations and semantics still exist in Ada95. This situation prompted the definition of a subset of Ada tasking suitable for use in high integrity systems, which was a major output of the 8th International Real-Time Ada Workshop. The subset was named the "Ravenscar Profile" and is fully defined in the proceedings [ACM 1997]. The profile is included in an ISO report giving guidelines for the use of Ada in high integrity systems. The major goals that governed the subset definition are:

- Increased efficiency by removing features with high overheads

- Elimination of features with non-deterministic execution semantics

- Elimination of features with non-deterministic timing semantics

- A small and simple runtime system suitable for formal certification

The Ravenscar Profile subset of Ada95 can therefore be considered particularly suitable for a wide range of embedded systems applications, for example:

- Those requiring a small runtime system due to memory constraints

- Those requiring a fast runtime system due to performance constraints

- Hard Real-Time Systems requiring timing analysis to prove that deadlines are met

- High integrity systems requiring static analysis of the code to prove that it correctly meets its formal specification

- Safety-critical systems that require formal certification, even to levels as high as DO-178B Level A

4. THE CONCURRENCY MODEL

The concurrency model assumed by the Ravenscar Profile matches the typical set of elements found in a real-time system:

- A fixed number of concurrent activities (we will use the Ada term "task" to denote an independent concurrent activity)

- Each task has a single invocation event, but has a potentially unbounded number of invocations

- The invocation event can either be temporal, or a signal from another task or the environment. (A high-integrity application may restrict itself to temporal events.)

- Task interaction is only via shared data. Access to this data must be atomic.

This model can be implemented using the Ravenscar Profile subset of Ada95. A simple mapping exists from the elements above to the corresponding Ada95 code templates. Execution of the model is based on Ada's fixed priority task scheduling (either preemptive or non-preemptive).

Non-preemptive (or "co-operative") scheduling may be required by systems with the highest level of criticality since the switch to a new task executing on the processor can only occur at well-defined points of execution. This added determinism may reduce significantly the cost of testing, and can also reduce the size and complexity of the runtime system.

Preemptive scheduling on the other hand is usually required by real-time systems requiring a high degree of responsiveness to events. In particular, preemptive scheduling is required in systems that must be proven to meet deadlines. Since preemption can occur at any time, it is not possible to test all possible preemption points. Rather, it is necessary for the run-time system to guarantee that interrupts or preemption does not affect the functional behavior of a task. For a high-integrity application requiring preemptive scheduling, evidence to support this guarantee would need to be provided by the supplier of the run-time system, generally in terms of certification testing material.

Analysis of the program can be achieved using the following techniques:

- The functional behavior of each task can be verified against its formal specification using tools and techniques associated with static analysis of sequential code (e.g. [Barnes 1997]). Shared data access is viewed as merely environmental input for this analysis. Timing analysis can be used to ensure that such data is appropriately initialized and temporally valid.

- The timing behavior of the system as a whole can be verified for meeting of all deadlines using tools and techniques associated with fixed-priority schedulability analysis (e.g. [Klein 1993]) following the assignment of temporal attributes to each task (period, deadline, priority etc).

5. MAPPING ADA TO THE RAVENSCAR PROFILE

5.1 Decomposition

The application must be decomposed into a number of separate processes, each with a single thread of control, with all interactions between these processes identified. Each process is implemented as a separate Ada task. The tasks are categorized as *cyclic* (meaning that they execute periodically using a statically assigned rate), or *event-driven* (meaning that they execute in response to an asynchronous event).

In addition, Ada95 protected objects [RM section 9.4] are used to provide mutually-exclusive access to shared resources (e.g., for concurrent global data access) and to implement task synchronization (e.g., via some event signalling mechanism). This decomposition is normally the result of applying a design methodology suitable to describe real-time systems, such as the Unified Modeling Language (UML).

5.2 Static Analysis Properties

Tasks In order to be suitable for schedulability analysis, the task set to be analyzed must be static. This implies that all Ada tasks in the program are created at the outermost *library-level* and never terminate.

Memory In order to meet the deterministic memory-size requirement necessary to ensure that the application cannot fail due to running out of dynamically-acquired memory, the model requires all task stacks to have a static size (which can, of course, vary from task to task), and does not provide a default heap management system for dynamic acquisition of memory. However in recognition that some real-time systems do require the controlled allocation and deallocation of dynamic objects, user-defined heap management systems can be written using Ada *Storage_Pools* [RM section 13.11]. The model does not place any restrictions on the declaration of dynamic-sized Ada objects.

General Execution In order to meet the deterministic execution profile requirement necessary for static analysis of the source code, use of Ada *exception handlers* [RM section 11.4] is prohibited. If an exception is raised at runtime, control is transferred to a user-supplied procedure for remedial action.

Interrupts Interrupt handlers are supported by the profile and map to the standard mechanism of an Ada protected procedure [RM section C.3].

5.3   Code Templates

The profile does not require the application to use any particular coding style for the tasks, protected objects, and interrupt handlers. However if the application is required to undergo schedulability analysis, certain task templates and coding styles are useful in defining the activities that are to be analyzed. These are described below:

Cyclic Task The task body for a cyclic task typically has, as its last statement, an outermost infinite loop containing one or more "delay until" statements [RM section 9.6]. (The basic form of a cyclic task has just a single delay until statement either at the start or at the end of the statements within the loop.) The model supports only one time type for use as the argument - Ada.Real_Time.Time [RM section D.8] - which maps directly to the underlying system clock for the maximum precision. Note that task termination is a bounded error condition in the Ravenscar profile; hence the loop is infinite.

Example

```
task body Cyclic is
   Next_Period : Ada.Real_Time.Time := First_Release;
   Period : Ada.Real_Time.Time_Span :=
                  Ada.Real_Time.Milliseconds(50);
   -- other declarations
begin
   -- Initialization code
   loop
      delay until Next_Period;
      -- Periodic response code
      Next_Period := Next_Period + Period;
   end loop;
end Cyclic;
```

Event-Driven Task The task body for an event-driven task typically has, as its last statement, an outermost infinite loop containing as the first statement either a call to an Ada protected entry [RM section 9.5] or a call to wait for the state of an Ada "Suspension Object" [RM section D.10] to become true.

The suspension object is used when no other effect is required in the signalling operation; for example, no data is to be transferred from signaller to waiter. In contrast, the protected entry is used for more elaborate event signalling, when additional operations such as data transfer must accompany the resumption of the event-driven task.

Example

```
task body Sporadic is
   -- Declarations
begin
   -- Initialization code
   loop
      Ada.Synchronous_Task_Control.
         Suspend_Until_True (SO);
      -- Event response code
   end loop;
end Sporadic;
```

Shared Resource Protected Object A protected object used to ensure mutually exclusive access to a shared resource, such as global data, typically contains only protected subprograms as operations, i.e., no protected entries. Protected entries are used for task synchronization purposes. A protected procedure is used when the internal state of the protected data must be altered, and a protected function is used for information retrieval from the protected data when the data remains unchanged.

Example

```
protected Shared_Data is
   function Get return Data;
   procedure Put (D : in Data);
private
   Current : Data;
   -- Protected shared data declaration
end Shared_Data;

protected body Shared_Data is
   function Get return Data is
   begin
      return Current;
   end Get;
   procedure Put (D : in Data) is
   begin
      Current := D;
   end Put;
end Shared_Data;
```

Task Synchronization Primitives Task synchronization, in the form of a wait-for/signal event model, can be achieved using either a protected entry or a suspension object. The suspension object is the optimized form for a simple suspend/resume operation. The protected entry is used when extra operations are required:

a. Data can be transferred from signaller to waiter atomically (i.e., without risk of race condition) by use of parameters of the protected operations and extra protected data.

b. Additional code can be executed atomically as part of signalling, by use of the bodies of the protected operations.

Example

```
protected type Event is
    entry Wait (D : out Data);
    procedure Signal (D : in Data);
private
    Current : Data;   -- Event data declaration
    Signalled : Boolean := False;
end Event;

protected body Event is
    entry Wait (D : out Data) when Signalled is
    begin
        D := Current;
        Signalled := False;
    end Wait;
    procedure Signal (D : in Data) is
    begin
        Current := D;
        Signalled := True;
    end Signal;
end Event;
```

Interrupt Handlers An interrupt handler will often be used to trigger a response in an event-driven task. This is because the code in the handler itself executes at the hardware interrupt level, and so typically the major part of the processing of the response to the interrupt is moved into the task, which executes at a software priority level with interrupts fully enabled. The interrupt handler usually will store any interrupt data in its protected object and then release the waiting event-driven task by changing the state of the protected data Boolean used as the entry barrier in the same protected object.

In the Event example above, if signalling is to be achieved via an interrupt, then procedure Signal is identified as an interrupt handler by the addition of pragma Attach_Handler [RM section C.3.1]:

Example

```
protected Interrupt_Event is
   entry Wait (D : out Data);
   procedure Signal;
private
   pragma Attach_Handler (Signal,<interrupt_id> );
   Current : Data;   -- Event data declaration
   Signalled : Boolean := False;
end Interrupt_Event;

protected body Interrupt_Event is
   entry Wait (D : out Data) when Signalled is
   begin
      D := Current;
      Signalled := False;
   end Wait;
   procedure Signal is
   begin
      Current := <interrupt data>;
      Signalled := True;
   end Signal;
end Interrupt_Event;
```

6. IMPLEMENTING THE RAVENSCAR PROFILE

Ada compiler vendor Aonix has undertaken the development of an Ada95 compilation system which implements the Ravenscar profile, known as *Raven* [Dobbing 1998], hosted on Windows NT and Sparc Solaris, and targeting the PowerPC, 68K and Intel range of processors. This section describes some of the key elements of this implementation.

The Ravenscar profile is a subset of the concurrency features of Ada95. To provide a complete Ada language subset requires support for sequential components of the language. The sequential part of the language subset that Raven works to is based on the purely sequential subset supported by our Ada83 Certifiable Small Ada RunTime (C-SMART) products with the addition of the new

Ada95 sequential extensions (mainly the OOP and additional hierarchical support features).

6.1 Development Practices

The principle goal of the implementation was to develop a runtime system for Ada95 restricted as per the Ravenscar profile, which was suitable for inclusion in:

- A safety-critical application requiring formal certification
- A high-integrity system requiring functional determinism and reliability
- A concurrent real-time system with timing deadlines requiring temporal determinism, e.g. schedulability analysis
- A real-time system with execution time constraints requiring high performance
- A real-time system with memory constraints requiring small and deterministic memory usage

Consequently a rigorous set of development practices was enforced based on the traditional software development model, including:

- Documentation of the software requirements
- Definition and documentation of the design to meet these requirements, including traceability
- Formal design reviews
- Formal code walk-throughs of the runtime implementation
- Definition and documentation of the runtime tests to verify that the implementation of the design meets its formal specification
- Documentation of the formal verification test results
- Capture of all significant items within a configuration management system

6.2 Requirements

The software requirements include the following elements:

- The runtime design shall support both the preemptive and non-preemptive implementations of the Ravenscar profile.
- The runtime design shall optimize a purely sequential (non-tasking) program by not including any runtime overhead for tasking.
- The design shall structure the runtime such that a library of additional runtime Ada packages which have not undergone formal certification can be supplied as a stand-alone "extra", for applications which require the extra functionality but not the rigors of certification.
- The runtime algorithms shall be coded such that the worst case execution time is deterministic and as short as possible

- The runtime algorithms shall be coded such that the average case execution time is as short as possible

- The runtime algorithms shall be coded so as to miminize the use of global data, and so as not to acquire memory dynamically. (The total global memory requirement of the runtime system shall be small and deterministic.)

- The runtime algorithms shall be coded so as to conform to the certification coding standards

- The runtime algorithms shall be coded so as to conform to the Ravenscar profile plus the implementation-defined sequential code restrictions

- A coverage analysis tool shall be provided for certification purposes

- A schedulability analyzer shall be provided which implements standard algorithms used in fixed-priority timing analysis.

- Enforcement of the Ravenscar profile, plus other restrictions on sequential constructs, shall be performed at compile-time wherever possible. (This eliminates runtime code to perform the checks, and the risk of runtime exceptions being raised in the event of check failure.)

- The runtime kernel shall be verified using the verification tests written to validate the correct implementation of the requirements.

6.3   Design Considerations

Restriction Enforcement   This is achieved at compile time using the Ada "pragma Restrictions" [RM section 13.12]. Some new restriction identifiers were defined to cover restrictions not considered by the Ada standard. The International Standards Organization Working Group is currently considering these new identifiers for standardization responsible for the Safety and Security annex of the Ada standard.

Worst Case Execution Time   In order to perform accurate schedulability analysis, it is necessary to input the runtime execution overhead (see [Katcher 1993]). For hard real-time systems, in which the failure to meet a hard timing deadline is catastrophic to the entire system, worst case execution times are generally used in the computations.

For the application code itself, the user can obtain worst case execution times either by analyzing the Ada code (e.g. [Burns 1996]) or measuring the times using tests that exercise the various code paths. But for the runtime system operations, the user has no direct way of knowing which scenario will produce the worst case time, unless the runtime source code is available and also documentation to describe the criteria which determine the execution path at each decision point. Thus for every runtime operation supported by the model, the vendor must provide "metrics" [RM section D (2)] which define its worst case execution time. For the runtime tasking kernel implementing the Ravenscar profile, this set of metrics will include:

- Overhead for protected operations, with and without a protected entry
- Overhead for processing of the **delay until** statement
- Overhead in handling timer interrupt and user interrupts
- Rescheduling overhead, including the time to perform a context switch

Clearly, this imposes strict constraints on the algorithms used to implement these operations such that their worst case execution time is not overly excessive. For example, use of a linear search proportional to the maximum number of tasks in the program would be unacceptable for a program with a large number of tasks. So, the runtime contains optimizations to minimize critical worst case timings.

Performance Several techniques are used to improve the performance of the runtime. Simple and very short runtime subprograms can be defined as having calling convention "Intrinsic" [RM section 6.3.1], which means that their code is built into the compiler and is used directly in place of the call. Typically this is used for immutable code sequences such as arithmetic and relational operators for the Time type [RM section D.8] and for highly time critical simple operations such as getting the identity of the currently executing task.

Other short subprograms can be defined as being "inlined" [RM section 6.3.2], which gives similar performance gain by avoiding the procedure call and return overhead, but without having to actually build the generated assembler code into the compiler code generator.

Early indications of the performance of the runtime system are very encouraging and are listed in Table 1.

PIWG T test (Microseconds)	Rendezvous (VxWorks)	Protected Object (VxWorks)	Protected Object (Ravenscar)
T000001	67.54	8.24	1.8
T000002	96.03	8.48	1.2
T000003	84.31	8.26	1.5
T000004	113.77	8.30	1.2
T000005	107.81	8.30	1.1
T000006	121.87	8.17	1.1
T000007	97.49	8.20	1.8
T000008	245.44	16.32	1.2

Table 1 – Runtime Performance on Ultra 604 133MHz

Runtime Size The runtime was designed and coded to minimize the size of both the code and the data. For example, an important optimization in the Ada pre-linker tool (the "binder") is elimination of uncalled subprograms from the executable image. But this optimization is only fully effective if the code is structured in a very modular way. For example, there is the requirement that no runtime code or data which is specific to Ada tasking should be included in the executable if the program does not use tasking.

The major component of the runtime data is the stack and Task Control Block (TCB) which is required for each task's execution. Each application program is required to declare the memory areas to be used for the stacks and TCBs in the Board Support Package. This provides a simple interface to tune the stack sizes to the worst case values, whilst also giving full application-level determinism on the amount of storage which is reserved for this purpose. Early indications of the size of the runtime system are very encouraging and are listed in Table 2.

(K-bytes)	Code	Data	Stack
Null program	3.7	0.45	0.81
Hello World	4.2	0.52	0.86
Minimal Tasking	12.1	1.10	1.80

Table 2 – Runtime System Sizes (Power PC)

6.4   Testing

The testing activity is split into two components:

- Use of the standard Ada validation test suite (ACVC) to verify the validation status of the compiler, binder and code generator support routines
- Development of a specific test suite to certification level for the runtime system.

ACVC Testing   Since a substantial number of ACVC tests violate Ravenscar profile restrictions, particularly relating to the tasking tests, it is not possible under current rules to validate such a subset. However by use of the same compilation system tools linked to a full Ada95 runtime system for the same target processor family, it is possible to run the full ACVC suite, thereby validating the compiler, binder and common code generator support routines (e.g. block move).

Certification Tests   A test suite has been created to verify the runtime code, thereby complementing the ACVC testing (which was not able to test this fully), whilst also ensuring the level of reliability specified by the requirements. The test suite has been developed to meet the safety standard DO-178B Level A. This is discussed further in section 8.

7. ADDITIONAL SUPPORTING TOOLS

The additional tools, which have been included in the implementation to support certification and schedulability analysis, include:

- Condition code and Coverage Analysis tool

- Schedulability Analyzer and Scheduler Simulation tool

DO-178 identifies two categories for tool qualification (not certification): development and verification.

Development tools are any tools which can induce an error in the application (i.e., the compiler). Given this, development tools if qualified, must be qualified to the same level as the application. It is currently beyond the state-of-the-art to qualify a Compiler to meet the requirements for development tool qualification for use to the highest levels of criticality of DO-178B.

Verification tools do not introduce errors but they can however mask errors. Verification tools have a less onerous requirement for qualification. To qualify a verification tool we do the following to meet the Do-178B guidelines:

- Put all components under configuration management control

- Produce a Tool Operational Requirements (TOR) document

- Produce a Tool Qualification Document (TQD)

- Produce tests to show compliance to the TOR

7.1 Coverage Analysis

Under the DO-178B guidelines, it is necessary to perform coverage analysis to show that all the object code (both the application program part and the Ada runtime system) has been executed, including all possible outcomes of conditions, by the verification tests. The entire runtime system is subjected to coverage analysis as part of its auditing process. For the user application code, the tool "AdaCover" is provided to assist in formal certification.

AdaCover is in two logical parts:

- A target-resident monitor which records the execution of every instruction in the program, including the results of every decision point

- A host-resident tool which annotates the compiler-generated assembly code listings with the results of part 1, thereby providing the user with a report of coverage at either the object code or the source code level for the set of executed verification tests.

AdaCover is a qualified verification tool so its results can be used for your certification.

7.2   Schedulability Analysis

The "PerfoRMAx" tool embodies classic schedulability analyzer and scheduler simulation functionality. Given a definition of the actions performed by the tasks in the application in terms of their priority, execution time, period and interaction with shared resources, plus certain runtime system overhead times, the tool performs analysis of the schedulability of the task set based on a user-selectable scheduling theory, for example Rate Monotonic Analysis (RMA) [Klein 1993].

The tool is also able to provide a graphical view of the processor load based on a static simulation of the scheduling of the tasks by the runtime system, thereby giving clear indication of potential regions of unschedulability. If such regions exist, the tool outputs messages highlighting the cause of the unschedulability together with suggestions for corrective action.

PerfoRMAx has not been qualified. However it still provides useful support during development of concurrent applications.

There are two stages in the development cycle where perfoRMAx can be used, during the Design and during Testing.

During design the tool is used with estimates of the scheduling events, task periods, execution time estimates and so on. The tool helps a user to work out the priorities of tasks and their interactions to show that there will be no missed deadlines. During this process users are arranging the execution profile through the use of priorities periods and so on. The tool will use a set of published formulae to determine the schedulability of the system, based on the user estimates.

When the system is constructed, the user can develop tests which force the tasks to execute their worst case paths. This requires the user to use some form of analysis to determine what these paths are.

The other way to determine the worse case execution time is to run the program through the various candidate paths and to measure the times. The measurements could be captured using hooks we provide in the run-time. Analysis of the paths and the times would yield a data set which when fed back into PerfoRMAx would confirm the schedulability calculated during design.

Once the schedulability was shown to be satisfactory, the calculations could be repeated by hand using the published formulae. The formula could be calculated using calculators and spread sheets i.e. some diverse means to show that the calculations are not in error. (Statistical diversity.)

By using this approach the PerfoRMAx tool does not need to be qualified. However it still serves a useful function in the development stages and does produce a schedulability analysis result, but the result must be confirmed using another technique.

8. CERTIFICATION

When selecting tools to use on a high integrity system, consideration has to be given not only for how these tools can help in developing the system but also what components it introduces into the delivered system. In the case of a runtime system, this introduces library routines that become part of the system that may require certification. If certification is required then the runtime system library routines need to be certifiable to, at least, the same level of criticality as the application code.

For DO-178B when a system is certified then the system as a whole must be certified, including any runtime library routines that are part of the flight system. Therefore we do not claim that our runtime is certified (as a standalone product) to DO-178B but that it is certifiable in a complete system. We provide all the materials, which are needed by the certification authority, to show that the runtime has been developed and tested to the necessary level. We believe that this approach is the safest as a component may be tested as a standalone item, but be used in an inappropriate environment, which causes the component to fail.

8.1 Certification Materials

Aonix provides the required material for supporting the certification of our runtime system in our customers safety-critical system. This material includes the documentation set, listed below, that maps onto the RTCA DO-178B standard and is sufficient for level A (catastrophic) certification.

Plan for Software Aspects of Certification

Software Development Plan

Software Verification Plan

Software Configuration Management Plan

Software Quality Assurance Plan

Software Requirements Standards

Design and Coding Standards

Software Requirements Specification

Software Hazard Analysis

Version Description Document

Software Development Folders (for each module)

Software Accomplishment Summary

Along with the above documents a number of sources of data are also required to provide certification evidence. This set is listed below:

Software Requirements Data

Design Description

Source Code

Executable Object Code

Software Verification results (test results)

Software Verification Cases and Procedures

Software Life Cycle Environment Configuration Index

Software Configuration Index

Problem Reports

Software Configuration Management Records

Software Quality Assurance Records

Where a customer is certifying to a standard other than DO-178B then we augment this documentation set with a Mapping document from the other standard to either sections in our existing DO-178B documentation set or to additional information provided in the mapping document itself.

8.2   Verification

We use the DO-178B Definition of verification.

> Verification is not simply testing. Testing in general cannot show the absence of errors.

> As a result the verification typically consists of a combination of reviews, analysis and testing

For the testing of our runtime routines we perform both black box and white box testing.

The black box testing is the traditional requirements based testing with no knowledge of the internal implementation. It includes tests in the typical problem areas (such as zero, large numbers, small numbers and boundary values) to show that the documented requirements are satisfactorily met.

The white box testing is used to ensure full coverage and boundary value testing.

The coverage testing uses requirements based tests to ensure coverage of all of the runtime kernel code at the machine code level. It also requires that all branches are taken in each direction at least once.

The boundary testing that is also performed in white box testing involves testing all objects values just in range, just out of range and with special case values.

When all the tests are completed then the Software Accomplishment Summary can be completed. This records traceability from requirements through design, source code, object code and test results to show compliance to the Software Aspects of Certification.

9. CONCLUSION

This paper describes state-of-the-art software to address the needs of embedded systems, particularly those with high integrity or safety critical requirements. The Ada language is recommended as the natural choice for such systems, and a tasking subset of Ada that is recommended by an ISO working group for use in high integrity applications is presented. Finally, details are given of an implementation of the subset by leading Ada vendor *Aonix*, with encouraging indications of it meeting the stringent requirements.

The Aonix Raven implementation is available with the necessary components to show its certifiability to safety-critical standards at the highest levels of criticality.

This important new advance opens the way for high integrity applications to take full advantage of the static semantic analysis and checking inherent in the Ada language and its supporting tools, including the use of some of Ada's rich concurrency features.

REFERENCES

[ACM 1997]   "Proceedings of the 8th International Real-Time Ada
                  Workshop", A.J.Wellings (editor), ACM Ada Letters
                  (September 1997)

[AJPO 1987]   "Reference Manual for the Ada Programming Language,
                  ANSI/MIL-STD-1815A", Ada Joint Program Office U.S.
                  Department of Defense (January 1983). ISO Standard
                  ISO/8652, 1987

[Barnes 1997]	"High Integrity Ada – The SPARK Examiner Approach", J. Barnes, Addison Wesley Longman Ltd (1997)
[Burns 1996]	"Combining Static Worst-Case Timing Analysis and Program Proof", A. Burns et al, Real-Time Systems 11(2):145-171, Kluwer Academic Publishers (September 1996)
[Dobbing 1998]	"The Ravenscar Tasking Profile for High Integrity Real-Time Programs" B. J. Dobbing et al. In Reliable Software Technologies – Ada-Europe '98, Lecture Notes in Computer Science 1411 (June 1998)
[IEC 1986]	IEC-60880, "Software for Computers in the Safety Systems of Nuclear Power Stations," International Electrotechnical Commission (1986)
[IEC 1999]	"IEC-61508, Functional Safety - Safety Related Systems", International Electrotechnical Commission (April 1999)
[Intermetrics 1995]	"Ada95 Reference Manual", ANSI/ISO/IEC-8652:1995, Intermetrics Inc. (January 1995)
[Katcher 1993]	"Engineering and Analysis of Fixed Priority Schedulers", D. Katcher et al. In IEEE Trans. Software Engineering 19 (1993)
[Klein 1993]	"A Practitioner's Handbook for Real-Time Analysis : A Guide to Rate Monotonic Analysis for Real-Time Systems", M. H. Klein et al, Kluwer Academic Publishers (1993)
[MISRA 1994]	"Development Guidelines for Vehicle Based Software", MISRA (November 1994)
[MISRA 1998]	"Guidelines for the Use of the C Language in Vehicle Based Software", MISRA (April 1998)
[RM]	See [Intermetrics 1995]
[RTCA 1992]	"Software Considerations in Airborne Systems and Equipment Certification", RTCA/DO-178B/ED-12B. RTCA Inc (December 1992)
[Storey 1996]	"Safety-Critical Computer Systems", N. Storey. Addison Wesley Longman Ltd (1996)

Assessing the Safety of Integrity Level Partitioning in Software

John A McDermid and David J Pumfrey
Department of Computer Science, University of York
York, UK

Abstract

In order to exploit the capability and performance of modern processors in safety critical applications, it is desirable to be able to run software of differing integrity levels on the same processor. To do this safely, however, requires the ability to enforce partitioning between these different integrity levels. For certification, there is a need to demonstrate the effectiveness of these partitioning mechanisms. In practice, this means analysing the hardware, e.g. memory management units, and software, e.g. operating system functions, which implement the protection mechanisms – and analysing the hardware-software interactions. This paper describes a method, known as LISA, developed to analyse low-level hardware-software interactions in multiprocessor computer systems, and draws some conclusions from experience of applying the method on a complex avionics system.

1 Introduction

Traditionally, safety critical computer systems have tended to be bespoke developments, with custom-written software, very often hand-crafted in assembly code, running on a unique hardware platform. Although it has not been the primary reason for building systems this way, safety engineering has benefited from the bespoke approach. Every part of the system is specified, designed and implemented for the application, and this allows a very high degree of visibility of, and control over, both process and product.

It is becoming generally accepted that completely bespoke development is no longer viable except for the most critical of applications. The primary reason for this change is economic; as hardware costs have fallen, development (particularly software development) costs have become dominant, even in products with high sales volumes. There is also a desire to find ways to allow safety critical systems to follow the general computing "power curve". Because of the need to use components with a good track record of reliable operation, safety critical systems projects have typically been restricted to using hardware that is no longer state of the art even when design begins. By the end of a lengthy development, the product may be a couple of generations behind leading technology, leading to a perception of poor performance when compared to contemporary non safety critical systems.

Possible approaches to reducing development costs and addressing performance issues include:
- moving to program generators
- increased use of standard components and hardware
- increased reuse of software components
- use of commercial-off-the-shelf (COTS) software.

All of these potentially offer significant benefits, but all also pose new challenges for achieving and assessing safety.

Essential to many of these changes will be the use of system architectures more similar to those found in general computing systems, implying the use of operating systems which can provide flexible scheduling, guarantee independence of separate processes on the same processor, and provide cross-platform commonality to allow applications to be migrated to new or upgraded hardware. Already, a number of operating system vendors offer products which they claim are suitable for use in safety critical applications, although these claims are not universally accepted (see for example, the debates on the selection of operating systems in the archives of the hise_safety_critical mailing list [hise_safety_critical 1999]).

The design and analysis of operating systems presents many new challenges for safety engineers. Significant progress has been made in some areas, notably in the guaranteeing of timing properties of different scheduling schemes on a range of architectures – see, for example [Audsley 1995; Joseph 1996; Kopetz 1997] – and in static analysis techniques for analysing the use and protection of critical data. However, most of these techniques assume perfect execution of the operating system software. There are few techniques that can provide evidence about independence of processes, protection of critical data or timing behaviour once potential unintended behaviour of the underlying hardware is taken into account.

In current industrial practice, the most common method of including computer hardware failures in safety analyses is simply to assume that any failure within the computer system will be sufficient to cause any failure mode of concern at the computer's outputs. Thus, in system level fault trees, it is common to see a basic (or undeveloped) event called simply "computer hardware failure" (see, for example, the fault trees for inadvertent aircraft braking developed in ARP 4761 Appendix L [SAE 1996]). Whilst this is clearly a conservative assumption sufficient to ensure safe treatment at the system level, it is of no use to software designers, who need to know what the symptoms of various hardware failures will be in order to develop detection and protection strategies.

Safety engineering always starts by identifying hazards at the platform level, and propagating safety requirements down to system and component level. It is clearly not possible to construct a complete safety argument for any operating system supplied as a "stand-alone" component (i.e. without knowledge of its eventual application context). However, it should be possible to develop "sub-arguments" – effectively, a description of a set of properties that the operating system is claimed to guarantee, together with the evidence to support the claims. Even this will require a combination of several different techniques, covering different aspects of correct behaviour and appropriate management of a range of failure modes.

Although superficially similar to designing any other engineered artefact (such as, say, a pump or valve), the main problem with operating systems is one of complexity. The designer of a pump may not know what systems his component will eventually be used in, but its capabilities and failure modes can be expressed relatively simply in familiar engineering terms, and the system designer can select a pump that meets his requirements.

It is perhaps better to compare an operating system with, say, the electrical power supply to a complete plant, rather than with a single component. The selection of electrical power supply characteristics will determine some of the requirements for components – suitable operating voltage, for example. A complete electrical system failure could disable all of the controlled components in a plant, or perhaps cause common damage to all of them through excessive voltage or current. In a similar way, selection of an operating system will set requirements for the development of other software components, in terms of interfaces, scheduling model etc., and operating system failures have the potential to disable or interfere with the behaviour of every other software function in a system.

This analogy is over-simplistic, but helps to identify further characteristics of operating systems that make them particularly problematic:

- *Unknown behaviour in case of hardware failure*
  The sheer complexity of computer hardware makes it impossible to predict all of its potential failure behaviours, or to guarantee continued correct behaviour of software if the underlying hardware fails. However, operating systems compound the problem due to the level of indirection between application code and hardware.
- *Lack of independent action in components* (all tasks rely on the operating system)
  The designer of the plant in the electrical example above could attempt to ensure that individual components were designed to behave in the safest way possible in the event of anticipated problems with the power supply – for example, fitting springs to make valves self-closing when un-powered. This sort of independent protection within components is not possible with software, as it is not possible to guarantee any specific behaviour of software in the event of hardware or operating system failure.
- *Un-needed functionality*
  The more general a computer, the fewer of its capabilities will be required by any particular application. This means that complete analysis of an operating system in any given context must include demonstration that the functions that are not wanted cannot in any way interfere with the required behaviour.

Thus, the major obstacle to a detailed combined safety analysis of hardware and software is how to manage complexity. Since the state space of even simple programs is very large, there can be no tractable approach (at least for manual analysis) based on evaluating the effect of individual hardware failures in every possible system state. This rules out analysis techniques based on conventional event or state models. The challenge for safety analysis is to find meaningful ways of identifying the critical parts of the system and modelling the potential impact of hardware failures at a more abstract level. We have developed an approach to this problem that we call Low-level Interaction Safety Analysis.

2 Low-level Interaction Safety Analysis - Principles

In a presentation to the International System Safety Conference in 1998 [McDermid 1998] we described the principles of an analysis method called Low-level Interaction Safety Analysis (LISA). This paper briefly reviews those principles, defines a complete method for the technique, and presents further results from a large-scale industrial trial.

LISA was developed specifically to study the way in which an operating system manages system *resources*, both in normal operation and in the presence of hardware failures. Instead of analysing the system functionality, the LISA method focuses on the interactions between the software and the hardware on which it runs. A set of *physical resources* and *timing events* is identified, and a set of projected failure modes of these resources is considered. The aim of the analysis is to use a combination of inductive and deductive steps to produce *arguments of acceptability* demonstrating either that no plausible cause can be found for a projected failure, or that its consequences would always lead to an acceptable system state.

The method starts from an identification of critical code to identify and classify resources. Critical code consists of safety critical application functions, plus any parts of the operating system that are essential to the correct operation of these application functions. (Note that if there is no partitioning, then all of the application code must be considered to be critical.) The criticality of resources is then determined by whether, and how, they are used by critical code.

2.1 Identifying and Classifying Resources

Physical resources consist of the processor registers, memory locations, I/O and other special registers. This is the programmer's model of the computer. Hardware features such as buses, arbitration logic etc. are considered in terms of the registers that control them. Physical resources are partitioned into five classes based upon the *criticality* of the resource usage:

- *intrinsically critical*
  resources that are used by critical application processes, or which contain data essential to the continued correct functioning of the operating system itself. For a general purpose operating system, it may be necessary to regard all memory locations that are available to application processes as intrinsically critical.

- *primary control*

  these are resources which directly control the use or function of an intrinsically critical resource; examples include memory management unit (MMU) registers, I/O control registers etc.

- *secondary control*

  resources which either provide a backup to primary controls (e.g. a secondary MMU giving redundancy in memory protection), or control access to primary resources (for example, "key" registers which must be set to particular values before protected locations can be altered).

- *non-critical*

  resources which are never used by critical software, and do not affect the correct functioning of the operating system itself.

- *unused*

  locations in the memory map which do not correspond to a physical device. The importance of these locations is that there should be no attempts by any part of the software to access them; such an attempt indicates a failure, and must be trapped and handled safely.

The model of time used in the analysis is based on the identification of discrete timing *events* that have associated hardware actions. Examples of these include interrupts, the use of system timers and counters, and synchronisation actions. Timing events can be identified as either critical or non-critical, depending upon whether they affect the execution of critical code. Note that there will be a set of primary (and possibly some secondary) control resources associated with each timing event. For example, the primary resources associated with a timer-generated interrupt will include the control registers for the timer, and the CPU registers that determine the response to the arrival of the interrupt.

From the descriptions of the resource classes, it is clear that there are dependencies between resources; that is, the state of one resource affects the behaviour of another. Indeed, this is explicit in the definition of primary and secondary control resources. However, there are other, less direct dependencies. The most significant of these is that, in most systems, there must be an initialisation phase, in which the software configures the hardware to the state required for the execution of the main body of the application.

A complete safety argument for the system must therefore demonstrate that the system powers up in a safe state, and respects minimum safety requirements throughout every stage of initialisation. To guarantee the correct execution of the application, it must also be shown either that successful completion of the initialisation guarantees that the hardware is correctly configured, or that it is impossible (or at least extremely improbable) that the main body of the software could fail to detect, and safely respond to, any incorrectness in its execution environment.

2.2 Failure mode identification in LISA

It is infeasible to consider every type and cause of failure of each device in a computer system individually, so it is necessary to make an abstraction. Experience applying HAZOP and related techniques to computer systems [McDermid 1995] has shown that a small set of fairly general guide words can be used to prompt consideration of many aspects of computer system failure provided that it is interpreted carefully in each new system context. The set of general guide words used as a basis for LISA is:

- *Omission* – a necessary action does not occur
- *Commission* – an unwanted action is performed (i.e. a perfectly functioning system would have done nothing)
- *Early* – an action is performed before the time (either real time, or relative to some other action) at which it is required
- *Late* – an action is performed after the time at which it is required
- *Value* – the timing of the action is correct, but the data it is performed with or upon is incorrect.

2.3 Arguments of acceptability

An argument of acceptability states why the normal use of a resource, and the way in which potential failures are detected and handled, result in acceptable safety properties at a system level. Suitable argument structures will vary from project to project. If the system to be analysed is being developed specifically for one application, and hazard and safety analyses are available, the LISA acceptance arguments will be able to relate low-level behaviour to system level effects. For systems that are being developed as components without detailed knowledge of the eventual application, the acceptance criteria will depend upon the target integrity level of the system, and might typically include requirements to demonstrate that:

- the intended usage of a resource does not allow low-integrity processes to access / alter high integrity data;
- no plausible cause can be found for a suggested failure;
- a suggested failure has been shown to be mitigated by a completely independent mechanism (i.e. different hardware and independently coded software);
- a suggested failure has been shown to produce no effect on the correct operation of the critical functions of the system;
- a suggested failure may have an adverse effect on the correct operation of critical functions, but the failure can be reliably flagged to application code, which can implement acceptable handling or mitigation.

2.4 Selection of analysts

As with all hazard and safety analyses, many factors will influence the selection of appropriate people to conduct a LISA analysis. This is a very low-level technique, requiring extremely detailed knowledge of both the software and hardware design; case study experience has shown that this is difficult and time-consuming for an outsider to obtain. However, LISA is intended to be a demonstration of achieved safety, and it is reasonable to expect that LISA analysts will be required to be as independent as possible.

Industrial experience has shown that easy access to members of the design team is vital, and our recommended way of applying LISA is to have a member of the design team working in an explanatory role, together with an independent analyst whose responsibility is to produce the final report and conclusions.

3 LISA Method

This section outlines the conduct of a LISA analysis.

Step 1: Agree principles for acceptability
Section 2.3 above explains the purpose of, and identifies some possible structures for, arguments of acceptability.

Step 2: Assemble source material
The minimum required source materials for LISA are:
- an overall description (specification or design) of the intended operation of the system, including strategies for managing expected failure modes;
- a complete system memory map;
- definitions of the purpose and usage of all special device registers, I/O etc. This may take the form of programmers' manuals for each hardware device in the system;
- a specification or design document which describes all the timing events in the system;
- specification or design documents which define the system start-up, initialisation, exception handling and normal and emergency shutdown procedures.

Additional sources that may be necessary or useful for some analyses include subsystem specification or design documentation, hardware failure data, and program source code.

Step 3: Analyse timing events
From the system documentation, identify all the timing events which involve a hardware / software interaction. These will include all uses of interrupts, system timers, counters or clocks, inter-processor synchronisations and time-dependent interactions with external devices or other systems. Care must be taken to ensure that events used in every mode of system operation, including initialisation, shutdown etc., are included.

For each event identified, describe its intended operation, including the preconditions necessary for the event to be generated (e.g. programming of timers) and the correct response(s) to the event. Ensure that the intended behaviour defined does not in itself create potential safety problems (e.g. check that context switches initiated by interrupts cannot leave critical data in an inconsistent state, that interrupt mask levels in the new context are appropriate etc.)

Step 3.1: Suggest deviations from intended behaviour of events

Use the guide words *omission, commission, early* and *late* to prompt consideration of possible deviations from the expected operation of each event. Each guide word may suggest more than one deviation.

Omission – the failure of an event to occur. Possible cases of omission to consider include:

- Source (writer) omission
  All events will have a single source, which in this case fails to produce the expected event. Depending on the type of source, it may be necessary to consider whether it is plausible for the source to proceed to its next expected action, or whether it experiences a fail-stop condition. A special case of this is *precondition* omission, in which the event is generated when a set of preconditions is satisfied, and the preconditions are never true.

- Transmission omission
  The medium through which the event is transmitted "loses" the event.

- Destination (reader) omission
  The destination process(es) or object(s) that was (were) expected to recognise and respond to the event do(es) not do so, e.g. through being in the wrong state or having incorrect interrupt masks. In a multiprocessor system, where events affecting more than one processor are possible (e.g. broadcast interrupts or synchronisation events), it is necessary to consider symmetric (where no recipient responds to the event) and asymmetric (one or some recipients respond) omission.

Commission – the spurious occurrence of an event. Source, transmission and destination may apply as for omission, and it may also be necessary to consider:

- Number of commission errors
  A single unintended event may have a different effect to multiple repetitions

- Repetition *vs.* insertion
  An expected event that is repeated may have a different effect from a completely unexpected event. This particularly applies when events are expected in a predetermined sequence, which is violated.

Again, there may be symmetric and asymmetric cases to consider in a multiprocessor system.

Early and *late* may be interpreted either with respect to real time, or as prompts to consider incorrect ordering (relative timing). They may also prompt consideration of jitter (i.e. where supposedly regular periodic events actually occur at irregular intervals). It should also be noted that it is important to define the boundary between an event that is late, and one that is considered to have failed entirely (omission), and similarly for early / commission.

Step 3.2: Investigate possible causes of event deviations
For each of the deviations suggested in step 3.1, identify possible causes, making certain that both direct hardware failures and indirect causes in software (e.g. incorrect programming of control registers) are considered. If no plausible cause can be found for a deviation, this should be noted.

Step 3.3: Investigate effects of event deviations
Investigate the effects of each deviation for which plausible causes were found in step 3.2. Consider how the deviation will be detected and handled by the system, and ensure that this will result in a safe system state. If there are no detection and handling mechanisms for the deviation, consider what its ultimate effect on system safety will be.

Step 3.4: Produce arguments of acceptability
Decide which of the principles of acceptability agreed in step 1 is appropriate for each suggested deviation, and produce arguments of acceptability showing how the system design meets the principles. These arguments do not need to be extensive, but should be sufficient for a reviewer reading the analysis to identify all of the components and mechanisms involved. If a suitable argument of acceptability cannot be found for a suggested deviation, this is an indication of a possible flaw in the system design.

Record the investigation of the deviation, and repeat for each suggested deviation of every identified event.

Step 4: Analyse physical resources
Identify physical resources in the system. The primary information source for this is the system memory map, although it may be necessary to consult processor, device and subsystem documentation to identify the function of all of the registers within the blocks allocated to each device. As for events, describe the intended usage of each resource, ensuring that start-up, initialisation, shutdown and other modes are considered, and check that the intended use does not in itself create safety problems.

Step 4.1: Group resources by common factors
There is no need (and, indeed, it would be impractical) to analyse every aspect of every resource separately. Resources should therefore be grouped by common characteristics so far as possible. For example, access permissions are typically assigned to blocks of memory locations; the effects of granting inappropriate access (or denying access where it is requires) can be examined for the whole block of locations. Similarly, access timing properties will usually apply to all of the locations within a single hardware device; again, these can be examined once for all locations within the device. If the initial suggested grouping is not correct,

this will become apparent as the analysis proceeds; either identical results will be obtained for many resources, suggesting they should be grouped, or the analysis of a block will show that the effects of deviations vary for different locations within the block, showing that it must be split.

Step 4.2: Classify resources

Resources are classified as *intrinsically critical, primary control, secondary control, not critical* or *unused* (the definition and implications of each of these classes is discussed in section 2.1 above).

Step 4.3: Suggest deviations from the intended use and operation of each resource

Use the guide words *omission, commission, early, late* and *value* to prompt consideration of possible deviations from the expected use and function of each resource. Each guide word may suggest more than one deviation.

- *Omission* and *commission* are interpreted as access permission violations. An omission failure occurs if a process that should be able to access a resource is denied permission. Commission failure occurs where a process is granted access to a resource that it should not have.

- *Early* has two interpretations in the case of a physical device such as memory, both leading to (unpredictably) corrupt data:
  - the processor reads from a location in the device, and attempts to latch the data from the bus before it is stable, or
  - the processor writes to a location in the device, and de-asserts data before the device has latched it correctly.
  These may seem unlikely failures, and only possible with poor hardware design. However, there are systems in which parameters such as the number of wait states inserted on accessing a particular device are programmable; the system can dynamically alter its own timing characteristics. In such systems, this type of timing failure is plausible and extremely important.

- *Late* refers to delay in accessing the resource, arising either from effects such as contention for a shared bus, or from the same type of configuration fault that could lead to *early* failures. Unlike *early* failures, lateness cannot cause data corruption. Excess wait states in a device access will merely extend the cycle and result in reduced performance; the data will be held stable until the end of the cycle. Late latching of data being read by the processor (i.e. after it has been de-asserted by the device being accessed) is highly unlikely, since the processor itself generates the timing control signals that the control the device. In general, therefore, *lateness* is only of interest in our analysis if the delay is great enough to be treated as an *omission*, e.g. by triggering a bus timeout.

- The *value* of a resource is its data content. For control resources, the correct value can often be determined in advance, and the effects of changes predicted. In the case of memory (RAM or ROM), the effect of unwanted changes can usually only be determined with knowledge of the application software.

Step 4.4: Investigate possible causes deviations in resource use or function
For each of the deviations suggested in step 4.3, identify possible causes, making certain that both direct hardware failures and indirect causes in software (e.g. incorrect programming of control registers) are considered. If no plausible cause can be found for a deviation, this should be noted.

Step 4.5: Investigate effects of deviations in resource use or function
Investigate the effects of each deviation for which plausible causes were found in step 4.4. Consider how the deviation will be detected and handled by the system, and ensure that this will result in a safe system state. If there are no detection and handling mechanisms for the deviation, consider what its ultimate effect on system safety will be.

Step 4.6: Produce arguments of acceptability
As with the event analysis, decide which of the principles of acceptability agreed in step 1 is appropriate for each suggested deviation, and produce arguments of acceptability showing how the system design meets the principles.

Record the investigation of the deviation, and repeat for each suggested deviation of every resource. It is helpful to produce two tables to record the analysis for each block of resources, one containing the investigation of properties such as access permissions and timing that apply to all resources in the block, and one that records deviations, effects and arguments which are specific to a single resource. As generic arguments become apparent (i.e. those that are used repeatedly), a separate table of these should be compiled to reduce the volume of the analysis.

4   Industrial Application of LISA

LISA has now been successfully applied to the development of a large, multiprocessor avionics system. The relative proportion of critical software to that of lower integrity levels, together with the relatively high levels of data sharing between the classes of software, meant that the conventional approach of partitioning out the critical software to separate processors would have resulted in very inefficient use of resources in a heavily loaded system. The design team therefore took the decision to implement a partitioned software system, with a core of critical software operating on all processors to implement initialisation, communication and scheduling / synchronisation tasks.

Although this was a completely bespoke development, the critical software effectively provided some of the functions of a rudimentary operating system. These included:
- memory and I/O protection
- synchronisation of activity across all processors
- scheduling

The critical software did not provide the uniform interface to hardware that would be expected of a full conventional operating system (i.e. application functions were able to access hardware directly).

Evidence was required that the partitioning system genuinely provided an acceptable level of independence between the critical functions and the rest of the system. No existing analysis technique could be identified which could provide this evidence so, with the agreement of the certifying authority, it was decided to develop a new approach. It was decided that the critical software that implemented the partitioned software environment should be analysed independently of the rest of the system. In effect, it was to be treated as an operating system to be analysed in isolation, without detailed application knowledge. The primary reason for this decision was that it was hoped to make the analysis of the critical code completely independent from the rest of the software, so that changes could be made to non-critical parts of the system without the need to repeat the complete safety analysis.

4.1 Case Study Safety Principles

In discussion with system developer, the primary requirements identified for acceptability of the partitioning scheme were:

1. Data flow corruption must be prevented
   - Modification of critical data by software of lower integrity levels shall not occur

2. Control flow corruption must be prevented
   - No action of the low integrity software shall prevent the critical software from executing when it should
   - Modification of critical code by software of lower integrity levels shall be prevented

3. Corruption of the execution environment shall not occur
   i.e. corruption of processor registers, device registers and memory access privileges shall not occur.

From these a further, secondary, requirement was identified:

4. If any of the primary requirements 1 to 3 is violated, this shall be detected, and the system caused to shut down promptly, setting a failure flag so that a stand-by unit can assume control.

Note that requirement 2 must be interpreted carefully, in that requirement 4 means that execution errors in the non-critical software may cause a shutdown, thus preventing further execution of critical code. This is acceptable, as it is the defined safe state of the system. However, the self-shutdown procedures, which are executed if any hardware failures or internal inconsistencies are detected, are a part of the critical software, and this gives a further derived requirement:

5. The ability of the self-shutdown procedures to run to completion (i.e. safe shutdown) must be guaranteed regardless of the state of the non-critical parts of the software.

It was further agreed that requirement 4 applied only to cases of single failure, i.e. the analysis did not need to consider cases of multiple simultaneous or near-simultaneous failures. This limitation was justified by two arguments:

1. Self-shutdown procedures were very quick and simple. It was considered that, provided that the first failure did not prevent the shutdown procedures from being initiated, the probability of a second, independent failure occurring that could prevent their completion was negligible.
2. In the case of multiple, coincident failures of sufficient severity to prevent orderly detection and shutdown, it was considered that the behaviour of the system would be sufficiently incoherent to be readily detectable by other systems or operators.

In order to meet the requirement that the analysis produced should be as independent of the application software as possible, it was decided that analysis should proceed by assuming that all non-critical application software would always behave in the worst conceivable way. This was interpreted as meaning that any failure of protection, synchronisation or scheduling would always result in the non-critical software causing the maximum possible interference to the operation of the critical functions. If satisfactory protection of the critical functions could be demonstrated under this assumption, no future change to the non-critical software could invalidate the safety arguments.

The LISA analysis of the system was carried out by one of the authors with considerable assistance and support from the project team, and also from Dr. Neil Audsley, who carried out a timing analysis of the system which was included in the final report. The case study extended over an elapsed period of approximately 30 months, during which time it received about 10 man months of direct effort. Of this, approximately 4 months was dedicated to developing an initial detailed understanding of the design and intended operation of the system. The initial analysis took approximately 2 months of effort, and there were then a number of updates of the design that necessitated repeating or updating parts of the analysis. The final report took a further two weeks to write.

Arguments of compliance with the safety principles were considered complete when either:

- the failure had been shown to be mitigated by two or more independent mechanisms
- the failure had been shown to produce no effect on the correct operation of the partitioning system or critical application software

or

- the failure had been shown to produce no effect on the correct operation of the partitioning system, but there were potential effects on the critical application software. In this case, the need for subsequent application software analysis was noted.

The complete final report contained 98 pages of safety analysis, including 7 tables of event analysis, which occupied 22 pages, and 18 tables of physical resource analysis, which occupied a further 20 pages. The report also contained 22 pages of Functional Failure Analysis, which was produced for comparison with the LISA results. The comparison showed that the LISA analysis contained every failure mode considered in the FFA, plus a significant number of additions, and much more detail (FFA, of course, does not consider the causes of the failure modes it examines).

In conducting this analysis, it was found that the method was extremely good at highlighting areas where the design intent was not clearly expressed in the available documentation, and several recommendations were made for improvement in the specification and supporting documentation. No safety related problems were found in the actual design at any stage, although completing the arguments of acceptability for some items required quite extensive investigation, including requests for additional information from subsystem suppliers. In a number of cases, the analysis also suggested additional tests that could be incorporated into the built in test (BIT) routines to improve the detection of certain classes of deviation. Most of these suggestions made use of self-test capabilities already present in the hardware, and all of the suggested additional tests were incorporated into the system. The LISA analysis was also used to investigate the iteration rate required for some of the continuous built-in test (CBIT) routines to meet the worst-case detection and shutdown response times agreed in the safety principles.

In a number of cases where particularly complex mechanisms were involved in the detection and handling of faults, the analysis recommendations also included bench tests involving fault injection to prove that the system response would be as predicted. It was also found that, when design changes were required for other reasons (e.g. to improve system performance), the results of completed parts of the analysis were valuable in developing modifications and in selecting between alternatives.

The final conclusion of the report was that the system was suitable and sufficiently robust for its intended use. However, this was strongly qualified by a number of limitations and exclusions. These included:

- The analysis was conducted on the design *as presented*; there was no attempt to verify that the implementation matched the design, and that this was a task that was essential to ensuring the accuracy and applicability of the report's conclusions.

- Throughout the analysis, it was assumed that previous hazard and risk assessments were correct, i.e. that the hazards were as described, and that the identified safe states were acceptable.

- The safety principles outlined at the start of this section were assumed to be sufficient to guarantee safe operation of the system. No attempt was made to ascertain, either quantitatively or in broad qualitative terms, the availability or reliability of the system. It was noted that extremely low levels of reliability or availability could invalidate the conclusions about the acceptability of the "fail stop" safe state.

The report was presented to customer representatives at the Critical Design Review, at which the analysis was described as thorough and credible. The customer representatives have formally requested that the LISA analysis is maintained as the system progresses through the remaining stages of development and commissioning to in-service status.

4.2 Sample analysis output

The tables at the end of this paper contain samples of the three types of tables produced by the case study. Due to the sensitive nature of the case study, details in the tables have been altered, but the style and technical nature of the entries is representative.

Table 1 contains a sample of the timing event analysis, in this case for the master interrupt that prompted Processor 1 to start a new cycle of the schedule. Table 2 contains samples of the generic arguments developed for blocks of physical resources, which were then used in the analysis tables as shown in Table 3. Note that, as so much information was contained in the generic arguments, or the whole device arguments in the top part of the table, the entries in the address-specific sections of the table were mostly extremely brief, as shown here. The only exception to this was in the analysis of special device registers, where complex arguments were frequently required.

5 Conclusions

This paper has presented an overview of some of the safety analysis problems associated with the transition to safety critical systems designed around conventional operating systems. It has presented a method for safety analysis of the hardware / software interactions in such a system, structured around study of the system *resources* (timing events and physical devices).

As a basis for analysis, this model has several advantages:
1. it is possible to ensure that the set of resources analysed is complete (i.e. includes the entire memory map, all non-mapped devices such as processor registers, and all interrupts and synchronisation events);
2. the model is familiar to the system's designers and programmers, so it is possible to discuss safety analysis in well-understood terms;
3. although potentially large, the set of resources in any system is of a fixed and predetermined size, so the effort required for analysis can be predicted reasonably accurately in advance.

Overall, we believe that the approach represents an important step towards the analysis of more complex architectures, such as integrated modular avionics, which are being proposed for future generations of systems.

References

[Audsley 1995]   Audsley, N. C., Burns. A, Richardson, M.F., Tindell, K. and Wellings, A.J., "Fixed Priority Preemptive Scheduling: An Historical Perspective", Journal of Real-Time Systems 8(2): 173-198, 1995.

[hise_safety_critical 1999] Archives of the hise_safety_critical mailing list, ftp://ftp.cs.york.ac.uk/hise_reports/sc.list/archive99.txt

[Joseph 1996]   Joseph, M., "Real-Time Systems: Specification, Verification and Analysis", Prentice-Hall, 1996.

[Kopetz 1997]   Kopetz, H., "Real-Time Systems: Design Principles for Distributed Embedded Applications ", Kluwer Academic, 1997.

[McDermid 1995] McDermid, J. A., Fenelon, P., Nicholson, M. and Pumfrey, D. J., "Experience with the Application of HAZOP to Computer-Based Systems", COMPASS '95: Proceedings of the Tenth Annual Conference on Computer Assurance: 37-48, 1995.

[McDermid 1998] McDermid, J. A. and Pumfrey, D. J., "Safety Analysis of Hardware / Software Interactions in Complex Systems", Proceedings of the 16th International System Safety Conference, Seattle, Washington: 232-241, 1998.

[SAE 1996]   "ARP 4761: Guidelines and Methods for Conducting the Safety Assessment Process on Civil Airborne Systems and Equipment", Society of Automotive Engineers, Inc., 1996

Master (start of cycle) Interrupt – periodic, 20ms, processor 1 only				
Guide Word and Deviation	**Cause**	**Effect**	**Detection / Protection**	**Argument of Acceptability**
Omission No master interrupt (more than 5ms late, as this is the limit imposed by the protection mechanism)	• Hardware failure • Programmable timer or interrupt control not programmed correctly • Interrupts remain masked during application code execution	Processor 1 will remain in application mode indefinitely	Back-up interrupt programmed for 25ms on Processor 2, which is reset when Processor 2 receives a start of cycle synchronisation message from Processor 1. If this interrupt occurs, Processor 2 will run the system shutdown procedure.	• Failure will be detected and shutdown initiated on first occurrence. • Backup mechanism uses completely diverse hardware (i.e. different processor, no reliance on shared bus)
Commission (single) Excess master interrupts (interrupt occurs less than 20 ms after preceding interrupt)	• Hardware failure • Programmable timer not programmed correctly	If Processor 1 is executing operating system code, no effect until context switch to application code, since interrupts are masked. In application mode, will cause immediate re-entry into operating system, resulting in shortened (no) time for application software. Result will be single-cycle application mode over-run.	Single spurious / early interrupts may not be detected.	• All resource protection mechanisms will function as intended despite mis-timed cycle.
Commission (multiple) Excess master interrupts	As above.	As above, except multiple-cycle application mode over-run is certain.	Multiple spurious / early interrupts will be detected by the application mode software completion detection mechanism. Repeated short application mode time slots be detected and will result in shutdown.	• Failure will be detected and result in shutdown within a maximum of 4 cycles. • Backup mechanism relies on Processor 1 hardware, but not on timer hardware, which is most plausible cause of failure.
Early Master interrupt early by less than the slack time in application schedule	• Hardware failure • Programmable timer not programmed correctly	Small reduction in master cycle time. Possible slip before effects become as commission on slack in application mode schedule.	Will not be detected.	• All resource protection mechanisms will function as intended despite mis-timed cycle.

Table 1 – Sample of LISA event analysis

Arg	Applies to	Justification
G1	Unused location (no hardware present)	• Attempted accesses to non-existent hardware indicate program corruption, and will result in system shutdown via one of the following mechanisms: • These locations are mapped out by MMU, and accesses will result in bus error on read or write; this will result in an exception in either application or operating system code, which will be handled to shutdown. • CPU bus timer provides a redundant mechanism; if an erroneous access is not refused by the memory protection hardware, an access to a non-existent device will result in the bus timer generating a transfer error signal; again, the result will be an unexpected exception handled to shutdown.
G2	Processor MMU functionality duplicated by second MMU	• This applies to access permissions to all locations • The two MMUs are always run in parallel, and both must give permission before a location can be accessed. This is 'fail safe', in that both devices have to grant permission for access; if either one denies it, a bus error handled to shutdown will result. • The MMU mapping tables are set up by separate sections of initialisation code.
G3	Read-only device register enforced by hardware	• Writes to these locations are ignored by the device (have no effect). • An attempt to write to such a location is indicative of software error, but it cannot further damage the system state.
G4	Program code area	• Given the degree of synchronisation within the operating system schedule, and the mechanisms which exist to detect erroneous application code behaviour, it is extremely unlikely that corrupt program code could execute for any significant period of time before causing a detectable failure. This also applies to mapping tables etc., as corruption of these will cause similar effects. The only plausible undetectable failure would be omission of a section of application code, so functions include cross-checks on successful completion (normal defensive programming techniques are sufficient).
G5	Application RAM area	• No corruption of application data can lead to violation of operating system integrity, as the worst case behaviour that can be produced is the malicious application code behaviour already assumed.
G6	Unused location (device register)	• Attempted reads from unused registers return 0, thus no detection at this level • Attempted write accesses to unused registers will cause a bus error, which will result in an unexpected exception handled to shutdown.

Table 2 – Examples of generic arguments applicable to many resources

EEPROM: Arguments applying to whole device:

Guide Word	Deviation	Causes	Argument of Acceptability
Omission	Denial of read access to application or operating system software, or operating system write permission during loading	Failure of one MMU	• G2 applies
Commission	Granting of write permission except during loading	Requires simultaneous failure of both MMUs	• G2 applies
Early	Processor attempts to latch data off bus before it has stabilised	Incorrect number of waitstates inserted on access	• See note 1 in discussion of timing analysis.
Late	Excessive latency between device access and data read	Incorrect number of waitstates inserted on access	• Local device - no system bus arbitration • See note 1 in discussion of timing analysis.

EEPROM: Address - specific comments:

Start Address	End Address	Description	Criticality	Reason	Argument of Acceptability
		Operating System Area			
010000	01FFFF	Operating System translation tables	Intrinsically critical	Tables used to initialise CPU MMU at initialisation. Define boundary between operating system and application software	• Region is check-summed and validity checked at initialisation • G4 applies
020000	03FFFF	Run-Time System	Intrinsically critical	Run time system code used by all code including operating system software	• As above
040000	0FFFFF	Operating System software	Intrinsically critical	Operating system software	• As above
		Application Area			
1D0000	1DFFFF	Application mode translation tables	Not critical	Non-critical application area	• G4 applies
1E0000	2CFFFF	Application mode software	Not critical	Non-critical application area	• G4 applies
2D0000	3BFFFF	Application mode subsystem software	Not critical	Non-critical application area	• G4 applies
3C0000	3FFFFF	**NOT USED**	Not used	-	• G1 applies

Table 3 – Sample of LISA physical resource analysis (simplified)

Guardian agents: a role for artificial intelligence in safety-critical systems?

John Fox
Imperial Cancer Research Fund
Lincoln's Inn Fields
London WC2A 3PX, UK
(44) 171 269 3624   jf@acl.icnet.uk

1. ABSTRACT

"Intelligent agents" are a hot topic in current computing. As the technologies mature agent systems will be increasingly deployed in applications that are safety or otherwise critical.. We have developed a general agent technology for use in medical and other safety-critical applications and have adopted a number of techniques to increase confidence in their soundness and safety in operation. Some of these techniques are adapted from standard software and safety engineering, but agent technologies also offer a novel approach to safety management, in which the agent reasons explicitly about hazards and their management as they occur. These "guardian agents" may also offer benefits as components of conventional software systems.

2. INTRODUCTION

The Advanced Computation Laboratory at the Imperial Cancer Research Fund has for some years been developing "intelligent agents" to support healthcare professionals in the management of cancer and other medical conditions. Our aim is to apply artificial intelligence and knowledge engineering techniques to achieve systems that are versatile and natural for healthcare professionals. In order to maximise quality and safety the techniques are being used in combination with established methods from software engineering.

By "intelligent agents" I mean software systems that are capable of emulating clinical expertise in complex situations and responding adaptively to unexpected and potentially hazardous events, potentially without requiring the participation of a human supervisor. A response may be a simple action, or a plan made up of sequences of actions over time. If a patient should suddenly have a clinical crisis, for example, medical staff will execute standard actions or care plans, possibly with some *ad hoc* problem solving. The selection and execution of care plans, whether routine or *ad hoc*, will often entail considerable uncertainty. There will be uncertainty about the interpretation of events, and the most preferred responses.

Treatment may also require repeated changes to plans if circumstances unfold unexpectedly, or if actions fail to achieve their intended goals.

We want our software to be able to support at least the routine parts of this process, in order to help minimise the errors and omissions that are increasingly difficult to avoid under the pressures of modern clinical practice.

The idea of using mathematical methods and computers to assist in clinical decision making has been discussed for many years. The concept achieved prominence with the appearance of "expert" or "knowledge based systems" (KBSs) which emerged as a side effect of attempts to construct AI systems that can solve non-trivial problems without human assistance. KBSs introduced a number of influential ideas:

1. *Emphasis on symbolic computation.* The term "symbolic" is commonly used in AI to distinguish *qualitative* from more traditional *quantitative*, or numerical, forms of computation. KBSs may use exclusively symbolic representations (such as representations based on mathematical logic) or hybrid methods which combine logical with numerical calculation.

2. *Explicit, declarative representation of knowledge.* Knowledge of a domain (e.g. the medical domain of diseases and drugs) is represented explicitly, and sharply separated from the processes that use it (e.g. problem solving, decision making and planning processes). Declarative representations capture what an agent needs to know without assuming how that knowledge is to be used.

3. *Domain-specific heuristics rather than general algorithms.* Heuristics can be thought of as formalized "rules of thumb" which often prove useful in practice but are not guaranteed to be valid, and may not have a clear theoretical justification.

4. *Generic tasks not one-off methods.* Generic tasks are generalized methods for achieving similar types of goal in a variety of domains. For example, we may have a generic "diagnosis" method that can be used in medical diagnosis or for explaining faults in electronic devices and other man-made equipment.

These and other innovations have given AI technologies a distinctive character, though they have also attracted some suspicion from more mainstream software developers due to their reputation for being somewhat "flaky". In recent years, however, there has been some convergence as both schools learned lessons from each other's successes.

The current state of this work is reported in detail elsewhere [Fox and Das, *in press*]. There we describe PRO*forma* a general technology for the design and implementation of intelligent systems, the theory of the RED agent [Das et al, 1997] and a number of medical applications are described in [Fox and Thomson, 1998]. The second reference also provides the formal details of the underlying agent theory that guarantees various soundness properties of the technology.

Throughout the work we have been concerned to take advantage of systematic development methodologies and, wherever possible, formal design techniques from software engineering. In return we believe that agent techniques can add value to conventional software by including "intelligence" for active safety management.

3. LESSONS FROM SOFTWARE ENGINEERING

Nowadays large software systems are commonly developed within structured lifecycles. These help to achieve quality by systematically organizing the design, development, testing and maintenance of the system. Structured lifecycle models are increasingly being used in the development of AI systems as well, as in KADS, a well known methodology for knowledge based systems that provides tools and techniques to support design, specification, knowledge acquisition, knowledge reusability, verification etc. [Wielinga, Schreiber and Breuker, 1992].

Figure 1 illustrates the agent development lifecycle that we have adopted. This covers the basic design, development and operation that we have found to be well suited to the development of agent systems in medicine, and potentially other domains.

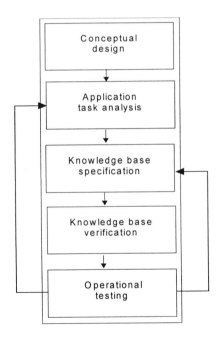

Figure 1 A development life cycle for intelligent systems. The first step requires the development of an integrated set of design concepts. Later steps are analogous to conventional software engineering, but take advantage of the expressiveness and clarity of the logical foundations.

156

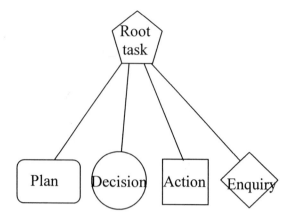

Figure 2: The PRO*forma* task ontology. Agent expertise models are composed out of these networks, forming networks of tasks carried out reactively in response to events (actions, decisions etc) and deliberatively to acheve goals (plans). The PRO*forma* method and toolset is described in Fox et al, (1997) and see exmaple A at end of article. The underlying formal agent model is described in Das et al (1997).

There has also been growing interest in applying techniques from formal software engineering to AI in recent years. Some researchers have explored the use of mathematical techniques for specifying and proving the soundness of knowledge based systems, inspired by formal specification languages such as Z, VDM, etc. These have been developed to meet the specific needs of AI applications e.g. $(ML)^2$ [van Harmelen and Balder, 1992] and DESIRE [Treur and Wetter, 1993].

The motivation for developing formal design techniques has been the desire to remove many of the informal design practices associated with AI systems development, and to provide techniques for automated verification and validation of the system knowledge base.

We have adopted both these methods in the PRO*forma* technology.

PRO*forma task analysis* is the development of a model of agent expertise (here clinical expertise) in terms of the data, decisions, actions and plans that are required in order to achieve a goal (e.g. the therapeutic goals inherent in a medical care plan). The core of our method is a collection (strictly an ontology) of *generic task models*, which are illustrated in Figure 2. Tasks are formal software objects which can be composed into networks representing plans or procedures which are

The task specification tools generate a definition of the application knowledge base in a formal knowledge representation language called R^2L [Fox and Das, *in press*].

Since we have a formal model of the general properties of decisions, plans and other tasks, and the relationships between them, there is considerable scope for automatically identifying many problems and potential problems in an R^2L specification with simple logical checks, including:

- critical missing values
- concepts referred to in inference rules but not defined
- inconsistent constraints (e.g. scheduling or temporal constraints)

A task analysis is not sufficient to build a complete application since the detailed knowledge that is required to enact each component task must also be provided. This is carried out in the next step of the method. The PRO*forma* task set is supported by a set of reusable software components that can be assembled or composed into a task network, using specialised CASE tool (Figure 3). Each task is modeled in an object-oriented style using a tabular format to represent the attributes of the task object, where values are typically logical conditions or rules associated with a task.

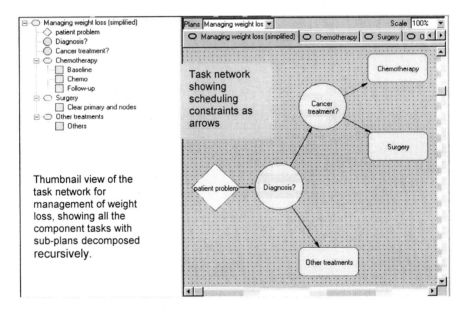

Figure 3: The PRO*forma* task analysis tool being used to develop an agent model for cancer diagnosis and treatment [Fox et al, 1997].

Once all the recognizable syntactical and other logical errors have been removed it is possible to execute the specification in order to test the medical adequacy of the agent's behavior and the correctness of its knowledge base. This is carried out with a software engine that interprets the R^2L task definition. Tasks are enacted according to a well-defined control regime in which tasks pass through a sequence of states, the particular sequence being determined by the situations and events that are encountered by the agent.

4. LESSONS FROM SAFETY ENGINEERING

"The goal of system safety is to design an acceptable safety level into the system before actual production or operation. ... "

N. Leveson, *Safeware*, 1996

The need to design quality into software from the beginning of the development lifecycle is now generally accepted in software engineering, and an analogous view is increasingly taken of software safety.

Traditional safety engineering involves several activities: (1) analyzing faults and other sources of hazards, (2) incorporating techniques to reduce the occurrence of hazards, and (3) preventing hazards turning into disasters. [Leveson, 1995] translates these activities into a special lifecycle for safety critical applications. Safety needs to be considered throughout the lifecycle; and it should be considered explicitly and separately from the normal engineering issues of functionality, efficiency and so forth. The same lessons apply to AI systems. Figure 4 extends our agent development lifecycle in figure 1 by including a separate safety design path.

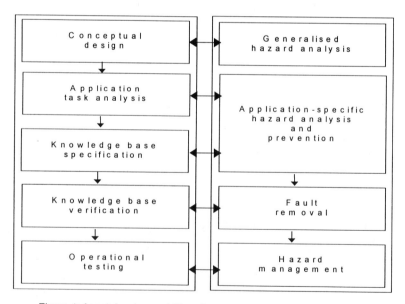

Figure 4: Agent development lifecycle augmented with a parallel safety lifecycle involving hazard analysis and removal.

5. CAN SAFETY ENGINEERING LEARN ANYTHING FROM AGENT ENGINEERING?

"The old admonition about 'the best-laid plans of mice and men' also applies to the best-laid plans of computers"
David E. Wilkins, 1997, p 305.

The standard view of software safety is that it is primarily a design problem. It should do precisely what the designers intend under all circumstances, and nothing else. Engineering a system to be safe broadly consists of trying to anticipate all the hazards that might arise, whether due to internal system faults or the environmental threats that can occur, and building appropriate responses into the hardware and software to ensure continued safe functioning, or failsafe shutdown.

With the wide range of techniques now available, much can be done to ensure that an operational system will continue to operate as intended, though we can rarely, if ever, guarantee it. Even with a rigorous design lifecycle that incorporates explicit hazard analysis and fault eradication techniques, however, there is a residual weakness for both AI and conventional software. The strategy depends upon the design team being able to make predictions about all the circumstances that may hold when the system is in routine operation.

In addition to the residual engineering problem that software cannot be guaranteed to be fault free and reliable, there is another important problem facing us. This is that software reliability is not the same thing as software *safety*. The software may be of high quality and generally operate as intended, but if deployed in complex environments it may not have a sufficiently comprehensive protocol to cover all the hazards that can arise.

In some fields it may be possible to anticipate most of the hazards that can arise, but in medicine and other complex settings this seems to be out of the question. The scope for unforeseen and *unforeseeable* interactions is vast. The environments in which the software is used may be quite different from those envisioned by the designers. There may be unexpected side effects if actions are correctly carried out but in unanticipated conditions, or two or more actions taken for independently justifiable reasons may have dangerous interactions. It is simply not possible to guarantee that all possible hazards will be exhaustively identified for substantial applications.

It is precisely these kinds of "ill-defined problems" that AI has always been concerned with. To deal with the safety problem we would benefit from additional approaches and AI may offer some novel opportunities. We are exploring the idea that safety-critical applications should be equipped with an explicit safety manager that operates in parallel with the primary systems. This would bring all the reasoning, decision making and planning capabilities to bear on the problems of detecting, interpreting and responding to hazards that it brings to its primary functions. Systems may incorporate "intelligent" components that have the explicit role of detecting, recognizing and remediating hazards at run time, to complement the standard methods of hazard analysis and error correction at design time.

Rather than try to anticipate all the specific hazards that can arise, an alternative strategy may be to provide the software agent with the operational ability to predict hazardous consequences prior to committing to actions, and to veto actions or preempt hazards when a potentially dangerous trend is recognized. The agent can then apply general or specialized problem-solving methods to find remedies that are appropriate to the context [Fox, 1993].

An early example of this approach was the "safety bag expert system" [Klein, 1991] which was designed to manage the routing of rolling stock through the shunt yards at Vienna station. The system's goal was to plan safe routings for rolling stock being moved through a busy rail network.

Planning the shortest or other minimum-cost route through a rail network is clearly hazardous[1]. A section of the route may have other wagons on it, or points (switches) might be set such that another train could enter the section. Klein's safety bag expert system had a dual channel design in which one program proposed viable routes through the tracks and points while a second system monitored the proposed routes and assessed them for potential hazards.

The safety bag is a rule-based system in which the rules' conditions embody knowledge of the safety regulations that apply at Vienna station. The actions of the rules are to veto (or commit to) routes proposed by the route planner as in the following examples.

```
If      there is a request to check for global locking and
        all switches in the route are correctly positioned and
        all switches in the route are interlocked and
        all switches in the route are flank protected and
        the status of the route is admissible
Then    commit the request and change the status to locked

If      there is a route element of shunting route and
        the new route is a train route and
        the start signal of the shunting route is not
        contained in the new route
Then    the route is not admissible
```

The use of rules to express what is, and is not, acceptable behaviour brings together the documentation and implementation of a safety-critical system. The "safety policy" embodied in the rules is explicit and readable for both the original designers and independent inspectors. The rule set is also executable, and the software will operate according to these rules so we can be more confident that the

---

[1] In the light of the recent horrific tragedy at Paddington Station in London this example seems particularly timely, though that was an error in plan execution rather than in route planning.

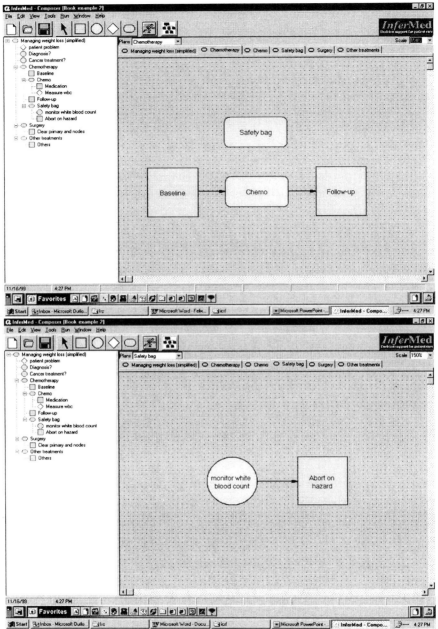

Figure 5: Cancer chemotherapy component from Figure 4, consisting of repetitive administration of cytotoxic drugs and monitoring of white blood count and an autonomous safety agent that executed in parallel with this process. This agent consists of a decision and an action (bottom)

safety policy will be followed than if the rules were no more than the designers' documented intentions.

Figure 5 is based on the same medical problem as the cancer example given above. However we have now attached a safety agent to our expertise model (top panel). This is an independent plan that is activated as soon as chemotherapy is started. (If the treatment decision is to treat the patient surgically, or the diagnosis is not cancer and no treatment is required then the safety agent will be dormant throughout execution.)

The safety agent itself consists in this simple example of a continuous *decision process* (the circle) and an *action* to abort chemotherapy if it is decided that there is a hazard (figure 5, bottom). The main "chemo" task consists of a cyclical process of administering cytotoxic drugs followed by measurement of the patient's white blood count. The white blood count (WBC) is recorded in the system's database which is being monitored by the safety agent, and in particular the "monitor white blood count" decision in the safety agent. The conditions of the agent's decision rules include functions to compute whether or not there is a hazardous trend present in the successive WBC values.

In this example the safety bag simply computes a running average though it could be any property of the data. If the average falls below some threshold value the decision is automatically taken to veto continuation of chemotherapy. The chemotherapy plan has an explicit abort condition: this matches the veto posted by the safety agent and the chemotherapy task halts. The safety agent is a novel approach to ensuring that software can be made safe. However, the concept as described so far has three significant limitations.

First, the rules simply say "if such and such is true then do this, but if such and such then don't do it". The rationale behind the rules and the safety goal(s) that are implied are not explicitly represented. If a rule turns out to be inappropriate for some reason, the agent has no way of knowing it.

Secondly, the rules of the protocol are "special case" regulations that are specific to the domains of trains and chemotherapy: they do not capture *general principles.* It would be desirable to have a generalized collection of safety rules that could be applied in a range of applications.

Ideally, we would like a *general theory of safety* which would provide the foundations for specifying general safety protocols that might be used in any domain, from medicine to train routing, to autopilots to robots [Fox, 1993]. There would be significant benefits if we could formalize general safety knowledge from an agent's domain-specific knowledge. This would simplify the task of proving that an agent design is safe and sound. Practically, it opens up the possibility of constructing a standard "guardian agent" as a reusable component for many applications.

Hammond recently reviewed a large number of cancer treatment protocols with the aim of establishing general principles of good care and capturing them in a logic (Prolog) program. Not only did he succeed in doing this [Hammond et al, 1994] but the principles that he identified seem to be potentially applicable in a wide range of domains. Among the general rules that he describes are the following:

ANTICIPATE: Prevent or ameliorate known hazards before executing essential actions.

AVOID AUGMENTATION: Avoid (extraneous) actions likely to exacerbate hazards due to essential actions.

AVOID DIMINUTION: Avoid (extraneous) actions likely to undermine the benefits of essential actions.

MONITOR: Monitor responses that herald adverse events or hazardous situations.

SCHEDULE: Schedule actions in time for best effect and least harm.

In more recent work we have taken this further, by formalizing intuitive concepts of *safety, safety constraints, obligations* as specialised modalities which modify propositions in the logic of R^2L [Fox and Das, *in press*].

6. CONCLUSIONS

In recent years knowledge engineers have become much more concerned with quality of design and implementation than traditionally, and they have learned much from conventional software engineering in this process. In return AI may have some novel techniques to offer which could add a further level of trust to safety-critical systems by adding "intelligence" into the designs. Alongside the pursuit of formal lifecycles, rigorous specification of software etc. we have investigated the idea of active safety management techniques which deal with hazards that arise unexpectedly during system operation.

If we are to achieve complete trust in any safety-critical technology it is not enough to prove that it is technically sound. We must also demonstrate, so far as is possible, that it is safe. Our proposal is that medical systems and, perhaps, other kinds of safety-critical software as well, might be equipped with guardian agents which exploit AI techniques. These agents would bring "intelligence" – the abilities to reason, make decisions and plan actions over time - to the problems of recognizing hazards and actively managing dangerous situations if and when they occur.

7. REFERENCES

Das S, Fox J, Elsdon D and Hammond, P "A flexible architecture for general agents" *Journal of Experimental and Theoretical Artificial Intelligence*, 9, 407-440, 1997.

Fox, J. "On the soundness and safety of expert systems." *Artificial Intelligence in Medicine*, **5**: 159-179, 1993.

Fox J and Das S *Safe and Sound: Artificial Intelligence in Hazardous Applications*, AAAI and MIT Press, in press.

Fox J and Thomson R "Decision support and disease management: a logic engineering approach" IEEE Transactions on information technology and biomedicine, 2 (4), 217-228, 1998.

Hammond, P., Harris AL, Das SK and Wyatt JC. (1994). "Safety and Decision Support in Oncology." *Meth. Inf. Medicine* 33(4): 371-381.

Klein, P. "The safety bag expert system n the electronic railway interlocking system Elektra" *Expert Systems and their applications*, 3, 499-506, 1991.

Leveson, N. *Safeware. System safety and computers.* Reading, Massachusetts, Addison-Wesley, 1995.

van Harmelen, F., Balder, J. "(ML)^2: a formal language for KADS models of expertise." *Knowledge Acquisition* **4**: 127-161, 1992.

Treur, J and Wetter T *Formal specification of complex reasoning systems,* Chichester: Ellis Horwood, 1993.

Wielinga, B. J. S., Schreiber, A T and Breuker, J A "KADS: A modelling approach to knowlege engineering." *Knowledge Acquisition* **4**(1): 5-53, 1992.

Wilkins, D. E. "That's something I could not allow to happen": HAL and planning. *Hal's Legacy.* D. G. Stork (Ed). Cambridge, MIT Press: 305-331, 1997.

Declaration of interest: The PROforma development environment has been commercialized under the Arezzo® trademark by InferMed Ltd, London.

SAFETY IN TRANSPORT

Framework for the Safety of Intelligent Transport Systems

Peter H Jesty, Keith M Hobley
and Oliver M J Carsten
University of Leeds, Leeds, UK

David D Ward and Mark Fowkes
MIRA
Nuneaton, UK

Abstract

The Department of the Environment, Transport and the Regions is funding a series of studies on how to apply Intelligent Transport Systems for Urban Traffic Management and Control (UTMC). Safety issues have been the subject of project UTMC22 which enquired into the current situation and how key stakeholders viewed the medium term. It also performed a preliminary safety analysis on the UTMC architecture and proposed a framework for the development and assessment of safety-related UTMC systems. These proposals, should they be adopted, will require a number of changes to be made to the current methodology for ensuring the safety of the road traffic environment.

1 Introduction

The Urban Traffic Management and Control (UTMC) programme is an initiative funded by the Department of the Environment, Transport and the Regions (DETR) to study the implications of using integrated telematic applications for the management and control of all aspects of road transport in an urban environment. A Technical Specification has been produced [DETR 1997] which provides information on the functions that can be expected, and an overall architecture for their deployment. Whilst the contents of this document has been influenced by, and taken data from, the results of the first two Telematics for Transport research programmes (DRIVE I and DRIVE II) funded by the European Commission, some interpretation has been necessary to make it applicable to the UK environment. The UTMC programme has funded a number of projects to study the various issues associated with the subject and one project, UTMC22, has had the task of reporting on the safety issues associated with the UTMC Technical Specification, and this paper describes the results.

The UTMC22 project consisted of three main phases:

- Fact-finding - an enquiry into the current situation and of how key stakeholders viewed the medium future;
- The undertaking of a Preliminary Safety Analysis (PSA) of the UTMC architecture based on the information given in the Technical Specification [UTMC22 1999a];

- The production of a Framework for the Development and Assessment of Safety-Related UTMC Systems [UTMC22 1999b].

A particularly important feature of this project was that the team included experts from each of the three areas of safety associated with road transport, namely Functional System Safety, Traffic Safety and Human Machine Interaction (HMI). These three aspects of safety were identified and treated as different subjects during DRIVE I (1989-91) [DRIVE 1991], and whilst they continued to be developed separately during DRIVE II (1992-95), their respective experts have now started to undertake collaborative work. The relationship between the three aspects of safety is shown in Figure 1.

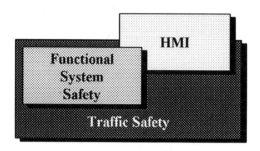

Figure 1 - Relationship between the Three Aspects of Safety

- **Functional System Safety** is primarily concerned with the analysis of the reliability of a piece, or pieces, of hardware and/or software. The analysis should identify the aspects of design, operation or failure of the system that may generate malfunctions and lead to dangerous or un-anticipated modes.
- **HMI** is concerned with how a human user interacts with a system via an interface. The targets of analysis are normally the visual, auditory and tactile interfaces within the vehicle, at the roadside and in the control room, and their ability to be used effectively and safely.
- **Traffic Safety** is concerned with the safe operation of the traffic system as a whole. It covers the outcome of both Functional System Safety and most HMI problems (with the exception of those related solely to customer satisfaction), for the system and the user, and the malfunctions that may lead to accidents. It also covers the ways in which a system might affect road user behaviour so as to alter the interaction between the driver, the vehicle, the road infrastructure and other road users (including vulnerable road users such as pedestrians and cyclists) such that they no longer use road transport in a safe manner.

2 Fact-finding

Six visits were undertaken to Local Authorities, Consultant Engineers, a Manufacturer and the Highways Agency. Since the project was only planned to be of a short duration (six months) it was necessary for the project team to approach these visits in a planned way, acknowledging that it had previously studied many of the problems, and already had ideas for some of the solutions. The details of these solutions were then modified in the light of the information discovered during the fact-finding exercise.

There is a general agreement, indeed many European research projects in the field of transport telematics (also known as intelligent transport systems, or ITS) have already demonstrated that more benefit will be obtained by integrating traffic management and traffic control functions, rather than by using them in isolation. This changes the very nature of the safety problem in two fundamental ways:

- Traditionally, regulatory agency approval for road transport equipment has been performed using a Type Approval process. It was devised when equipment consisted only of mechanical and electrical components, and thus a series of tests was a valid and sufficient exercise to demonstrate safety. The additional use of software now means that testing alone is not sufficient to prove correctness.
- An integrated system exhibits emergent properties that are not present in the individual items of equipment; indeed this is why they have been integrated. It is therefore necessary to consider the safety hazards that may result from the emergent properties of the system, as well as the specific hazards associated with the equipment of which it is constituted.

The fact-finding process found that, whilst neither of these two basic issues were well understood; as might have been expected, those who had some experience of ITS as part of the various European research programmes were more aware of the issues.

There has been a general assumption that the only real safety issue in traffic management and control is in connection with traffic signals (i.e. "traffic lights"), and that provided they do not give unsafe commands, e.g. simultaneous green on conflicting arms of the junction, the main cause of all other accidents is assumed to be the result of driver error. This is despite the fact that many studies in both Traffic Safety, e.g. [Carsten 1989], and HMI, e.g. [Sivak 1985], have shown that there are many other factors that can create traffic safety hazards. It should be noted that not all traffic safety hazards will automatically result in an accident, most are "conflicts" between one or more vehicles which are resolved by the drivers braking and/or taking avoiding action; it is only when these measures fail that an accident will occur. However since the difference between "conflicts" and accidents may only be a small fraction of a second, or a few millimetres, they are still undesirable, and measures should be taken to avoid them whenever this is possible.

The lack of recognition of the potential problems associated with ITS can be explained, in part, by the fact that few have been deployed so far. Until now changes in the technology for traffic control have been slow, and traffic management is very much in its infancy. As a result most deployment plans are based on historical precedent, and there is a definite need to provide some form of education on the characteristics of the new ITS in general, and their implications for safety in particular.

In fact the authorities, in the guise of the Highways Agency, have been working on this issue for some years and two documents have been produced, one still in draft form. The draft Code of Practice [COP 1998] is intended to be part of the *Design Manual for Roads and Bridges* (a document in many volumes). It covers all public roads except motorways (for regulatory reasons), and is concerned with the safe and consistent design methodology of traffic control systems and providing an awareness of the life-cycle procedures. The Code of Practice is clearly concerned with many of the issues covered in the Framework produced by the UTMC22 project [UTMC22 1999b], which is intended to supplement, not supplant, it. Thus, whereas the Code of Practice provides the overall framework for the deployment of ITS, the Framework is concerned, in particular, with the more detailed engineering requirements of the development part of the life-cycle. The other document is concerned with the formal assessment of equipment [TRG 0500B 1996] and is discussed further in Section 5.

Early drafts of the Code of Practice included major sections on the use of Safety Integrity Levels (SIL), a concept that was then being introduced in early drafts of [IEC 61508 1999]. Unfortunately the process that was recommended for their use was considered inapplicable and unworkable, and thus not only has it been rejected, but there is now antipathy within the industry towards the entire concept of SILs.

This industry currently certifies its safety-related equipment using a Type Approval process but, based on its experience of ITS in the European research programmes [Hobley 1995a], the project team felt that the future regulatory process for ITS should be moving towards "self certification" by the manufacturer or systems integrator (see Section 5). It was very interested to discover that none of the four groups of stakeholders wanted to see an end to a formal regulatory process and, for different reasons, all wanted something that would continue to provide an "official seal of approval".

- **Manufacturers** face competition from some companies which, in their ignorance, view the traffic control market as being easy to satisfy. They therefore want a formal mechanism to demonstrate that their equipment does indeed satisfy the regulations.
- **Local Authorities** do not have the expertise to judge the technical quality of the equipment that they purchase. They therefore want a formal mechanism to demonstrate that the equipment they purchase does indeed satisfy the regulations.

- **Consultant Engineers** find that it is very much to their advantage to be able to recommend the use of "approved" equipment both in their national and international operations, because this helps to "guarantee" the quality of their work. The use of "approved" equipment also absolves them from legal liability should a failure occur.
- **The Highways Agency** is responsible for ensuring that the roads are safe for public use. They want a formal mechanism to help it maintain the regulations.

3 Preliminary Safety Analysis of UTMC

The Preliminary Safety Analysis (PSA) of the UTMC architecture was undertaken to identify all the types of hazards that may be associated with a complete implementation of the UTMC Technical Specification. Whilst this activity will not necessarily find all the hazards of a specific implementation, and so cannot replace the PSA of any proposed UTMC system, nevertheless many hazards can be identified to highlight where special effort needs to be taken during any design.

The PSA was undertaken using the PASSPORT methodology for PSA [Hobley 1995b]. In order to provide a target for the systematic identification of hazards, a tabular version of a PASSPORT Diagram for the full UTMC specification was created showing the inputs, outputs and the functions that related one to the other [UTMC22 1999a]. The main source of information came from the list of 24 functions and 116 sub-functions that the current UTMC architecture is intended to support. This list was extracted from a larger list produced during the Transport Telematics research programmes [Gaillet 1997]. Unfortunately, whilst the form of this list may be suitable for high level plans and discussions, there is little solid information upon which to base an engineering analysis, even at a high level of abstraction. A typical example is:

> 420 Direct vehicle speed control
> (limiting vehicle speeds to within mandatory speed limits)

Note that it does not specify the input or output terminators, i.e. the links between the UTMC system and the outside world, nor does it provide a complete description of what the function actually does. Since a system safety hazard can only occur outside the boundary of that system, in order to identify the safety hazards associated with UTMC systems, it was necessary to make assumptions about the functions and their corresponding input and/or output terminators. Some functions may not be connected directly to a terminator, but they may still have an effect on it as part of an emergent property.

Function 420 also has a variety of different implementations to satisfy this one top level description, and we are aware of at least four principal techniques that satisfy this sub-function, three of which have been studied in the External Vehicle

Speed Control project [Jesty 1998]. (The PSA during that project showed that many of the hazards varied with the technology being used.) There is thus the potential for some systemic faults to arise due to the diverse interpretations of the top-level Technical Specification [DETR 1997] that are possible. (A systemic fault is similar to a systematic fault except that it pervades the whole system, normally because it is deliberately designed into the system due to a major misinterpretation, or misunderstanding, of the requirements. It is a particular characteristic of complex systems.) It should be noted that when the current EC Transport Telematics project KAREN (TR4108) has completed its Framework Architecture for Intelligent Transport Systems (ITS) it should be possible to specify the UTMC architecture in a less ambiguous manner.

The principal hazards identified during the PSA were associated with traffic management and traffic control. In addition to the basic safety hazard associated with any individual set of traffic signals, e.g. simultaneous green on conflicting arms of the junction, when the controllers are integrated to provide co-ordinated instructions along a traffic corridor it is possible to disrupt the flow of traffic as well as to make it more coherent. Such disruption will result in an increased number of conflict situations and even accidents.

The use of variable message signs (VMS) can also introduce some hazards. If they cannot be read or understood easily then they will be a distraction to the driver. They must also provide consistent information when a number are being used in an integrated system. The potential severity of the hazard increases when VMS are used to provide commands to drivers rather than advice or information.

It was not possible to provide more than rather generic safety requirements at this stage, given the large number of possible ways in which a UTMC system is likely to be created. For example, the setting of the message on a VMS can be a manual operation with a controller choosing from a number of pre-set messages, to a fully automated system where the controller is only informed as to what has been done. An attempt was also made to allocate SILs [IEC 61508 1999] to the various systems that would produce the hazards, but on most occasions it was only possible to state a range, since the precise value would depend on the exact deployment being proposed. Examples were found at all four SILs.

Probably the most important result of the PSA is that it demonstrates that there are very many potential hazards in a UTMC system over and above those related solely to the basic safety of a road junction controlled by traffic signals. In addition it will be necessary to perform PSAs on each and every planned deployment in order to identify the precise hazards associated with the desired applications, and hence to confirm the SIL(s) for the equipment that will comprise a particular UTMC system.

4 Development Life-Cycle

UTMC systems are one set of applications that will make use of ITS, but it does not make sense to try and categorise a system as belonging to UTMC or not. Not only might this place *ad hoc* restrictions on what can be deployed, but the safety aspects of an application might be ignored because it is not an "official" part of a UTMC system. In addition, there is a growing need for ITS to work across the urban/inter-urban boundary. Nor does it make sense to distinguish between Traffic Control Systems and Traffic Management Systems; whilst the former are normally obviously safety-related, the latter may also contain some longer term Traffic Safety hazards. It is therefore essential to consider each function in its application, and for this reason the Framework [UTMC22 1999b] is really addressed at all ITS.

The obvious basis for the Framework is a life-cycle model to highlight the various stages when particular processes should be performed. This proved to be particularly difficult for three important reasons.

Firstly, the development of a UTMC system does not normally have a beginning or an end; it evolves over time using existing equipment where possible, and purchasing new equipment only when the funding becomes available. Indeed, according to some strict definitions, it could be said to be in a permanent state of maintenance.

Secondly, the word "system" can be used in many senses, and it is important to be able to distinguish between them. Figure 2 shows that a typical UTMC system may be built up from a variety of types of unit. Each unit performs one or more functions, e.g. location determination using the Global Positioning System, and may be used in more than one application, e.g. route guidance or hazardous goods monitoring. Some units, such as a traffic signal controller, need to receive a formal Type Approval certificate (see Section 5), whilst others, such as a control room computer system or closed circuit television, may be available "commercially off the shelf" (COTS). The more novel applications may need to have equipment specifically designed and built to support them but, because they are so new the regulations concerning them have not yet been created; this was the situation when the system was developed for the speed controlled section of the M25. A large manufacturer may offer a UTMC system as a package, whilst some towns or cities may wish, or need, to organise their own integration of units.

When a city installs a UTMC system a number of parameters will have to be set in order to satisfy the constraints of that environment, and it then becomes a unique deployment of that system. For example, Type Approval for a traffic signal controller includes the need for the equipment to check at all times for the "green light conflict", but the timing of the phases between different arms of a junction,

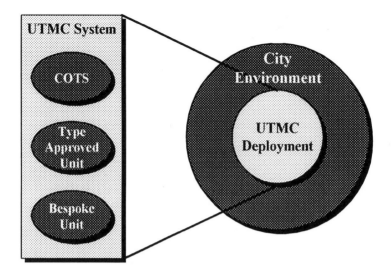

Figure 2 - System and Deployment

or between junctions, is programmable. This complexity of deployment means that, not only do the safety issues vary throughout the life-cycle, but so does the person who is responsible.

The third major difficulty occurred because the project team was writing a Framework that covered all three aspects of safety at the same time. Traditionally they have been covered by different academic and professional disciplines, whose terminology has developed independently of each other. It turned out that, not only had the same words been given different meanings, but their respective system life-cycles highlighted different issues. Thus, for example, whilst for Functional System Safety the term "test" is used to describe the process of supplying known data to confirm an expected result during equipment development, in Traffic Safety the word "test" can be used to describe the process of "let's see what happens" during a Field Trial.

When comparing the three approaches it became clear that most, though not all, of the Functional System Safety and HMI issues were connected with the development of particular items of equipment, whilst Traffic Safety experts are primarily concerned with effects of the integrated systems. Two rather large life-cycle diagrams were then created that showed when all the main safety activities should take place. Although we believe that they do conform to the safety life-cycle of [IEC 61508 1999], this has not been demonstrated explicitly in the Framework due to the current scepticism in the applicability of this standard for ITS.

4.1 Life-Cycle Phases to Assure the Safety of an ITS

The basic philosophy of the Framework, which is summarised in Figure 3, is that not only must there be an understanding as to what needs to be done but, once it has been completed, there must also be a demonstration that it has been done correctly. This demonstration must be performed with a degree of rigour that will provide the necessary confidence in the safety of the final system. Thus, if a system has been allocated a high SIL then more work will be necessary to demonstrate that the desired safety properties have been achieved than for one with a lower SIL.

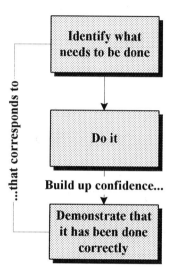

Figure 3 - Building Confidence

The basic safety activities are summarised below, not necessarily in consecutive order; the framework provides further explanation but refers to source documents for the details. It should be noted that whilst the sub-sections indicate the areas of expertise that will be needed to perform the detailed work, the needs of each expert should be understood by the others, and there should be regular communication between them.

4.1.1 Safety planning and assessment

In order to be able to demonstrate the safety of the final system a plan must be made so that the correct tasks are undertaken from the beginning.

- **Begin System Safety Plan**: The process of creating a plan as to how the safety of the system will be assured. This plan should be continually reviewed and modified as further information is obtained.

- **Begin Unit Safety Plan**: The process of creating a plan as to how the safety of the sub-system or unit will be assured. This plan should be continually reviewed and modified as further information is obtained.
- **Equipment Type Approval**: The process of approving a unit or sub-system for use in a limited range of applications.
- **System Certification**: The process of approving a specific installation in a specific application.

4.1.2 Functional System Safety

In order to assure the Functional System Safety of an ITS there should be a number of processes to identify the safety hazards, decide how to mitigate them, and then to demonstrate that this has been done satisfactorily.

- **Preliminary Safety Analysis**: The process of finding the safety hazards that are associated with the system concept, and the safety requirements needed to mitigate them.
- **System safety analysis**: The process of analysing the design, especially the interactions between the various individual units, or sub-systems, of which the system is to be comprised.
- **Hazard and risk analysis**: The process of identifying hazards directly associated with the unit or sub-system, or that propagate to becoming a hazard of the system.
- **Safety requirements allocation**: The process of allocating requirements to mitigate the effects of any safety hazard.
- **Detailed Safety Analysis**: The process of analysing the detailed design, both to identify any further safety hazards, and to demonstrate that design measures exist to mitigate all the safety hazards.
- **Safety validation**: The process of confirming that all tests and other processes have been performed to demonstrate that all safety hazards have been mitigated adequately.
- **Maintenance activities**: The process of performing the actions that are necessary to keep the system functioning correctly.

4.1.3 Human-Machine Interaction

Human factors design and development targets should be defined for the HMI aspects which can then be used as benchmark criteria in establishing the success or failure of a system during its development.

- **HMI specification**: The process of analysing the human factors issues associated with planned use of the system, and the expected ability of the users.

- **HMI validation**: The process of confirming that the desired HMI performance has been achieved.
- **HMI analysis**: The process of analysing the human factors issues associated with planned use of the unit or sub-system.
- **HMI requirements allocation**: The process of specifying the HMI attributes of the unit or sub-system.
- **HMI appraisal**: The process of testing a prototype to confirm that the desired HMI performance has been achieved.

4.1.4 Traffic Safety

The proposed solution to a traffic problem should be checked to ensure that it does not bring additional safety hazards, and the final installation(s) should be monitored for any unexpected effects.

- **Formulate Traffic Safety hypothesis**: The process of planning a solution to a traffic problem and assessing the safety hazards that might be associated with it.
- **Prospective Traffic Safety analysis**: The process of performing small scale off-road trials on prototypes or facsimiles (e.g. driving simulators) of the system in order to confirm, or otherwise, the basic hypothesis.
- **Retrospective Traffic Safety evaluation**: The process of performing full "before and after" field trials on the fully deployed system, usually when it is the "first of a kind", in order to assess the safety and other benefits.
- **Safety audit and monitoring**: The process of verifying that a specific installation is correct, and then monitoring the system for a long period of time in order to identify any long term problems or unexpected effects.

4.2 Rôles and Responsibilities

The fact-finding exercise had shown that the creation of a typical ITS was likely to involve many companies and organisations, but it also showed that, for many people, there were only two aspects of safety:
- The health and safety of the civil engineering construction workers, which is the responsibility of the construction company;
- The safe operation of the equipment, which is covered by Type Approval.

Whilst this works satisfactorily for the deployment of traditional traffic systems, ITS will require someone to be responsible for the overall "safety of the system". Each deployment of an ITS is likely to be different and possibly novel, both in terms of the functions used and in the way that the functions are integrated together. The final safety of the ITS is therefore likely to be the result of work carried out by a variety of people over a length of time. The Framework recommends that the overall responsibility for the safety of the final ITS must be allocated to one named person, the Safety Manager, who will co-ordinate all the activities according to a formal Safety Plan.

4.2.1 Competence of Persons

Whilst it is obvious that all personnel performing one of more of the tasks that will ensure the safety of an ITS should be competent, there are currently few people who can demonstrate that competence in an obvious manner. The main reason for this is that many of the techniques and methodologies that are now recommended have only been available for a few years, and few people have the experience of using them so far. It is therefore important that the Safety Manager ensures that all the key personnel are both aware of the new features, and the problems, associated with the advent of ITS, and that they have received suitable and adequate training in how to deal with them.

It is also important that a "safety culture" pervades all the organisations associated with the development of any safety-related system. Whilst it will be the responsibility of the Safety Manager to see that such a culture exists, he or she cannot do this effectively without the backing of his or her own senior management, and all the Authorities and Government Agencies associated with the creation of any ITS.

4.2.2 Operations

It is clearly a requirement for operating a safe ITS that all the relevant staff are suitably qualified. Staff need to have appropriate skills and competencies, and the organisations involved need to ensure that there are appropriate procedures in place to provide those skills and competencies. There is no specific qualification in ITS operation for which individuals can be certified, but there are arguments for creating such a competence. Certainly it is incumbent on system operators to ensure that their staff are appropriately trained. In addition, it should be pointed out that training is not merely a question of providing a background competence. Lack of training in system-specific operating procedures for emergencies was one of the factors that exacerbated the Channel Tunnel fire of 1996 [CTSA 1997]. Such training should be provided on a regular basis to ensure that emergencies are handled, as far as possible, on a proceduralised basis. Appropriate training should also accompany system modification. Here best practice would suggest that operating staff should be involved in the design process, e.g. for control room layout. Simulated prototypes of a new system, enabling operators to actually "use" the new system, have been shown to be helpful in the design of air traffic control systems [Carver 1999]. Whilst a new system is being installed, and before it goes live, it is vital that staff are given hands-on training in its operation. Feedback from such testing and training should be used to improve the operating procedures.

5 Assessment and Certification

5.1 Possible Processes

In general, an assessment process may take one of a number of different forms:

- **Type Approval**: the process of testing product-intent samples according to some defined strict criteria immediately prior to volume production.
- **Certification:** the process of obtaining regulatory agency approval for a function, equipment or system by establishing that it complies with all the applicable statutory regulations. There are normally two classes of regulations against which a certification process may be performed. The first ensures that the target of the certification process conforms to one or more standards so that it will be able to function correctly. The second ensures that the target will be able to function safely.
- **Conformity Assessment or Self Certification**: a process whereby a manufacturer can demonstrate that a product conforms to certain standards, etc. [90/683/EEC 1990] provides eight different possible processes.

Traditionally, regulatory agency approval for road transport equipment has been performed using a Type Approval process. It was devised when systems consisted only of mechanical and electrical components and thus the successful application of a series of tests was a valid exercise to demonstrate their safety. Such systems are now recognised as being "simple", i.e. their design is suitable for exhaustive simulation and test, and their behaviour can be entirely verified by exhaustive testing. ITS, however, are normally "complex", i.e. their design is unsuitable for the application of exhaustive tests, and therefore their behaviour cannot be verified by exhaustive testing [DEFSTAN 00-54 1999].

In order to gain the confidence required that a "complex" product does conform properly, a knowledge of the development process is also needed. Such certification is done in the aerospace industry by representatives of the notified body following the entire development process. Whilst such a process is likely to be perceived as being too expensive for the ITS industry in which cost margins are very tight, and SILs are normally low, there is clearly a need for a process which maintains the authority of the Type Approval, or full Certification process.

The Highways Agency also recognised the need for a change to the Type Approval process when it issued the *Statutory Approval of Equipments for the Control of Vehicular and Pedestrian Traffic on Roads* [TRG 0500B 1996]. It is essentially a four stage process:

1. The supplier must submit a number of documents to the Approval Authority in order to obtain an "agreement in principle" to their intentions.

2. The supplier must agree a test plan for the equipment with the Approval Authority which will be used to demonstrate the conformity of the equipment to appropriate standards.

3. The equipment is submitted for test. For functional performance the supplier is permitted to self-certify. If the functional performance includes safety, the test schedule has to be agreed with the Approval Authority as part of the second stage. The Approval Authority may require to witness any of the approval tests.

4. Upon satisfactory completion of all testing, and receipt and acceptance of final documentation by the Approval Authority, the equipment supplier is deemed to have completed the approval procedure and a Type Approval certificate is issued.

This process can be resource intensive for the Approval Authority, especially when applied to "complex" ITS and, during the fact-finding exercise, the project team came to the opinion that the Approval Authority was unlikely to be given the resources necessary to support its proper application during the nation-wide deployment of UTMC systems. A revised approach was therefore sought.

Module H of [90/683/EEC 1990] provides a form of "self assessment" whereby the notified body can monitor the activities of a manufacturer without having to perform all the verification and validation activities itself. The manufacturer must operate an approved quality system for design, manufacture and final product inspection and testing, and shall be subject to surveillance by the notified body. However the fact-finding exercise found that this approach does not have the support of any of the stakeholders in the UTMC arena who still want some kind of "official seal of approval", each for their separate reasons (see Section 2). It was therefore necessary to produce a scheme that combined the two approaches.

5.2 Proposal for UTMC System Certification

The project team proposed a new Approval process similar to that defined by [TRG 0500B 1996] for the assessment or certification of "complex" UTMC systems and their components (see Figure 4). It is based on a scheme devised by the DRIVE II project PASSPORT [Astruc 1995 and Hobley 1995a]. The process is essentially the same as TRG 0500B but with additional requirements for large systems. It has also been designed so that the Approval Authority can devolve work to accredited assessors at any stage that more detailed analysis is required than can be performed within the Authority. It should also be noted that whilst there is no basic engineering difference between an urban traffic management and control system and an inter-urban traffic management and control system, the regulatory environment in the UK is very different. The assessment process being proposed is therefore only for UTMC systems.

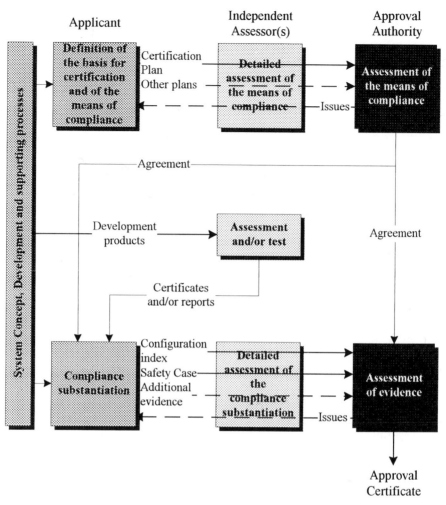

Figure 4 - Proposal for the Approval of "complex" UTMC systems

In order to deal with the issues associated with large "complex" systems, the "agreement in principle" stage is expanded. The applicant, typically a manufacturer or a system integrator, will be required to submit documentation to the Approval Authority that includes:

- A **Certification Plan** which defines the system, outlines the product development process, and identifies an acceptable means of compliance with the regulations. It should include a PSA of the system concept, and a preliminary SIL for the equipment or system.

- **Other Plans** may also be needed, e.g. for software or hardware qualification, and/or for the demonstration of compliance with a Technical Specification, e.g. UTMC.

Subject to the satisfactory resolution of any issues, the Approval Authority will agree the contents of the plan(s) as being suitable for the demonstration of compliance. If the system is too large and/or complex for the Approval Authority to check internally, it may require the Applicant to obtain a detailed assessment of the means of compliance from an Independent Assessor.

During the Development phase, products and groups of products will be passed to Independent Assessor(s), who will supply certificates and/or reports as appropriate. All those that relate to the safety of the system should be incorporated in the Safety Case. Once the Applicant believes that all the work has been performed in accordance with the agreed Certification Plan, the following documents are submitted to the Approval Authority:

- **Configuration Index:** the configuration identification of each item of equipment, software, inter-connections between equipment, required interfaces with other systems and sub-systems, and all safety-related operational and maintenance procedures and limitations. When applicable, any permissible interchange of alternative equipment within the ITS should be given.
- **Safety Case:** this should contain all the information necessary to assess the safety of a system, an application, or a specific installation, to the required SIL. A good Safety Case will provide information that will make the assessor comfortable with the reliability, availability and maintainability properties [Skogstad 1999].
- **Additional evidence:** For example, any deviation from the agreed plan should be described together with the rationale to substantiate the deviation. Also any Security, Environmental and Compliance to a Technical Specification data, for evidence that the system satisfies any non-safety-related regulatory requirements.

Subject to the satisfactory resolution of any issues, the Approval Authority will determine the adequacy of the data to show regulatory compliance. Once it is satisfied that all is in order, an **Approval Certificate** can be issued. If the system is too large and/or complex for the Approval Authority to check internally, it may require the Applicant to obtain a detailed assessment of the compliance substantiation documents from an Independent Assessor.

Many of the processes described above rely on the product and process information being obtained during the development of the ITS. Such data may not always be available for existing ITS, or subsequent modifications, or when COTS equipment is used. In this situation the Safety Case will have to be created using such data as is available to build up the necessary confidence, e.g. a history of successful working elsewhere, but this will need to be agreed in advance with the Approval Authority and may need independent verification.

5.2.1 Scope

One problem with a formal assessment mechanism, especially one that has legal status, is that it is first necessary to define what is, and what is not, an ITS. Unlike an aircraft or a nuclear power station, which are unmistakable, there is currently no legal definition of what is, and what is not, an ITS. In addition, and also unlike an aircraft or a nuclear power station, whose boundaries are well defined, many ITS, in particular UTMC systems, will be subject to continual:

- **Extension**: UTMC-like systems are likely to be subject to geographical extension as the funding becomes available. This will be done either with identical equipment to that already installed or, more likely, with new hardware that performs the same or similar functions.
- **Expansion**: Functional expansion of UTMC-like systems may be undertaken either with additional equipment or, possibly, by re-programming existing equipment.
- **Evolution**: An ITS can evolve in at least two ways:
  (a) It is possible for a safety-related system to emerge from a previously non-safety-related system by the addition of new functions and/or new types of data. For example, an ambulance dispatch system and a taxi scheduling system have very similar top-level functional requirements, or a commercial fleet of lorries may begin to carry hazardous goods.
  (b) It is possible for an application to change its required SIL over time. For example, a route guidance advice system becomes a command system if it is so good that the driver becomes accustomed to not having to check the safety implications of following the directions being given.

As UTMC-like systems increase in complexity the changes may also modify the total system behaviour as new emergent properties appear. It will therefore be necessary to define:
- What must be assessed, both for equipment and integrated systems
- When it must be assessed
- When it must be re-assessed.

6 Conclusion

The UTMC22 project has shown that there are a great many safety hazards associated with the various functions that might comprise an ITS; this is not only true for individual systems, but also for integrated systems that create the desired emergent properties needed to manage or control road traffic effectively. The project team found that many traffic engineers expected to be able to deploy ITS in the same manner as simple traffic control systems, relying on Type Approval to ensure the basic safety of controlled junctions. It was therefore necessary to produce a Framework for the development of ITS that not only stated what should be done, but that explained why it was necessary. The Framework covers all three of the main safety areas that affect road transport systems, namely Traffic Safety, HMI and Functional Systems Safety.

The project team also found that, whilst there was a clear need to ensure that the safety of such systems needed to be assessed before the public used them, the more obvious process of "self certification" was not acceptable to any of the stakeholders. It therefore proposed an Approval mechanism that would be controlled by the Approval Authority, but would not necessarily require that Authority undertake large quantities of detailed work.

The Framework introduces many new features and processes for the development and assessment of road-side systems, and it will be necessary to get the agreement of that industry sector in these proposals before they can be fully utilised. The use of SILs, in particular, is currently under debate. Another important feature is the use of Safety Cases in the proposed Approval process, and it will be necessary to identify exactly what the contents of such documents should be. The project team suggested an approach similar to that used for railways, but this needs to be validated. An ITS, in particular a UTMC system, will extend, expand and evolve over time and it will be necessary to identify when re-Approval is necessary without imposing unacceptable costs, but whilst maintaining the overall safety of the system.

It is clear that, from the way that the Framework has been received so far, the issues have only started to be resolved, rather than it representing a final solution. Much more work, in particular, in education and the undertaking of case studies, needs to be done before an agreed and satisfactory approach to the safety of ITS can be achieved.

References

[90/683/EEC 1990]   90/683/EEC: Council Decision, Concerning the Modules for the Various Phases of Conformity Assessment Procedures which are Intended to be Used in the Technical Harmonisation Directives. Official Journal of the European Communities (380), 1990

[Astruc 1995]   Astruc J-M, et al.: Towards the Certification of Advanced Transport Telematic Systems - System Safety Aspects. Deliverable N° 8, V2058 PASSPORT project of the Advanced Transport Telematics (ATT/DRIVE II) sector of the TELEMATICS APPLICATIONS Programme, Third Framework Programme (1991-94), 1995

[Carsten 1989]   Carsten O M J, Tight M R, and Southwell M T: Urban Accidents - Why Do They Happen?. Automobile Association for Road Safety Research, Basingstoke, 1989

[Carver 1999]   Carver E, Janssen W, and Franzén S: Traffic Information and Control Centres. Deliverable N° 4/5, HINT project of the Transport Research Programme of the Fourth Framework Programme, 1999

[COP 1998]   COP: Code of Practice for Traffic Control and Information Systems. Highways Agency, 1998

[CTSA 1997]   CTSA: Inquiry into the Fire on Heavy Goods Vehicle Shuttle 7539 on 18 November 1996. Channel Tunnel Safety Authority, 1997

[DEFSTAN 00-54 1999]   DEFSTAN 00-54: Draft Interim Defence Standard 00-54 - Requirements for Safety Related Electronic Hardware in Defence Equipment. Ministry of Defence, 1999

[DETR 1997]   DETR: Specification for Urban Traffic Management and Control (UTMC) Systems: Technical Issues. Department of the Environment, Transport and the Regions, 1997 {http://www.utmc.org.uk/utmc}

[DRIVE 1991]   DRIVE: Guidelines on System Safety, Man-Machine Interaction and Traffic Safety. DRIVE Safety Task Force, 1991

[Gaillet 1997]   Gaillet J-F: A Proposal for a Revised Transport Telematics Function List. Deliverable DSA7.2, TR1101 CONVERGE support project of the Transport sector of the Telematics Applications Programme, Fourth Framework Programme (1994-98), 1997 {http://www.trentel.org/index.htm}

[Hobley 1995a]   Hobley K M and Jesty P H: Analysis and Assessment of Advanced road Transport Telematic Systems. Proceedings of the 14th International Conference on Computer Safety, Reliability and Security (SafeComp '95), Belgirate, Italy, G. Rabe, Ed., Springer-Verlag, 1995, ISBN 3-540-19962-4

[Hobley 1995b]   Hobley K M, et al.: Framework for Prospective System Safety Analysis Volume 1 - Preliminary Safety Analysis. Deliverable N° 9a, V2058 PASSPORT project of the Advanced Transport Telematics (ATT/DRIVE II) sector of the TELEMATICS APPLICATIONS Programme, Third Framework Programme (1991-94), 1995

[IEC 61508 1999] IEC 61508: Functional Safety of Electrical/Electronic/Programmable Electronic Safety-Related Systems. International Electrotechnical Commission, 1999

[Jesty 1998]   Jesty P H, Easier Driving on Safer Roads. Traffic Technology International, UK & International Press, pp. 74-77, June/July 1998

[Sivak 1985]   Sivak M, Multiple Ergonomic Interventions and Transportation Safety. Ergonomics, Vol. 28, N° 8, Taylor and Francis, pp. 1143-1153, 1985

[Skogstad 1999]   Skogstad Ø: Experiences with Safety Case Documentation According to the CENELEC Railways Safety Norms. In Towards System Safety, Proceedings of the Seventh Safety-Critical Systems Symposium, Huntingdon, Springer-Verlag, 1999

[TRG 0500B 1996]   TRG 0500B: Statutory Approval of Equipments for the Control of Vehicular and Pedestrian Traffic on Roads, Issue B. Highways Agency, 1996

[UTMC22 1999a]   UTMC22: Preliminary Safety Analysis of the UTMC Architecture. , Department of the Environment, Transport and the Regions, 1999

[UTMC22 1999b] UTMC22: Framework for the Development and Assessment of Safety-Related Urban Traffic Management and Control Systems. Department of the Environment, Transport and the Regions, 1999

Digital Advanced Radio for Trains (DART)
The Safety Management & Engineering Case

Gerry Hansford

Siemens Transportation Systems Limited
Poole UK
gerry.hansford@poole.siemens.co.uk

Andy Harrison and Dr Andy Vickers

Praxis Critical Systems Limited
Bath UK
ajh@praxis-cs.co.uk, ajv@praxis-cs.co.uk

Abstract

This paper describes the safety management and engineering activities undertaken to develop safety requirements for the Digital Advanced Radio for Trains (DART) system. The project applied the principles of Railtrack's Engineering Safety Management System. Particular safety aspects of the project are highlighted and experience shared to support future projects.

1.   Introduction

In 1997, Railtrack contracted Siemens Transportation Systems Ltd (STSL) to undertake the design and development of the Fixed and Mobile Equipment (FME) for a new generation of nation-wide mobile rail communications, known as Digital Advanced Radio for Trains (DART). The DART system aimed to provide reliable mobile communications between train drivers and Railtrack control centres using the public GSM network, and would supersede current track to train radio systems such as National Radio Network (NRN).

Siemens contracted Praxis Critical Systems Limited to support the system design activity. This support included the development of safety requirements for DART FME. Railtrack required Siemens to undertake the safety management and engineering activity in compliance with the requirements of Railtrack's Engineering Safety Management System (ESMS) [Railtrack 1997]. First issued as a Railtrack document in 1996, and colloquially known as the 'Yellow Book', ESMS represents the continuous development of safety processes originally prepared for British Rail in the early nineties. In its current form, the Railtrack ESMS comprises 4 volumes. It defines Railtrack's approach to engineering safety, system assurance and system and traction and rolling stock acceptance. It also provides wide-ranging guidance on safety engineering practices and Railtrack's risk assessment methodology.

It should be noted that the DART Project is no longer under development. The project has been subsumed into the West Coast Route Modernisation (WCRM) Programme, as part of work aimed at delivering an EIRENE-compliant railway voice radio solution. Consequently, details of the DART system discussed within the paper should be considered in the context of the WCRM voice radio solution.

2.   Overview of the DART System

2.1.   System Architecture

DART aims to provide reliable mobile communications between train drivers and Railtrack control centres using the public GSM network. DART will be used to contribute to the mitigation of accidents potentially arising from the occurrence of operational railway hazards such as failure of the railway signalling system.

The DART architecture is shown in Figure 1. With Railtrack as systems integrator, the Siemens system design activity was limited to the following sub-systems:

- DART Fixed Terminal;

- Core Control Unit;

- Location Processor;

- System Managers Terminal;

- Cab Radio; and

- Portable Maintenance Unit.

DART Fixed Terminals (DFT) are fixed communications units, enabling signallers, zone controllers and other railway operators to initiate and respond to communications from cab radios and authorised DART hand-portables. Using a System Managers Terminal, a DART System Manager can configure all fixed and mobile equipment for use on the DART network.

DFTs are linked over the Public Service Telephone Network (PSTN) using ISDN to a Core Control Unit (CCU) Layer comprising two core control units and two Location Processors (LPs) configured in a master/standby configuration. A fail-over mechanism transfers control in the event of a single CCU or LP failure. Within this arrangement, a CCU routes communications between fixed and mobile units whilst the LP, which interfaces DART to Railtrack's Train Describer systems, enables communications to be routed correctly.

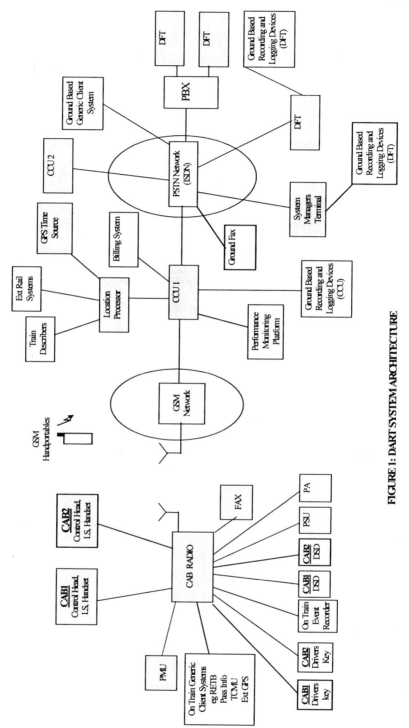

FIGURE 1: DART SYSTEM ARCHITECTURE

The CCU layer is linked to train cab radios (CR) or authorised DART hand-portables over the public GSM network.

Each CR comprises a processor unit and peripherals to enable an operator to initiate and respond to voice and data communications. On-board GPS can be used to update the CCU with the train's current position in the event of a failure of the interface with the Train Describer network. A Portable Maintenance Unit (PMU) configures CRs for operation on the DART network.

2.2. System Operation

2.2.1. Normal Operation

DART has two principal operating modes, secure and comfort in normal operation.

In secure mode, emergency calls from the cab radio are routed to the signaller controlling the train. In comfort mode, emergency calls made by the cab radio operator are received in the Railtrack Zone Control Room responsible for the route. For each cab radio, modes change based on the level of GSM coverage over specific routes and the availability of DART equipment to signallers controlling the route.

In normal operation, a cab radio logs onto the DART system at the start of a journey and then is able to initiate and respond to both voice and data communications with DFTs and other DART users. An emergency facility enables a cab radio operator to use a single button push to set-up a voice call with either the signaller or zone controller.

DFTs are configured to control specific signalling areas. As the train moves between areas, the position of the train is updated and the CCU uses this information to route communications between the cab radio and the correct, controlling DFT.

2.2.2. Failure Scenarios

There are a number of redundant features within, and external to, the DART system which provide safeguards against effects of failure of individual DART subsystems:

- If a cab radio fails, the train can be out of radio contact with the signaller or other DART users. Alternative methods of communication, for example, Signal Post Telephones, can be used instead.

- If a CCU or LP fails, the second CCU or LP will assume Master status, following implementation of the fail-over mechanism.

- The GPS facility fitted to cab radios will update the location of the train within DART should the Train Describer fail. If the GPS facility on the train is either failed or the train is not within a GPS area, the cab radio operator will be requested to supply manual updates of train position to the CCU at regular intervals.

- Failure of the GSM network will mean that DFTs are unable to communicate with either cab radio or hand-portables. DFT to DFT communication will still be possible and other users can be contacted over the railway Extended Trunk Dialling (ETD) system.

- Failure of the ISDN link will mean that DFTs are unable to talk to cab radios or other DFTs (except by other external means), however cab radios will still be able to communicate with ETD/PSTN users using the GSM network.

- Failure of a single DFT will cause emergency communications to be re-routed to a default DFT. A DFT area can be re-assigned to a second DFT area with either the agreement of the DFT operators or by the System Manager. In the event of a prolonged failure of a DFT, area re-assignment to a second DFT would provide a level of redundancy.

Whilst these fall back modes exist within the STSL supplied equipment, it should be recognised that failure of the ISDN and GSM networks simultaneously will represent a full failure of the DART system.

2.3.   System Design Approach

The initial phase of the project involved the system level design of the fixed and mobile equipment with the aim of establishing a full set of sub system requirements. As a number of these sub-systems were to be sub contracted externally, a complete set of requirements was essential. Siemens therefore undertook a rigorous and systematic system design process.

Based on the System Requirements Specification, system functions were modelled and documented within a System Functional Specification and Logical System Architecture Specification. These specifications were supported by a Physical Architecture Specification and a Communications Protocol Architecture Specification. Sub-system requirements were then allocated and specifications compiled. An audit of the system design activity provided confidence that the approach was consistent with the development process requirements for a SIL2 system as defined in IEC 1508 (now superseded by IEC 61508) [IEC 1999].

The safety management activities, culminating in the development of safety requirements, were an integral part of the system design phase.

3.   DART Safety Management and Engineering

This section summarises, and then goes on to discuss in further detail, each safety engineering activity with respect to the Railtrack ESMS requirements. The results obtained are summarised and an analysis of key issues that arose during the work is presented.

3.1. Key Issues

There were a number of key issues that the safety management activities had to address.

- In the early stages of the work, it was important to precisely define the boundaries of the system in terms of Siemens contractual responsibilities. This was necessary in order to ensure that safety engineering effort was focused in the most effective manner because whereas Railtrack, as DART operators, have responsibility for the operation of the system, Siemens had responsibility for ensuring that the risk associated with the sub-systems they supplied was reduced As Low As Reasonably Practicable (ALARP). The approach developed involved a holistic system safety consideration, based on the functionality and performance of the sub-systems for which Siemens retained responsibility which would support the later placement of safety requirements at the most cost-effective level within the whole DART system architecture.

- The approach to safety management had also to recognise that traditionally train radio had not been seen as a principal railway safety system. This role has been taken by the signalling equipment, which has been developed historically to the highest levels of safety integrity. This aspect was recognised by assigning a Safety Integrity Level (SIL) of 2 to the fixed and mobile equipment.

- The safety management activities also recognised the potential for changes both to the design requirements and external documents such as Railway Group and Railtrack Line standards. To counter the risks posed by this problem, an Impact Assessment process was developed to identify and track changes and ensure that the effect of change was analysed and assessed prior to implementation.

- The use of Commercial Off The Shelf (COTS) products was considered beneficial because of the potential for cost and timescale benefits. Although these benefits were recognised the potential for imported safety risk had to be assessed by an External Items Assessment activity.

3.2. Summary

The safety management and engineering activity within the system design phase of the DART fixed and mobile equipment project adopted a systematic and comprehensive approach, in line with the guidance provided by Railtrack's ESMS.

Initially, a Design Safety Plan was prepared to describe the safety management and safety engineering activities to be carried out during the project. The activities, which were then implemented in accordance with the requirements of the Safety Plan, comprised the following:

- Hazard identification, in order to identify DART fixed and mobile equipment hazards and to compare them with hazards identified previously during DART system level safety analysis;

- Hazard analysis and risk assessment, in order to better understand hazard causes and their relationship to the consequential railway accident scenarios. Subsequently hazard removal opportunities and hazard mitigation strategies were systematically developed;

- Safety requirements for fixed and mobile sub-systems were derived following hazard analysis and risk assessment, based on the identified hazard removal and hazard mitigation measures. Safety requirements were then incorporated into sub-system requirement specifications;

- A Hazard Log was established and maintained, in order to record evidence of the management of safety by the project;

- A Safety Audit and Assessment Plan was developed, showing the scope of all project safety audit and assessment activities, and implemented;

- An Impact Analysis Procedure was developed and implemented to ensure that the effect of project change on safety management and engineering was properly controlled; and

- A Safety Case (Design) was prepared, to provide evidence of the adequacy of derived safety requirements.

All safety deliverables were independently reviewed prior to delivery to Railtrack. In addition, Railtrack appointed a further Independent Safety Review team. The team assessed and approved safety deliverables as the project moved forward.

3.3.   Safety Planning

Railtrack's ESMS recommends a Safety Plan be developed prior to the commencement of safety work. The Safety Plan has to:

- Adequately address the scope of the work to be undertaken;

- Ensure roles and responsibilities are defined and competently implemented;

- Ensure safety activities support traceable safety requirements development;

- Define the role of relevant standards; and

- Define the requirements for independent review, audit and assessment.

For this project, a Safety Plan was developed and approved by Railtrack. It included details of:

- The safety organisation roles and responsibilities for the project, including evidence to show that persons undertaking key safety roles within the organisation were suitably qualified and experienced;

- The sequence of safety activities applicable to the system design phase of the DART FME project and the safety deliverables that would be produced. The safety lifecycle for the project is shown in Figure 2. The roles of standards within the project and the manner in which compliance would be demonstrated. Compliance against the recommendations of the Railtrack ESMS would be addressed through individual compliance reports for each safety activity. Compliance with the broad requirements of IEC1508 for a Safety Integrity Level (SIL) 2 system would be demonstrated through the use of a compliance matrix. Compliance with specific Railway Group and Railtrack Line standards would be demonstrated through the early identification of applicable Railtrack standards and subsequent monitoring and reporting against this report;

- Specific design safety controls for contractor management;

- Safety controls for all safety deliverables, including baseline standards and responsibility for review and approvals;

- Requirements to ensure that safety-related and other key project items were retained under configuration management; and

- The engineering competence of key members of the project team, including safety engineers and those with safety review or approval responsibilities, and the manner in which these competencies would be demonstrated.

The Safety Plan delineated safety responsibility, both upwards to the 'parent system' authority and also down to the sub-system suppliers. This boundary description was important in defining subsequent safety engineering activity.

Two particular aspects of the Safety Plan are worthy of note:

- The Safety Plan recognised that safe systems depend upon the entire project contributing to the project safety effort. As a means of ensuring whole team buy-in to the principles of Railtrack ESMS, the Railtrack ESM training course was run for the project development team, together with key members of the sub-system suppliers. This provided an efficient means of ensuring that all members of the organisation were able to see how the principles of ESMS could be applied, and to raise any concerns that they might have about safety on the project; and

- The Safety Plan required procedures to be written for each major safety activity. These procedures provided the means for management and engineering staff to share an understanding of the activities that were to be carried out.

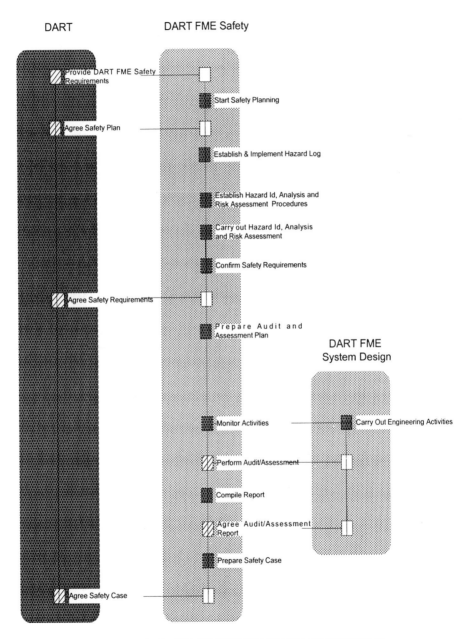

FIGURE 2: SAFETY ENGINEERING LIFECYCLE

3.4.   Hazard Identification

Railtrack's ESMS recommends that hazard identification should:

- Be carried out systematically;

- Include an assessment of the impact of external dependencies that could affect implementation;

- Identify the scope of system boundaries prior to hazard identification;

- Identify hazards that could lead to accidents;

- Use complementary hazard identification techniques; and

- Address life-cycle phases from installation to de-commissioning, considering all equipment modes.

Initially, a Hazard Identification Procedure was developed and reviewed by Railtrack. Hazard identification was based on a combined checklist and Hazard and Operability Study (HAZOP) approach, using technical groups, in order to ensure adequate coverage all technical disciplines.

Three hazard identification meetings were held. Two meetings identified equipment, human, machine interaction, environmental and lifecycle hazards, using a checklist approach. A third meeting identified functional hazards, using a HAZOP approach, based on the System Functional Specification and the System Requirements Specification. Whilst the hazard identification activity did not assess equipment outside of Siemens scope of supply, the failure of interfaces to external systems, was within the scope of the activity.

Based on an analysis of the information collected during the meetings, the DART fixed and mobile equipment hazards described in Table 1 were identified and logged, along with source information, within the project Hazard Log.

3.5.   Hazard Analysis and Risk Assessment

Railtrack's ESMS recommends an approach to hazard analysis and risk assessment such that:

- It is implemented following hazard identification;

- It includes consequence and causal analysis;

- Accident severity and likelihood are identified in a traceable manner;

- Risks are ranked according to a tolerability matrix;

- Results are recorded within a Hazard Log; and

- Rationale for the use of engineering judgement is recorded.

Hazard	Detailed Description
Misroute a Message	DART FME behaves in such a way that coherent, on-time information, with content as intended, is routed to some target destination other than that intended by the operator.
Wrong Message	An operator intends to communicate coherent, on-time information but DART FME behaves in such a way so as to cause unintended information to arrive at the desired target destination or DART FME behaves in such a way so as to cause a spurious message to be transmitted to a destination.
Meaningless Message	An operator intends to communicate on-time to the desired target destination, but DART FME behaves in such a way so as to cause the message to be meaningless.
No Message	An operator is unable to use DART FME (including FME failure) to communicate with a target destination.
Partial Unavailability of Functionality	An operator is only able to access a sub-set of the desired DART FME functionality.
Distraction	An operator is distracted from normal duties because of the behaviour of DART FME.
Personal Injury	DART FME exists in such a state that injury could be caused to an individual.
EMI with Other Equipment	DART FME exists in a state such that it can adversely affect the operation of other equipment through electromagnetic interference.
Physical Interference with other Equipment	DART FME exists in a state such that it can adversely affect the operation of other equipment through its physical presence.
Late Message	An operator communicates coherently, with information as intended, to the correct target destination, but DART FME retains the message so that it arrives at some time after it would normally be expected.

Table 1: DART Fixed and Mobile Equipment Hazards

Initially, a Hazard Analysis and Risk Assessment Procedure was developed and reviewed by Railtrack. This procedure involved applying cause-consequence analysis to the identified hazards.

In the consequence domain, protective, procedural and circumstantial accident sequence mitigation measures were identified for each identified hazards. These measures are barriers in that they reduce the likelihood of a hazard escalating to an undesirable consequence. For each hazard, worst case consequences were then ranked in terms of severity by project engineering staff, using engineering judgement, and classified. The analysis identified two types of unsafe consequences associated with DART FME hazards:

- Fixed and mobile equipment could initiate an incident through the existence of a specific fixed and mobile equipment hazard; and

- Fixed and mobile equipment could fail to mitigate an existing external incident.

Within the assessment of each fixed and mobile equipment hazard, only the Distraction hazard has the potential to cause, in the worst case, a catastrophic railway accident. This is possible if the fixed and mobile equipment distracts the driver from his primary safety tasks with respect to the signalling system. Other fixed and mobile equipment hazards can affect the progression of an incident originating from a source outside DART. A number of accident sequence barriers were identified which significantly reduced the likelihood of fixed and mobile equipment hazards either leading to an incident or contributing to an external accident sequence.

In the causal domain, significant work was undertaken to identify the sequence of hazardous events that could lead to the identified hazards. For each hazardous event, mitigation options were systematically identified, based on the following checklist:

- Design out the hazardous event;

- Add a safety feature;

- Add a warning device; and

- Implement a procedure.

Following the identification of mitigation options, an engineering assessment was undertaken for each hazardous event. The assessment isolated preferred mitigation options that either removed the hazardous event or reduced the likelihood of its occurrence. Following pre and post mitigation assessment of each hazardous event, the likelihood of each hazard occurring was estimated on the basis of the likelihood of the hazardous events that could lead to the occurrence of the hazard.

The risk associated with each fixed and mobile equipment hazard was assessed on the basis of the likelihood of the hazard occurring, taking into account the effect of the accident sequence barriers in reducing the likelihood of the hazard leading to an accident and the severity of the accident should it occur. The results of the assessment showed that all fixed and mobile equipment hazards, post mitigation, were tolerable or better.

The results were recorded within the project Hazard Log.

Five particular aspects of the hazard analysis and risk assessment activity are worthy of note:

- Within the causal and consequence analysis activity, the role of the human cognition specialist was retained to support the analysis. This expertise added an important dimension to the consideration of event sequences through the usability perspective and the likely effect on usability of mitigation measures;

- Whilst a fully quantified analysis was not justified for this project, for particular hazards system level fault trees were constructed as an aid to understanding the problem;

- Although a consequence diagram for each hazard was not a safety deliverable, sample consequence diagrams were produced as an aid to understanding the domain within which DART FME was to operate. A pessimistic view of external mitigations, and their contributions, was taken for each hazard. This enabled a worst case approach to hazard probabilities to be taken;

- Close liaisons with the client enabled mitigation measures to be considered that were outside the contractual boundary. The effect of this was to provide an opportunity to implement the most cost-effective set of holistic risk mitigation measures. The recognises the fact the an ALARP argument at the DART FME level contributes to an ALARP argument at the DART system level; and

- The role of professional judgement was important within the risk assessment activity. Particular care and attention was taken to ensure that those making such judgements were adequately experienced, in terms of technology, the rail domain and the operation of similar systems, and that this competence was recorded.

The assessment provided the necessary confidence that the adoption of specific mitigation options for each hazardous event introduced adequate risk reduction for each fixed and mobile equipment hazard. These mitigation measures, when combined with existing accident sequence barriers, provide confidence that the risk of the DART FME hazard leading to a worst case consequence has been reduced ALARP and is either negligible or tolerable. Further analysis at the system level will be required to show that risk associated with the DART system is ALARP.

3.6. Safety Requirements

Railtrack's ESMS recommends an approach to safety requirements definition such that safety requirements are:

- Traceable to identified hazards and risks; and

- Set so as to reduce eliminate or reduce risk ALARP.

Initially, a Safety Requirements Derivation and Confirmation Procedure was developed and reviewed by Railtrack.

Following hazard analysis and risk assessment, the selected mitigation options were been carried forward as safety requirements. Additional self-evident safety requirements were also derived from the hazard identification and impact analysis activities.

The safety requirements for fixed and mobile equipment were documented within a Safety Requirements Report and carried forward into the safety case. Traceability from hazard identification through hazard analysis and risk assessment to safety requirements derivation was maintained using the project Hazard Log. Assumptions connected with the development of safety requirements were also recorded within the Hazard Log.

Safety requirement types included:

- Random failure probability requirements;

- Systematic failure probability requirements;

- Hazard removal design requirements;

- Functional safety requirements; and

- Other safety requirements.

Traceability from the safety requirements to their source is included within the Safety Requirements Report. Safety requirements trace to one of the following:

- Directly to hazard identification and impact analysis (where self-evident safety requirements were identified); or

- Directly to a mitigation option identified in the hazard analysis and risk assessment.

The traceability of the derived safety requirements to the original analysis activity is shown in Figure 3.

The majority of safety requirements were included within the appropriate system design documentation and sub-system requirements specifications; others were exported to Railtrack to enable risk mitigation to take place in the most cost-effective way.

Three particular aspects of the safety requirements derivation process are worthy of note:

- Traceability of safety requirements through the development process is an essential activity. However, for large systems this problem can be very difficult to manage. The project Hazard Log was an essential tool in enabling this process to be undertaken successfully;

- Safety integrity levels were not used within DART FME safety requirements as claim limits but rather to support process assurance; and

- The agreement of the client to accepting safety requirements derived during the fixed and mobile equipment safety work supports a value engineered approach to safety to be integrated into the next phase of work.

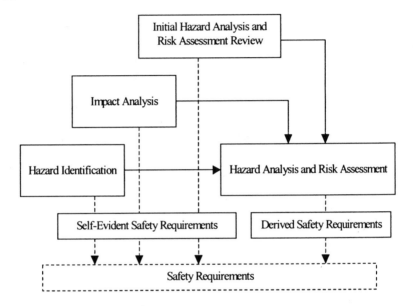

FIGURE 3: SAFETY REQUIREMENTS TRACEABILITY

3.7.   Safety Case (Design)

Railtrack's ESMS recommends that a safety case should show that:

- The safety plan has been implemented;

- Risks have been adequately addressed;

- Risks have been reduced ALARP;

- Adequate safety requirements have been set;

- Engineering techniques employed to meet the requirements are suitable; and

- Safety requirements have been met.

Following development of the project safety requirements, a Safety Case was developed to demonstrate the adequacy of the requirements. Initially, the Safety

Case was developed using goal structuring notation and then converted to become an essentially text based document.

The Safety Case provided evidence that:

- A full and thorough series of safety management and engineering activities had been carried out;

- A number of hazards had been identified and an assessment suggested that DART FME hazards contribute towards known DART system hazards rather than initiates new DART system hazards;

- Identified hazards had been subjected to a rigorous process of hazard analysis and risk assessment;

- A set of system and sub-system safety requirements had been derived from the analysis and any assumptions underlying the requirements explicitly stated; and

- The implementation of these requirements within DART FME, along with the implementation by Railtrack of other specified safety requirements, will reduce the risk associated with DART FME to as low as reasonably practicable.

The Safety Case recognised that further iterations of the argument would be necessary in order to show that the finally developed system met the safety requirements set for it. It should also be noted that in order for the DART system to be shown to be safe, a cascade of safety cases would be required. Sub-system safety cases would build to form the fixed and mobile equipment safety case, which in turn would be part of the complete DART system safety case.

Two particular aspects of the safety case production process are worthy of note:

- The initial use of goal structuring notation, whilst not appearing in the final safety case, provided a sound way of reviewing the adequacy of both the argument construct and the evidence available to support the argument. Developing a textual argument to follow a goal structured argument was straightforward; and

- The development of process procedures for safety activities, the clear recording of safety activity results and the use and maintenance of the project Hazard Log all served to make the Safety Case production process an evidence collation exercise.

3.8.   Hazard Log

For safety projects, Railtrack's ESMS recommends that a Hazard Log should be created and maintained. The hazard log should:

- Record and track to closure identified hazards;

- Reference the state of all project safety documentation;

- Be maintained as safety information evolves;

- Support the import and export of hazard information; and

- Support traceability.

A Hazard Log Procedure was developed and reviewed by Railtrack.

A project Hazard Log was created using an electronic database product and then maintained throughout the project. The role of the Hazard Log was crucial in supporting the management of information during the project and significantly eased the production of the safety case for the system.

One particular aspect of the hazard log process is worthy of note:

- The use of an electronic hazard log supported access by the engineering team to the latest safety engineering information.

4. System Assurance

4.1. Project Audit and Assessment

The Safety Plan required the production of a Safety Audit and Assessment Plan for the project. This plan identified a series of audit and assessment activities to be undertaken throughout the work, with the audit checking compliance against the requirements of the Safety Plan and an assessment checking the integrity of the engineering activity. The Safety Audit and Assessment Plan was approved by Railtrack.

The Design Safety Team was subjected to an independent audit and assessment, at a level of independence commensurate with SIL2 requirements.

Additionally, the System Design Team was subjected to an independent audit and assessment, at a level of independence commensurate with SIL2 requirements.

The audits and assessments were reported in Audit and Assessment Reports. All issues were categorised and actions put in place to resolve outstanding open issues in subsequent project phases.

4.2. Independent Safety Review

4.2.1. Siemens

Siemens appointed an Independent Safety Reviewer whose responsibilities were defined within the Safety Plan. The reviewer independently assessed all project design safety deliverables. The assessment was traceable and resulted in an assessment signature.

4.2.2. Railtrack

Railtrack also appointed an Independent Reviewer whose role was to observe safety activities underway within the project with respect to the overall DART System, assess safety deliverables and recommend Railtrack acceptance of safety deliverables.

Safety process documents were supplied to the reviewer for informal comment prior to formal submission in order to facilitate timely acceptance. by the project Subsequently safety deliverables were reviewed by the reviewer prior to acceptance by Railtrack.

The good working relationship developed between the Railtrack Independent Reviewer and the project was of significant benefit to the integrity of the work.

5.   Conclusions

This paper has discussed the safety management and engineering case for the DART Fixed and Mobile Equipment.   It describes the safety management arrangements implemented within this commercial systems development project and the safety engineering activities undertaken in support of the derivation of safety requirements for the system.

This paper has described the development of safety requirements for DART fixed and mobile equipment. In particular:

- The safety management arrangements in place within the project have been discussed;

- Safety engineering activities and the results of the activities have been described;

- The assurance mechanisms have been outlined; and

- A case for the safety of the work undertaken has been made.

The requirements of the Railtrack ESMS and the way in which these requirements were implemented within the project have been described.

The paper has described several interesting safety features of the project including:

- The value engineering approach to system safety within a commercial systems development project;

- The maintenance of safety controls at contractual interfaces through close liaison with the customer ISA; and

- The benefits of explicit consideration of human factors issues within the hazard identification and hazard analysis and risk assessment process.

At the end of the Design Phase, fixed and mobile equipment safety requirements have been derived by following a rigorous and systematic safety engineering programme. All hazards, foreseeable at this stage of the project, have been identified and adequate requirements identified to ensure that, following implementation of the requirements, the risks associated with identified hazards have been reduced ALARP.

6.   Acknowledgements

We would like to acknowledge the assistance of Railtrack and the DART FME project team in supporting the project safety engineering activities and in the preparation of this paper.

7.   References

[Railtrack 1997] Engineering Safety Management, Railtrack 1997

[IEC 1999]   Functional Safety of E/E/PES, IEC 61508, IEC 1999

SAFETY STANDARD IEC 61508 AND RECENT SECURITY STANDARDS

The Application of IEC 61508: An Industrial Perspective

David Boulton
ERA Technology
Leatherhead, UK

Abstract

The last decade has seen significant changes in the way that safety is dealt with where complex electronic systems are concerned. A number of industry sectors have developed standards in order to provide both guidance and also a more uniform approach to the safety of complex electronic systems, and in particular software. Arguably the most important standard in this area is IEC 61508 'Functional Safety of Electrical/Electronic/Programmable Electronic Safety Related Systems'. This standard is generic in that it is intended to address all appropriate industry sectors, and sets out an approach to addressing functional safety throughout all aspects of a system's lifecycle. In order to assist industry's understanding of this standard, the DTI has sponsored a number of projects under the Sector Challenge initiative. This paper provides some of the initial results of one such project, 'Assuring Programmable Electronic Systems' (APES), which was set up to look into the practical issues relating to the application of IEC 61508. The project will complete in January 2000, at which point a more comprehensive report on the project results will be made available. For more details of the activities and results of this project, the reader is referred to the APES web site (http://www.era.co.uk/apes/apes.html).

1. Introduction

1.1 Background

Compliance with national and international standards has become a feature of vital importance in the marketing of products. Products which are safety related carry especially heavy burdens of compliance and this trend is likely to increase in the future as industry exploits increasingly sophisticated technologies to gain competitive advantage in the market-place. However, the trend is also towards a rationalisation of standards to mitigate the burden on industry whilst ensuring that safety standards are not compromised.

Given this role of standards it is an important business requirement that companies are able to comply with relevant international standards and have competent and well trained staff able to use them. In some areas there is a distinct shortage of experience in using standards relating to the development of safety related Programmable Electronic Systems (PES), and in addition there are a number of technical and interpretation problems with these standards. The most important standards influencing the development of PES at the moment are draft standard IEC 61508 (Ref. 1).

The sector challenge project 'Assuring Programmable Electronic Systems' (APES), was initiated in order to look into some of the problems experienced by industry in the application of standards relating to the safety of PES based systems. The project began in early 1998 and will complete in January 2000. Whilst the project is still going, this paper provides a description of the aims and objectives of the project, the activities undertaken, and some of the results obtained to date. By February 2000 a more comprehensive presentation of project results will be feasible.

1.2 The APES Project

1.2.1 Objectives

The main objectives of the APES project were to achieve a wider understanding of the problems associated with the application of IEC 61508, and to propose ways of addressing at least some of them. The seven part standard contains a large amount of information and requires the reader to be familiar with principles and associated activities relating to functional safety. Therefore, to achieve the project objectives two main activities are being undertaken:

1. highlighting and resolution of some of the technical issues arising from the use of IEC 61508 (Ref. 1) and machine safety standards for developing safety critical programmable electronic systems (PES);

2. development and dissemination of technology transfer material relating to the use of these standards and the methods and techniques that underpin them.

While some evidence is available concerning the use of the standard, for example from the SEMSPLC (Ref. 2) project, no systematic study has been undertaken looking at the application of the approach to real applications. This project has carried out a study of the application of IEC 61508 through the conduct of trial applications, and also through gathering the experiences of the project participants. This collected body of experience will be made available to industry at large, and will also be fed back to both regulators and the standards bodies responsible for IEC 61508. Communicating the results to the standards bodies is considered to be one of the most important for the project to fulfil.

Previous experience has shown that small manufacturers have difficulty in devoting resources to developing and refining infrastructure skills. Thus, the advent of regulations such as those deriving from the Machinery Directive, or new safety standards such as IEC 61508 and IEC 61511, pose problems to small companies and are often seen as imposing additional costs on industry without exhibiting commensurate competitive advantages. Such standards can be seen in another light for, by accommodating them, manufacturers can produce and market demonstrably safer products and can help exclude inferior products from the marketplace. In such circumstances, technology transfer material can be particularly helpful.

1.2.2 Project Organisation

The project is led by ERA Technology. Other participants in the project include developers of safety systems, influential users of these systems, regulators, professional societies and the UK's Safety Critical Systems Club. There is also input from trade associations. For a full list of all organisations participating in the APES project please refer to Appendix A. Collectively this consortium is in a position to bring the results of this project to the attention of the UK's safety community and to effect a change in the way that the community approaches the development of safety products and systems containing PES.

1.2.3 Main Activities of Project

The are three main activities which are being undertaken within the APES project and a short summary of each of these is given below. More details of these activities may be found in Section 2.

Conduct of Trial Applications
Three trial applications are being carried out, one related to transport, one to the machinery sector (i.e. under the machinery directive) and one related to the offshore oil and gas sector. Each trial involves the application of IEC 61508 to a real project, and focuses on the issues arising as a result. Each carries an

emphasis on different aspects of the standard in order to provide greater coverage of the issues which can arise in the application of IEC 61508.

Development and Delivery of Training/Technology Transfer Material
Based on the experience gained in conducting the trial applications and additional issues arising during the APES project, technology transfer material is being developed, essentially to drive a series of training courses which have the aim of providing a basic level of understanding of IEC 61508. A five day training course program is now being developed, based on material generated by the project. Three days of the five have been run at the time of writing.

Dissemination Activities
Three dissemination events will be run with the specific aim of making the results of the APES project known to a wider audience. The three events are:

1. a workshop day at which specific issues relating to IEC 61508 will be discussed (held on 18 October 1999)

2. an event run through the safety critical systems club, where some aspects of the project will be presented (scheduled for 6 December 1999)

3. a final presentation of the results of the project to be run through the DTI (scheduled for 27 January 2000)

In addition, under the heading of dissemination, the results of the project will be fed back to the standards bodies and to regulators as appropriate. All material released under the APES project is available at the APES project web site (http://www.era.co.uk/apes/apes.html).

1.3 Contents of Paper

Section 2 of the paper provides a more detailed description of the activities undertaken on the APES project, and also indicated those project activities still to be undertaken at the time of writing. In section 3, the issues which arose in the course of these project activities are highlighted, along with the conclusions reached in respect of these activities. Concluding thoughts are provided in Section 4. A list of the organisations participating in the APES project is provided in Appendix A. Note that this paper does not present the final results and conclusions of the project, as these will follow only at the end of the project.

However, it will be possible to report on the final conclusions at the Safety Critical Systems Club Symposium in early 2000.

2. The APES Project

2.1 Conduct of Trial Applications

The objective of this work package was to carry out three trial applications, to monitor and advise on the methods and techniques deployed on the trials and to discuss and resolve any problems that may arise. A focus group was established for each trial application consisting of those participating in the trial and other related bodies such as users and regulators. The output from each application was submitted to the relevant focus group for comment and consideration of ways to resolve particular technical problems. Each of the applications is discussed below.

Machinery Application

This trial application related to the manufacture of light guards, and specifically the re-engineering one such product in the timescale of the APES project. A light guard is a protective piece of equipment used to shield hazardous machinery. The principle of operation is that a series of light beams is generated and if any are interrupted, for instance by the hand of an operator, power is remove from the hazardous machinery. The objective of this task was to understand how to produce a model Technical File, taking into account the requirements of IEC 61508. Technical File is a term from the machinery directive, and is the documentation which demonstrates the adequacy of the light guard in terms of safety. It can be seen as a type of safety case. The work also involved the use of standards specific to the machinery sector, including EN 954-1, EN 1050 and EN 61496. Issues to be considered in this application included how to assign priority to IEC 61508 in an environment where several standards may apply, and also to examine the impact of IEC 61508 on an environment in which it has not previously been applied.

SCADA Application

The project used for the APES project related to the supply of SCADA equipment for a light railway system. The SCADA equipment is required to control power distribution to the line, as well as controlling additional auxiliary services such as tunnel ventilation.

The objective of this task was to examine two specific issues relating to this type of system. The first issue concerns demonstrating conformance to IEC 61508 when the system in question incorporates a significant Commercial Off The Shelf (COTS) software element, in this case Windows NT. The second issue relates to specifying a SIL for such a product, and consideration of the factor that unaware customers sometimes specify needlessly high SILs for a product, without understanding the implications of such a requirement for the supplier.

Offshore Process Control Application

The project selected for study related to the development of an emergency shutdown system for use on an offshore storage platform. The objective of this task was to undertake a trial implementation of IEC 61508 in the context of an application area where products are sold internationally and where, as a consequence, a range of guidelines and standards are in use.

It is noted that there resourcing problems have been experienced in connection with this trial application, and for this reason, no results are presented in this paper.

2.2 Development of Training/Technology Transfer Material

The aim of this task was to address some of the issues of complexity associated with IEC 61508 and to enable newcomers to the standard to achieve a basic level of understanding. The factors involved in determining appropriate material for inclusion in the material to be developed were:

1. issues considered to be of importance by project members

2. issues which arose during the trial applications

3. issues arising from technical discussions held during the project.

Some of the questions requiring consideration included the following:

1. Should sector specific material be developed? Whilst the view was advanced that this material would be of value, it was decided that uncertainty over audience and limitations on available effort precluded development of this material.

2. Given the size of the standard, on which areas should effort be concentrated? A course covering all aspects of the standard in detail could last for months. The only realistic answer to this question seemed to be to focus on principles, with forays into detail where they could be accommodated.

3. Should course material concentrate on the principles of the standard or achieving conformance (not always the same thing)? The choice in this instance was to try to provide an understanding of principles, since once this had been achieved, it would be possible to understand what is required for conformance.

4. Who is the target audience for the training course material? The target audience was deemed to be composed of a number of categories. The main categories were:
    a) developers with limited experience of safety systems
    b) more experienced developers of safety systems with limited experience of IEC 61508
    c) users/purchasers of safety related systems.

The eventual format chosen for the material a series of 4 courses, one of which has 2 day duration, all others being a single day. These courses are being run as part of the APES project, and feedback from the participants will be used to finalise the material before it is made publicly available. The four course titles are:

1. Risk Analysis and IEC 61508 (basic introduction to standard and the principles behind it)

2. Hazard Analysis and Risk Management (expands the requirements of part 1)

3. System Architecture Design and Analysis (expands the requirements of part 2)

4. Software Design and Analysis (expands the requirements of part 2)

Delivery of the courses will be complete by the end of November 1999.

2.3 Dissemination of Lessons Learnt

External Dissemination

Three dissemination events are planned as part of the APES project and these are outlined below.

1. Workshop Activity, IEE, 18 October 1999. This activity, the only dissemination event to have taken place at the time of writing, involved gathering users, suppliers and regulators of safety related system together in order to discuss some key issues relating to IEC 61508. The issues discussed were SILs, levels of risk reduction and development of systems incorporating COTS elements or other similar elements. Results from this activity were not available at the time of writing.

2. Safety Critical Systems Club Event, 6 December 1999, London. Three papers from the APES project will be presented at this event. One will provide an overview of the APES project (in a similar way to this paper), one will discuss the issues relating to SILs and there will be a talk from Transmitton relating the issues arising from that trial application.

3. Final Project Presentation, DTI, 27 January 2000. This event will provide an opportunity for presentation of the completed results to all interested parties. In particular it is intended that the standards bodies will be represented in order that first hand experience of IEC 61508 may be passed on. There will also be an opportunity for wider discussion of issues raised by the project.

Feedback to Standards Organisations

As stated in the previous paragraph, the final dissemination event will provide one opportunity to give project feedback to the standards organisation. In addition, a project report will be produced explicitly for the standards organisations, and it is also intended to meet with the appropriate representatives in order to discuss project results.

3. Practical Issues Arising

In this section we consider some of the issues which have arisen during the APES project, and present interim conclusions where they are available.

3.1 Machinery Sector Trial Application

1. **Understanding the impact of IEC 61508.** The trial application illustrated the problem which will affect many SMEs of dealing with the impact of IEC 61508. For an organisation with its own existing internal development practices, changing these to conform to IEC 61508 and the additional educational activities which may be required for staff are non-trivial exercises, and the costs involved in such exercises may exclude a number of organisations from the market sector. In addition, the degree of software involved may be relatively small (but bring in all software related requirements) and typically the number of staff involved is small too.

2. **Which standard should be followed?** There are several standards in this sector which apply to the development of electro-sensitive protective equipment, some of which make reference to IEC 61508. It is not clear which of these standards takes priority, and how much recognition of the requirements of IEC 61508 is needed. During the course of the trial application the standard prEN 61496 (Ref. 3) was revised and became an EN, thus making it an appropriate standard to follow in order to demonstrate conformance to the machinery directive. However, the degree to which IEC 61508 should be taken into account remains indeterminate.

3. **Lifecycle based approach.** The approach adopted in the trial application was to follow a development lifecycle which contained the most important elements of IEC 61508 and which may be regarded as standard practice anyway. Such an approach was deemed to be most suitable in terms of minimising the costs which may accrue from such activities whilst reducing non-conformance to IEC 61508 and at the same time including aspects of best practice in the development. The key factors involved in such an approach were safety planning, hazard analysis, documentation of design activities and appropriate verification.

4. **Incomplete Knowledge of Final System.** With respect to devices such as light guards, it was noted that not all of IEC 61508 is applicable, in that the supplier cannot take into account the final application and thus has no

knowledge of the final system of which the light guard will constitute one element. No detailed risk analysis can thus be performed as the consequences of failures cannot be determined. The hazard analysis has therefore to be geared around the level of protection which the light guard can provide. Additional work would be required once the application is known to determined if the level of protection afforded is appropriate to the application.

3.2 SCADA Application (Transport Sector)

In the course of this trial application Safety Integrity Levels (SILs) were discussed at length. A number of issues arose, some relating to the trial application and others outside it. Issues relating to SILs are listed below.

1. **Performance of Risk Assessment.** Conduct of the appropriate hazard analysis and risk assessment is a prerequisite to assessing the appropriate SIL which should apply to a given protection system. Instances where inadequate analysis supported the choice of SIL or even where an arbitrary SIL was imposed on a supplier were mentioned. This issue highlighted the difficulty commonly experienced of producing an adequate risk assessment and also the inadequate understanding of what a SIL is across different parts of the supply chain. This area of safety analysis appears to be one of the least well understood. It is noted that there is almost no guidance on either hazard analysis or risk assessment within IEC 61508, although it requires that both are done.

2. **Use of numerical failure rates in associate with SILs.** Throughout discussions on SILs, the benefits of using the numerical targets associated with a SIL remained unclear. Two main issues arose. Firstly it was not uncommon to find that risk analyses or reliability analysis were obviously geared towards generating the 'right' answer. Strange mitigating factors or unusual numerical quantities may be introduced to ensure that the failure on demand target for the system conforms with the appropriate SIL, leading to a masking of the areas where the real risk may lie. Secondly, where software is concerned, the reliability figure for a given SIL is often entered (erroneously) into the failure rate calculation in the absence of any other data for software failure rates. Whilst using a target figure to demonstrate achievement of a target figure is clearly wrong, it was note that there is no

obvious solution to the problem of applying a failure rate to software functions.

3. **Explanation of SIL in IEC 61508.** In discussing the points above, the question 'what is a SIL?' frequently arose, and the first port of call in these cases was IEC 61508. SILs are dealt with in most detail in part 5. The best answer arising was that a SIL is 'a measure of the amount of risk reduction which a protection system is able to supply'. However, it was felt that there were inconsistencies in the description provided in part 5 of IEC 61508, and that given the difficulties experienced in applying this concept, a clearer description would be of significant benefit.

The issue of COTS software was also discussed within this trial application. The main points raised are listed below.

1. **COTS guidance in IEC 61508.** With respect to the use of COTS software, it was felt by the project that the requirements given in IEC 61508 are minimal and overly prescriptive (see Annex D, part 7 of Ref. 1). It is unlikely that the conditions specified for including COTS software in a safety related application will be commonly achieved. Strict compliance to IEC 61508 is likely to lead to the exclusion of COTS software from safety related applications.

2. **Use of COTS Software in high Integrity Applications.** The view which emerged from discussions of this issue was that it is feasible to argue that COTS software may be acceptably incorporated into lower integrity safety systems (corresponding to SIL 1 or perhaps SIL 2), although such systems may not confirm to a strict interpretation of IEC 61508 as it currently exists. However, for high integrity systems, say SIL 3 or SIL 4 systems, it was thought that the inclusion of significant COTS elements was unlikely to be feasible. The sort of conditions which may need to be applied to systems seeking to incorporate COTS elements are:

   • It must be demonstrated that the system as a whole provides defence against all possible failure modes resulting from the COTS software, i.e. the system must be fault tolerant and/or robust. In order to defend against such errors, it may be necessary to add additional hardware/ software components around the COTS component.

- A clear understanding will need to be demonstrate of the interactions that are likely to take place between the COTS software other parts of the system.

3.3 Awareness Survey

In order to understand the commercial environment in which IEC 61508 is positioned, an awareness survey was circulated to a wide range of organisations involved in the development or use of safety related PESs. The aim of the questionnaire was to understand how much awareness of the principles of IEC 61508 exists in the industrial community and how well these principles are being applied. The questionnaire was circulated to just over 100 individuals and 47 replies were received and processed. Some of the key points arising from the survey are summarised below:

1. **Experienced Respondents.** Respondents were people experienced in their industry sectors, with almost half having more than 15 years experience in their sector. Industry sectors covered include transport, defence, nuclear and oil and gas.

2. **Incomplete Control of Process.** The survey showed that awareness of safety principles is high but a significant minority of respondents reported that certain aspects of safety lifecycle processes are not well controlled. Aspects to which this conclusion apply include:
   a) customer requirements
   b) documentation of procedures
   c) availability of information from previous projects
   d) risk management
   e) use of test plans
   f) measurement of technique effectiveness.

3. **Non-conformance to IEC 61508.** The points listed in 2 above do not necessarily mean that organisations to which these points apply are producing unsafe products, but more that safety, if it is achieved, is not achieved in a way which is compliant with IEC 61508. However, points such as d) and e) are likely to raise the odd eyebrow.

4. **Demonstrating Technique Effectiveness.** Point f) as listed in 2 above shows that technique effectiveness is not commonly measured This raises the question as to how selection of techniques can be improved without any

information to inform the decision? Further, how can the effectiveness of the standard as a whole be demonstrated without such measurement? Clearly it is not straightforward to define the measurement metrics for many techniques, but the question as to how to demonstrate value in the absence of such measures remains. Demonstrating value remains a particular problem where organisations or even countries are sceptical of the benefits of using IEC 61508.

5. **Changing Requirements.** Requirements change frequently in most projects, including those involving safety applications, throughout the lifetime of that project. This conclusion reinforces the need for tight change control in safety related projects, and for appropriate procedures to be developed to deal with the impact of such changes throughout the system lifecycle. Hazard analysis should be anticipated as a through life activity, albeit that under normal circumstances most will take place in the early stages of a project.

3.4 Additional Points

1. **Selection of Tools and Techniques.** The standard requires that certain tools and techniques should be applied during development in order to claim system conformance to a particular SIL (see parts 2 and 3 of Ref. 1). The view of the project is that the instructions on selection of tools and techniques is unclear. It is not always clear which combinations of tools and techniques will be acceptable given the wording of the standard and the view was expressed that a more pragmatic approach would be to ask the developer to present an argument as to why selection of a set of techniques was adequate. If more detailed guidance is to be provided, the appropriate place for such guidance is a sector specific standard which takes into account the particular practices and requirements of that sector.

2. **Use of Sector Specific Standards.** IEC 61508 is intended to be a generic standard from which sectors will develop their own industry specific standards. This process has happened at least in part in the oil and gas industry through the development of the UKOOA guidelines, and in the railway industry through the development of the CENELEC standards (Refs. 4 to 6). The view of the project is that the development of such sector specific standards is to be encouraged. They provide an appropriate place in which to document more detailed guidance and in addition allow sectors to preserve those aspects of safety practice which are inappropriate to document

in a standard such as IEC 61508. Both the oil and gas sector and the railway sector have mature safety practices, but practices which differ at least in part owing to the very different environments in which they operate and functions which they carry out. Under such circumstances it is sensible to try to preserve the beneficial aspects of sector specific practices in sector specific standards.

4. Conclusions and Remaining Work

The APES project is now nearing completion and conclusions are emerging from the work carried out, in particular from the trial applications. By the end of the project the achievements listed below will be complete.

1. A body of material relating to practical experiences from the application of IEC 61508 will be available. This material will be of use to those wishing to apply the standard, those interested in developing IEC 61508 further and also those involved in the development of sector specific standards.

2. A body of technology transfer material, suitable for use in a set of training courses will be available to all interested parties. This material should assist in understanding the principles behind IEC 61508 as well as providing help in demonstrating conformance.

3. The conclusions arising from the project will be assembled into a report suitable for delivery to the standard bodies with responsibility for the development of IEC 61508 in order that the results arising from the APES project may be taken into account in future versions of the standard.

The main conclusions emerging from the APES project with respect to IEC 61508 are listed below.

1. There is general support amongst suppliers and users of safety related systems of the system lifecycle and associated activities proposed by IEC 61508. The standard is seen to represent a recognised approach to dealing with functional safety and an important opportunity to settle on a unified approach to this area across industry.

2. The development of sector specific standards is seen as an important adjunct to the further development of IEC 61508. Sector specific standards allow best practice from a specific sector to be taken into account and also allow

more detailed guidance to be given to suppliers and users. Such detailed guidance is not appropriate in a generic standard such as IEC 61508.

3. It is necessary to look to other information sources to understand all the requirements of IEC 61508. This statement is particularly true with respect to hazard analysis and risk assessment. These items are mentioned as specific requirements in part 1, and are widely accepted in the safety community as essential elements of a credible safety management process. However, IEC 61508 offers no guidance as to how these activities should be undertaken. Other standards such as those used for military systems (Refs. 7 and 8) may be looked to for additional support in this area.

4. The current attributes associated with SILs and the associated definitions in IEC 61508 do not prevent their frequent misapplication, with misapplication being particularly frequent when considering the numerical properties of SIL. It is considered that some revision of part 5 of IEC 61508 would be of particular benefit in this area. A move more towards guidance in the selection of tools and techniques for a given SIL would also be helpful.

5. The conditions currently applied to COTS elements, interpreted strictly, are likely to lead to the exclusion of COTS elements from safety related systems. No recognised view as to how regulators deal with such issues was available to the project although it was noted that a more relaxed interpretation of the requirements of IEC 61508 may allow such elements to be used in lower integrity safety related systems. More study in this area may be needed to determine whether excluding systems with significant COTS elements from safety applications results in safer systems being installed instead, or needlessly excludes systems which could provide a cheaper, safer alternative to those available at present.

5. References

1. International Electrotechnical Committee
    Functional Safety of Electrical/Electronic/Programmable Electronic Safety-Related Systems, Parts 1-7
    IEC 61508, 1998-1999

2. IEE
    SEMSPLC Guidelines Safety-Related Application Software for

Programmable Logic Controllers
1996

3. BS EN 61496-1:1998
   Safety of machinery - Electro-sensitive protective equipment
   1998

4. CENELEC prEN 50126
   Railway Applications: The Specification and Demonstration of
   Dependability, Reliability, Availability, Maintainability and Safety (RAMS)
   European Committee for Electrotechnical Standardisation (CENELEC)
   November 1995

5. CENELEC prEN 50128
   Railway Applications: Software for Railway Control and Protection Systems
   European Committee for Electrotechnical Standardisation (CENELEC)
   December 1995

6. CENELEC ENV 50129
   Railway Applications: Safety Related Electronic Systems for Signalling
   European Committee for Electrotechnical Standardisation (CENELEC)
   May 1998

7. UK MoD, Defence Standard 00-56
   Safety management requirements for defence systems
   December 1996

8. USA Department of Defense, Military Standard 882C
   System safety program requirements
   January 1993.

Appendix A: APES Project Partners

The following organisations are participating in the APES project:

1. Adtranz

2. British Computer Society

3. Civil Aviation Authority

4. EJA Engineering

5. ERA Technology Limited

6. Gambica

7. Health and Safety Executive

8. Institution of Electrical Engineers

9. Institution of Mechanical Engineers

10. Keele University

11. London Underground Limited

12. MTE Ltd

13. Railtrack

14. Safety Critical Systems Club

15. Silvertech

16. Transmitton

17. United Kingdom Offshore Operators Association (UKOOA)

18. Westinghouse Signals (incorporating Institute of Railway Signalling Engineers representation).

Application of IEC 61508 to Air Traffic Management and Similar Complex Critical Systems

- Methods and Mythology

Derek Fowler CEng FIEE
CSE International Ltd
Scunthorpe, UK

Abstract

IEC 61508 is widely viewed as the best available international generic standard for the management of functional safety in the development, operation and support of electrical, electronic and programmable electronic systems (EEPES). It has its roots in the process industries, in which, typically, relatively simple protection systems are used to reduce the risks from large, complex and potentially dangerous industrial plants.

Despite the origins and generic nature of IEC 61508, it has been shown that the Standard is capable of adaptation to a range of other applications - the European railway industry is a good example.

In considering how effectively IEC 61508 could be used in the even more complex Air Traffic Management (ATM) environment, the paper, addresses the fundamental issue of identifying the *equipment under control*; discusses hazard- and risk-analysis techniques for the determination of SILs (including situations where the relationships between service provision and the risk of catastrophe are difficult to determine); describes, using a goal-oriented approach to *safety assurance*, how compliance to the Standard may be demonstrated and used to present a coherent safety case; and considers the feasibility and value of system certification and conformance.

1 Introduction

CSE International Ltd has provided consultancy services in the field of software-intensive, safety-critical systems since the Company was founded in 1983.
In recent years, the Company has expanded its area of activity to include the

management of all aspects of project risk on the basis that whether a system is critical from a safety, business or mission perspective the underlying processes should be the same. That philosophy has been applied very successfully by CSE on software-intensive systems for a wide range of applications from safety-critical vehicle management systems to large infrastructure projects, including Hong Kong's Chek Lap Kok Airport and the Channel Tunnel. The Company has also been heavily involved in the development of safety standards, especially IEC 61508, and in the design and delivery of safety training courses.

IEC 61508 sets out a generic approach for all safety lifecycle activities for systems that consist of electrical, electronic and/or programmable electronic systems (EEPES) and are used to perform safety functions. A key objective of the Standard is to facilitate the development of specific application-sector standards based on a rational and consistent technical policy.

The suitability of the Standard for use in relatively simple protection systems - typical of, say, the process and automotive industries – is fairly evident; indeed it is in such applications that the Standard has its roots. However, despite its origins, IEC 61508 has already been shown to be suitable for adaptation to quite different applications - the European railway industry for example.

This paper examines how IEC 61508 could be adapted to even more complex, safety-related environments such as Air Traffic Management (ATM). It examines two key areas: the derivation of *safety requirements/safety integrity levels* (on which the application of most of IEC61508 depends) and the relevance of the Standard to the *safety assurance* process (on which safety approval, of whatever form, is usually based). It also considers whether system conformance and or certification are meaningful concepts in such environments.

2 Definitions

The following terms are used in this paper:

- *Harm* - the end event which safety management seeks to avoid (eg loss of human life);

- *Hazard* - a situation which could give rise to harm (eg a system failure);

- *Risk* - a combination of the effect of a hazard and the likelihood that the effect will occur (eg the probability that loss of human life would occur as a result of a specified system failure);

- *ALARP* - the principle that any risk must be reduced to a level which is As Low As Reasonably Practicable, provided also that some net benefit would accrue from taking that risk.

3 IEC 61508 Fundamentals

3.1 System Delineation

It is a basic requirement of IEC 61508 that, in the specification of any potential safety related-system, three key elements be identified:

- *the equipment under control (EUC)* – "equipment, machinery, apparatus used for manufacturing, process, transportation, medical or other activities";

- *EUC control system* - "system which responds to input signals from the process and/or from an operator and generates output signals causing the EUC to operate in the desired manner";

- *safety-related protection system* - "designated system that ... implements the required safety functions necessary to achieve or maintain a safe state for the EUC [and where applicable its control system] and is intended to achieve .... the necessary integrity for the required safety functions".

3.2 Safety Requirements

3.2.1   Types of Requirement

It is a fundamental principle of IEC 61508 that safety-related systems (SRS) are those systems whose primary purpose is to reduce risk – not merely those systems which present a hazard if they fail. For example, a nuclear power station is not a safety-related system per se, but the protection systems within it are!

That point is most important, as is the fact that SRS safety requirements need to be specified in two, complementary forms – ie *direct* (function and performance) and *derived* (integrity).

Direct safety requirements comprise simply:

- a description of the functions to be performed by the SRS; and
- the performance required of each of those functions;

as necessary to reduce to an acceptable level the risks originating in the EUC.

The performance specification must include all the desired attributes of each *safety function* - eg data accuracy, resolution, response time, update rate, latency etc.

Whereas the *function and performance safety requirements* specify what the system is required to do, it is also necessary to identify and limit the undesirable (failure) attributes of the SRS, since the latter will detract from the risk reduction intended to be achieved by the *safety functions*. These *derived* requirements therefore specify the *integrity* of the *safety functions*.

The relationship between risk and the two forms of safety requirement is illustrated in Figure 1. R_u represents the level of risk from the EUC that would pertain in the absence of the SRS that we are attempting to specify, and R_m represents the level of risk after adding a hypothetically failure-free SRS. Therefore, the maximum theoretically possible reduction in risk $\{R_u$ to $R_m\}$ is determined entirely by the functions and performance of the SRS - ie by its *direct* safety requirements.

Provided R_m is less than the tolerable level of risk (R_t), as set by relevant safety policy, then the allowable probability of dangerous failure of the SRS is determined by the risk margin {R_m to R_t} – this means that the <u>lower</u> the performance of a *safety function,* the <u>greater</u> its integrity needs to be in order to achieve the same net level of risk reduction from the SRS (and vice-versa).

3.2.2   Safety Integrity Levels

Safety Integrity Levels (SILs) are a form of *derived* safety requirement and are defined by IEC 61508 in two ways:

- where the SRS is required to perform continuously (or on demand, at a <u>high</u> rate of demand), the SIL indicates the allowable probability of a dangerous failure of the SRS per hour; or

- where the SRS is required to perform only on demand, at a <u>low</u> rate of demand, the SIL indicates the allowable average probability of failure of the SRS to perform its design function on demand.

IEC 61508 (Part 1, para 7.5.2.2) also suggests that the SIL of a safety function stems directly from the *necessary risk reduction* to be achieved by that function – ie {R_u to R_t} on Figure 1. That view may be true in the specific case of a simple on/off protection system (ie an SRS which either works or doesn't) but is incomplete when considering an SRS whose performance is potentially a continuous variable – eg a car braking system – and is even less helpful in those applications for which it is difficult, if not impossible, to determine R_u. In both those situations, a more general interpretation, relating the SIL directly to the risk margin {R_m to R_t}, is necessary.

4   ATM Interpretation

4.1 Introduction

Correct interpretation of the EUC in the context of ATM is more than just a nicety in the application of IEC 61508; it is essential in order to start the hazard analysis at an appropriately high level.

This section proposes that the air traffic as a whole be considered to be the EUC and suggests how ATM - ie the means by which the risk of collision between two aircraft (or between a single aircraft and the ground) is reduced to an acceptable level – may usefully be subdivided into *control system* and *protection system* aspects.

4.2 ATM Safety Requirements

Figure 2 illustrates how the two main elements of ATM – ie *Airspace Management* and *Air Traffic Control (ATC)* - contribute to the reduction of collision risk.

The risk level R_u represents a hypothetical situation in which:

- there is no Airspace Management (ie no structure to, separation standards for, or rules established for operating within, the airspace); and
- there is no ATC (ie no independent means of maintaining separation between aircraft or between an aircraft and fixed obstacles);

In most circumstances this would represent a very high level of risk to the air traffic.

Risk reduction $\{R_u$ to $R_f\}$ is provided by Airspace Management alone and includes not only function (eg airspace structure and rules) but also performance (eg separation minima and aircraft navigation accuracy) and failure (eg human error) parameters. In this context it is useful to think of Airspace Management as the *control system*. IEC 61508 requires that a *control system* whose dangerous-failure rate needs to less than 10^{-5} per hour be considered to be an SRS – this would be the case, for example, in non-radar environments, and in the vertical plane even for radar environments, where a high degree of reliance has to be placed on Airspace Management to achieve a safe situation.

Where $R_f >> R_t$, the ATC service itself has to achieve a substantial further net risk reduction $\{R_f$ to $R_t\}$. From the model described in para 3.2.1 above, it is evident that the reduction $\{R_f$ to $R_m\}$ represents that provided by a hypothetically failure-free ATC service and is determined by the effectiveness and performance of that service. Assuming that $R_m < R_t$, then the risk margin $\{R_t$ to $R_m\}$ represents the allowable dangerous-failure rate (ie a measure of the SIL) of the ATC service.

4.3 Practical considerations

Here we meet the first major problems in determining safety requirements:

- how could we determine what the collision-risk probability would be without any form of ATM -ie R_u ?
- how could we determine what a tolerable probability of collision (R_t) would be - ie the Target level of Safety (TLS) ?
- how could we determine how much ATM could contribute to the necessary reduction in risk $\{R_u$ to $R_t\}$?
- how could we determine the relative contributions of Airspace Management and ATC to the achievement of the TLS ?

Although a TLS is relatively easy to decide, without complex, validated collision risk models, the other three questions cannot be answered absolutely; it is for this reason that most ATM system safety cases are argued incrementally from a historical base. This approach is based necessarily on the (often implicit) assumption that the means of delivering the ATM service is not substantially different from that on which the historical evidence of a safe service is based. However, the progression towards free-flight, for example, is likely to undermine that assumption, and the role of collision-risk models will then become an essential part of demonstrating that such new concepts will be safe !

Even where the means of delivering the ATM service is not substantially changed but the parameters within that service are changed, collision risk modelling may be required in order to show that the ATM service will remain safe. This has certainly been the case for the introduction of Reduced Vertical Separation Minima (RVSM) in the North Atlantic ATM Region (above 29 000 feet) in 1998 and its imminent extension to European airspace. The safety argument in these instances is that improved aircraft-navigation (ie height-keeping) accuracy could fully compensate for the lessening of the collision-risk-reduction caused by a halving of the minimum required vertical separation between aircraft. Such modelling still depends on historical data and is confined to the Airspace Management function – ie the problem of modelling the more complex ATC functions has been avoided here.

4.4 Specification of ATC Systems

4.4.1 Function and Performance Safety Requirements

The first step in specifying a new ATC system is to identify those (safety) functions which are needed in order to achieve the *necessary risk reduction* and to specify the performance required of those functions - data accuracy, update rate, resolution, response time etc. However, as discussed above, it is usually difficult to establish absolutely what the level of risk <u>would</u> have been in the absence of the ATC functions (R_f in Figure 2) or to quantify the risk reduction {R_f to R_m} provided by ATC. A common solution to this problem is to:

- require the new system to have at least as much functionality and performance as the system which it is intended to replace; and

- produce evidence to show that the ATC service which was supported by the old system was itself tolerably safe.

This at least places R_m below R_t, albeit by an unknown amount. However, it is also essential to identify which of the function and performance requirements of the system are safety related (and to what extent). The fact that this is a difficult task may explain why it often avoided! A pragmatic solution is to specify <u>all</u> the system function and performance attributes as <u>direct</u> safety requirements and require those which are not met in implementation to be assessed for their safety significance.

4.4.2 Derived Safety Requirements

Without knowing the risk margin {R_m to R_t}, we cannot determine the integrity requirements for the ATC safety functions by using the direct methods proposed in IEC 61508.

One popular way around the problem is to use a deductive risk-analysis approach, which works on the basis that $R_m < R_t$ and comprises two stages:

- assessment of the effect (consequence) of every possible failure mode of each ATC function; and

- determination of the maximum acceptable probability of failure for each function, using a Risk Classification Matrix (RCM).

There are a number of schemes used in ATC applications, a particularly useful one being that devised by the UK National Air Traffic Services (NATS) Ltd outlined below.

4.4.3   The NATS Approach to Deriving Safety Integrity Requirements

To get around the problem of not being able to model the risk of collision, the NATS approach is based on the risk of not being able to positively maintain the minimum required separation between aircraft. In other words, risk analysis focuses on the *hazard* (separation erosion) rather than on the *harm* (collision/loss of life), and leads to a slightly revised risk model, as illustrated in Figure 3.

Figure 4 is an illustrative sample of the output from the first stage of the process, in which a Functional Failure Analysis (FFA) technique is applied to two ATC high-level functions – communications and surveillance. In this example, only a 'loss' failure mode is considered, for which the effect on the ATC service has been assessed as shown. The most important but most difficult aspect is determining the consequence of failure – ie the Severity Category, as defined in Figure 5 - taking account of any mitigation that might be available. The analysis is based typically on brainstorming sessions, involving skilled and experienced ATC operational and technical staff.

The allowed probability of failure (per operating hour, per ATC sector) is then derived from a Risk Classification Matrix (RCM), as shown in Figure 6. The RCM is normally used by taking the assessed Severity Category for the particular failure mode and ascribing an allowed likelihood of occurrence of that failure mode, according to the Risk Class (ie tolerability) defined in Figure 7. A key feature of Figure 7 is that it embodies the ALARP principle - that risks shall be reduced to a level which is as low as reasonably practicable.   Therefore, when specifying an ATC system initially, the lowest risk level (Class D or, the case of a Category 1 failure, Class C) is normally used.

The question arises as to whether the allowed probability of failure of a safety function, thus derived, can be used to determine the required SIL of that function, using the table from IEC 61508 shown in Figure 8. As the NATS method uses the consequence of failure to determine the allowed probability of failure, it is clearly making an assessment of risk. Furthermore, as the assessment of risk of failure is relative to an assumed safe state (ie a level of risk R'_m in Figure 3), then it follows that we have made an assessment of the risk margin $\{R_m$ to $R_t\}$ – ie the SIL - QED!!

4.4.4   Caution!

If the foregoing weren't enough to deter all but the most single-minded IEC 61508 protagonists, the use of the techniques described comes with a number of "health warnings", in addition to the issues raised in para 4.3:

- the risk of collision and the absolute and relative contributions of Airspace Management and ATC vary according the spatial dimension and phase of flight under consideration – eg the method described above would not be suitable for approach and landing;
- the probability values presented in the RCM shown in Figure 6 are largely subjective and relate to risk of separation erosion not to risk of collision (though based on considerable historical safety evidence of UK ATM operations);
- the RCM probability values must, to some degree, depend on the pattern and density of the air traffic;
- the RCM probability values are based on operations in radar-controlled airspace – they are unlikely to be applicable to a non-radar environment such as that found in oceanic ATM regions;
- the RCM probability values are based on an assumed total number of ATC sectors in the airspace to which it applies;
- the RCM probability values apply to a single ATC sector – failures which affect more than one sector may invalidate the results particularly in respect of assumed mitigations;
- the RCM probability values shown apply at only one level in the system hierarchy (ie to a single major element of the ATC system) and make an assumption about the total number of such elements which could contribute to a particular failure in the service – if the technique were to be applied at a higher or lower level, the values should be adjusted accordingly;
- the Severity Categories defined in Figure 5 apply at the overall service level - therefore, for example, it is the probability of a Category 1 event which must more occur no more frequently than 10^{-7} per hour, not each separate cause of such an event.

There is also a problem in the application of the SIL concept to complex systems which is not adequately dealt with in IEC 61508. For example, we might determine that a particular failure mode of an ATC function should be SIL 2. However, as in most ATC examples, the function may comprise a number of sub-functions which in turn may be implemented in a system involving people, procedures and complex, software-intensive systems, and once the high-level integrity requirement (of a failure probability of 10^{-6} to 10^{-7}) has been decomposed to the lower-level components of the equipment, it is quite conceivable that the allowed failure probability would need to be one or two orders of magnitude lower. Thus to develop that system to a SIL 2 standard would be ignore the possibility that some of key components should be developed to SIL 3 or 4 standards.

4.5 Conclusions

It is suggested that the above discussion shows that it is possible to determine SILs for ATM applications and, therefore, it seems that IEC 61508 could be applied to such complex environments.

However, the safety analysis and specification process is so complex and based on so many (often hidden) assumptions that an application-specific interpretation of the Standard will be necessary if the many pitfalls are to be avoided.

5 IEC 61508 and Safety Assurance

5.1 Why Use a Standard ?

5.1.1 Legal Considerations

The safety environment is heavily governed by law, defining the roles and responsibilities of regulatory authorities, service providers and systems / component suppliers.

The use of best practice through the adoption of relevant, recognised standards can be a valuable "defence".

5.1.2 Technical Issues

It is impracticable to prove the integrity levels of any high-integrity system by testing alone (test time must exceed ~10 MTBFs). Furthermore, the *systematic* nature of software failures means that integrity of software-based systems is extremely difficult to predict quantitatively, and is at least as dependent on the processes used to develop the software as on any intrinsic (testable) attributes of its design.

The effective use of appropriate standards that govern, inter alia, the process of design and development of high integrity systems is important in gaining the necessary assurance that the system will meet its requirements.

IEC 61508 is certainly appropriate to safety-related systems – the question is how to ensure that its application is effective in the safety assurance process.

5.2 Safety Assurance Principles

The purpose of *safety assurance* is to ensure that the risks associated with the deployment of a system are tolerably low, and to provide positive evidence of that fact. For many projects, the task of demonstrating that a system is tolerably safe can involve a highly complex *argument,* each strand of which needs to be supported by adequate *evidence.* Furthermore, the degree of rigour required of the *evidence* should depend on the risks involved, and the *assurance* process therefore needs to focus on the higher-risk areas of the project.

The task of setting out a complete and consistent *argument,* and linking the strands of that *argument* to the vast array of *evidence* needed to support the *argument,* can be facilitated by techniques such as *Goal-structuring Notation,* described below.

5.3 Goal-structuring Notation

The basic Goal-structuring Notation (GSN) is illustrated in Figure 9. The logic involved is as follows:

- a *goal* is a statement of intent that a particular objective will be achieved;
- a *goal* can be broken down into *sub-goals*;
- a *goal* can be said to be have been satisfied if all its *sub-goals* can be shown to be have been satisfied; and
- further decomposition of *goals* can continue until we reach a level at which a *solution* to each lowest-level *goal* can be provided.
- *assumptions* may be used as a mitigation for an otherwise incomplete or unsubstantiated set of *goals* (but only if adequately validated);

In safety assurance work, *goals* are usually referred to as *arguments,* and *solutions* as *evidence*. This approach and the inherent characteristics of GSN make it ideal not only for the ultimate *assurance* objective of producing a well-constructed, complete and consistent case that the system is tolerably safe, but also for planning and managing the whole *assurance* process from the outset. Furthermore, because *arguments* and *evidence* structure can be mapped directly on to recognised international safety standards - such as IEC 61508 - GSN can be extremely effective in demonstrating that *best practice* has been applied rigorously throughout the lifecycle.

The following section illustrates these points by decomposing, in a GSN format, the highest-level safety assurance objectives for a new ATM system (NATMS).

5.4 ATM Safety Assurance Illustration

Figure 10 starts with the (first-level) *argument* that the NATMS will be [tolerably] safe. That argument can be said to be true if (and only if) the four second-level *arguments* can be shown to be true.

Figure 11 decomposes the safety-requirements *argument* such that the next-level *arguments* map on to the first five phases of the IEC 61508 safety lifecycle, and shows the type of *evidence* (also determined from IEC 61508) which could be introduced to satisfy *arguments* at that level. The fifth phase is further decomposed, and introduces a *strategy* symbol (parallelogram) - a "comment" facility that can be used, for example, to explain the rationale for sub-dividing a parent *argument* into further *arguments*.

The top-level *argument* on Figure 12 is complex and requires several layers of decomposition - Figure 13 provides the first level for the implementation of one of the major sub-systems (the Radar Data Processing System – RDPS).

The software aspects of the RDPS are further decomposed in Figure 14 to the lower levels of the IEC 61508 software lifecycle - ie the level at which the software process requirements of the standard are applied and *evidence* of compliance with the Standard is best obtained. The Standard sets out the requirements for each stage in the lifecycle (in many cases, depending on the SIL of the software) and specifies the type and quality of *evidence* necessary to demonstrate compliance with those requirements. Clarity of the *argument / evidence* relationship can be enhanced by including the relevant IEC 61508 references on the GSN structure – an example is given, on Figure 14, for software *code implementation*.

As the *evidence* is collected and shown to be adequate to support the related *argument*(s), the *arguments* can be aggregated up through the structure until finally the top-level *argument* - in this illustration that the NATMS is tolerably safe - has been shown to be true. Thus we have formed the basis of a rigorous, complete and consistent *safety case*.

In practice, the amount of data needed to manage safety and present an adequate *safety case* is likely to be enormous. However, tool support is available - eg the SAM 2000 tool developed by York Software Engineering Ltd, which provides not only an intelligent GSN capability but also includes a comprehensive, integrated set of hazard and risk analysis tools.

6 Conclusions

6.1 General

IEC 61508 is by its very nature a process standard rather than a product specification.

The Standard starts by specifying out the processes by which the safety requirements for an SRS should be derived; it recognises that such requirements are themselves determined by the risk reduction which the SRS has to achieve and that such risk reduction is itself determined by the characteristics of the EUC (and where applicable its control system). Because it is generic, IEC 61508 focuses on the integrity aspects (ie SIL) of the SRS rather than on function and performance, since the latter attributes are necessarily application specific.

The paper has shown that the parameters of the process for deriving a SIL for an ATC system are heavily dependent on the environment (airspace characteristics, phase of flight, spatial dimension etc) in which the system has to operate. Furthermore, because systems comprise not just equipment but also people and procedures (and what IEC 61508 refers to as "other technology"), the apportionment of the requirements to the equipment element is somewhat arbitrary.

The rest of the IEC 61508 specifies (but does not always mandate) design and development techniques and processes to be followed in the rest of the lifecycle, according to the target SIL. However, the paper has also shown that allocating SILs (and therefore applying the Standard) at system (or overall equipment) level can be misleading because the integrity required of the lower-level components depends on the design architecture and is often higher than the integrity required of the total equipment / system. The need to apply IEC 61508 selectively in complex systems is not very well explained in the Standard.

6.2 Conformance and Certification

It follows, therefore, that attempts at specific *certification* (or type approval) of ATM/ATC equipment against IEC 61508 face a number of difficulties, including the following:

- the operational environment (and therefore safety requirements) for ATM/ATC systems is very variable;
- equipment is only one element of the system – the safety requirements (ie function, performance and integrity) of the equipment depends on, inter alia, how those requirements are apportioned from the overall system requirements;
- IEC 61508 deals only with system integrity and cannot, by virtue of its generic nature, specify system function and performance – however, as has been shown, risk reduction provided by an SRS is determined as much by its safety function and performance as by its integrity, and therefore any certification statement in relation to IEC 61508 would give a wholly incomplete picture regarding the suitability of the SRS for the intended application;
- IEC 61508 does not address the issue of system complexity but rather assumes that the integrity of the lower levels of the system hierarchy would need to be no higher than the integrity of the overall system – this simplified approach does not work for complex systems;
- many of the requirements in IEC 61508 are not mandatory – on the contrary, it is left to the developer to decide on how much to apply the recommendations given in the Standard (although the onus is on the developer to justify ignoring them!);

Therefore, a goal of ATM equipment standardisation, however well intentioned, is unlikely to be achieved via *certification* against IEC 61508!

Conformance is a somewhat different issue and potentially much more meaningful than *certification*, if interpreted sensibly – ie if applied to the process of designing and developing a product, rather than directed at the product itself.

Consider the following statements:

Statement	Interpretation
This system has been developed fully in accordance with IEC 61508	A recognised safety management process, covering the whole system lifecycle, has been used in the development of the product
This system has been developed fully in accordance with IEC 61508, SIL 3	A recognised safety management process, covering the whole system lifecycle, has been used in the development of the product <u>and</u> techniques have been applied to the product design, development, verification and validation which are, at some level, appropriate to a product of required integrity SIL 3

Neither of those statements addresses the fundamental issue as to whether the product would be safe for its intended use – that still requires a well-structured safety argument, supported by appropriate and adequate evidence, specific to each application. However, both statements give us some assurance about the process which led to the product and, in the case of the second statement, about the properties of the product itself.

The value of demonstrating conformance to IEC 61508 lies, therefore, not in a guarantee that a product will be safe, but rather in lessening of the likelihood that it will be unsafe!

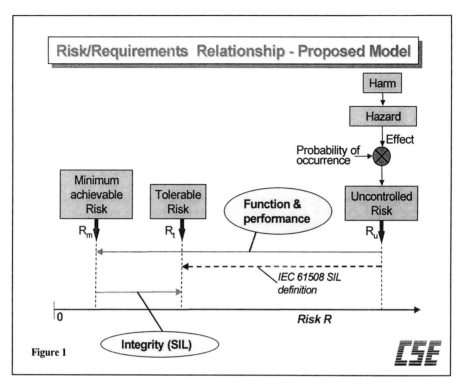

Figure 1

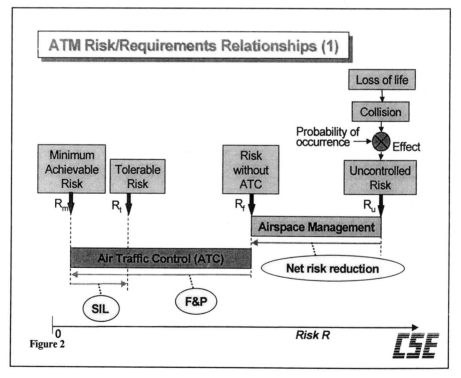

Figure 2

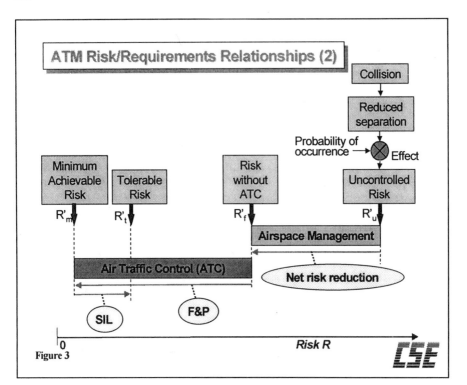

Figure 3

Illustrative Functional Failure Analysis

Function	Failure mode	Effect	Severity category	Mitigation
Air-ground voice communication	Loss	Inability to communicate between aircraft and ATC centre	1	Fallback procedures invoked. Traffic transfer to adjacent ATC sector
- - -	- - -	- - -	- - -	- - -
Radar data	Loss	Loss of displayed aircraft position and height data	2	Revert to voice control. Transfer traffic to adjacent ATC sector

Figure 4

CSE

Illustrative Severity Categories

Category	Definition
1	Sudden inability to provide any degree of air traffic control .... within one or more airspace sectors for a significant period of time
2	The ability to maintain air traffic control is severely compromised within one or more airspace sectors , without warning, for a significant period of time
3	The ability to maintain air traffic control is impaired within one or more airspace sectors , without warning, for a significant period of time
4	No effect on the ability to maintain air traffic control in the short term but [contingency measures may be required if the failure condition prevails].

Figure 5

CSE

Illustrative Risk Classification Matrix

Likelihood		Risk Classification			
Frequency	Probability	Severity Category			
		1	2	3	4
Frequent	$>10^{-3}$	A	A	A	C
Probable	10^{-3} to 10^{-4}	A	A	B	D
Occasional	10^{-4} to 10^{-5}	A	A	C	D
Remote	10^{-5} to 10^{-6}	A	B	D	D
Improbable	10^{-6} to 10^{-7}	B	C	D	D
Extremely improbable	$<10^{-7}$	C	D	D	D

Figure 6

CSE

Illustrative Risk Tolerability

Risk Class	Tolerability
A	Intolerable except in the most extraordinary circumstances
B	Tolerable only if risk reduction is impractical or the cost of reduction would be grossly disproportionate to the value of improvement to be gained
C	Tolerable if the cost of risk reduction would be greater than the value of improvement to be gained
D	Acceptable – the only safety measures necessary are those to maintain assurance that the risk remains in the class

Note: Risk classes B and C represent the so called ALARP region

Figure 7

IEC 61508 SIL Table

Probability of dangerous failure per operating hour	SIL
10^{-5} to 10^{-6}	1
10^{-6} to 10^{-7}	2
10^{-7} to 10^{-8}	3
10^{-8} to 10^{-9}	4

Note: Table applies to high-demand and continuous-mode systems

Figure 8

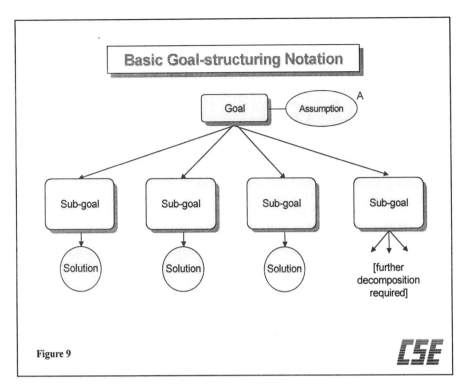

Figure 9

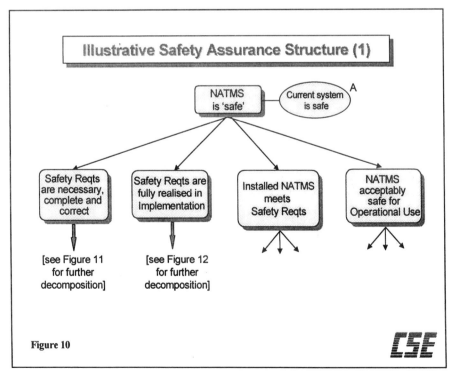

Figure 10

244

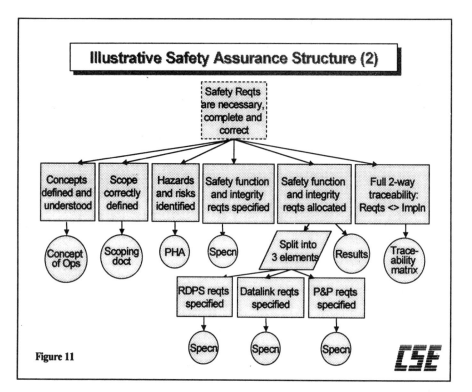

Figure 11

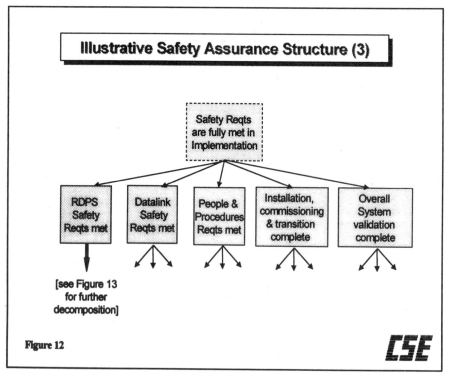

Figure 12

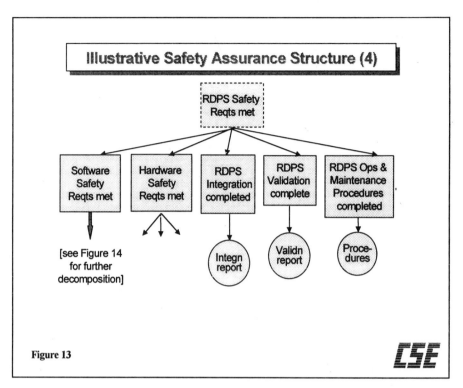

Figure 13

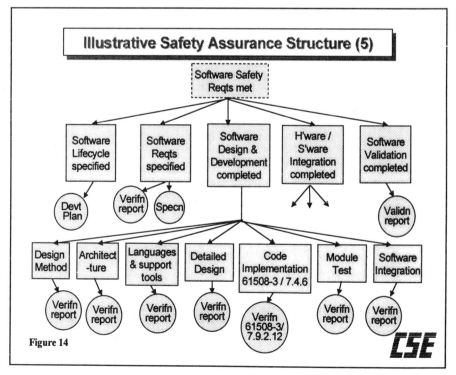

Figure 14

Ten Years On: Doesn't the World of Security have Anything to offer the World of Safety?

Dr. David F.C. Brewer

Gamma Secure Systems Limited

Diamond House, 149 Frimley Road, Camberley, Surrey, GU15 2PS, UK

Abstract

This paper revisits the question of whether there is anything in common between the world of security and the safety critical community. It reviews the two most important information security standards and highlights areas where that commonality might be developed.

1 Motivation

In the late 1980s there was a concerted effort to identify similarities between security and safety techniques, with a view to aligning the approaches where it made sense to do so. Two particular areas of commonality were identified. The first was termed "policy". It defines the reasons why security/safety features are required, for example to prevent the disclosure of secret information to an enemy, or prevent two trains from attempting to occupy the same space at the same time. The second was termed "assurance", which may be defined as "confidence that the security/safety features meet the security/safety policy and cannot be bypassed, deactivated, corrupted or otherwise circumvented". Although some research was performed in both of these areas, there is no evidence of any uniform take up of the ideas with the result that the two disciplines have remained separate.

Information security was discussed at a recent meeting (July 1999) of the Safety-Critical Systems Club, with invited speakers from the World of Security. It was observed that while the World of Security was becoming concerned with the threats of natural disaster and power failure, areas traditionally associated with safety, the World of Safety was becoming concerned with the threats of terrorism, an area traditionally associated with security. This led to the conclusion that the time is ripe for revisiting the two disciplines. The purpose of this paper is to provide an update on advances in security thinking over the past decade by reviewing the two most important security standards that have recently been published: the Common Criteria [ISO 99] and British Standard (BS) 7799:1999 [BSI 99].

2 An Overview of the two Most Important Security Standards

2.1 The Common Criteria

The Common Criteria for Information Security Evaluation [ISO 99] is an ISO standard for evaluating information security products. It provides a common language with which to describe the security claims of a product and how to substantiate those claims. It was first published in 1996 as a result of harmonising the European, US and Canadian evaluation criteria. A revised version was published in 1998 and soon afterwards adopted by ISO as an international standard.

There are three parts to the Common Criteria (CC):

- An Introduction and General Model (Part 1) that explains the philosophy behind the CC. It presents constructs for expressing IT security objectives, for selecting and defining IT security requirements, and for writing high-level specifications for products and systems (called "Protection Profiles" (PPs) and "Security Targets" (STs)). In addition, the usefulness of CC is described in terms of each of its target audiences.

- Security Functional Requirements (Part 2) establishes a set of functional components as a standard way of expressing the functional requirements, and catalogues the set of functional components into families, and classes.

- Security Assurance Requirements (Part 3) establishes a set of assurance components as a standard way of expressing the assurance requirements, and catalogues these into families and classes. It defines evaluation criteria for PPs and STs and defines a scale for rating assurance, called Evaluation Assurance Levels (EALs).

There are a variety of national evaluation and certification schemes and an international mutual recognition arrangement.

The evaluation and certification schemes are quite unlike the more familiar ISO 9000 process. The major difference is that the product, together with associated documentation and (in some cases) source code, will spend a long time in the evaluation laboratory (e.g. 1-2 years) before certification is achieved. A mutual recognition arrangement is in force between Canada, France, Germany, the US and the UK. This means that the results of evaluations conducted in one of these countries (currently up to and including EAL4) will be accepted by the others.

2.2   BS 7799:1999

British Standard (BS) 7799 [BSI 99] is the emerging international standard for security management. It addresses the standardisation of "Information Security Management". First published in 1995, BS 7799 is now used in the UK, South Africa, the Netherlands, Brazil, Australia and New Zealand. Norway has translated the standard into Norwegian, with the intention of adopting it as a national standard. Other countries, such as Denmark, Eire, Sweden, the US and Japan, are considering adopting BS 7799 as a standard. Indeed, the revised version of the standard BS 7799:1999 has just been formally proposed as an ISO standard.

There are two parts to BS 7799 and also a certification scheme for public and private organisations. The certification scheme has been designed to be strong enough and consistent enough with BS 7799 to be accepted reciprocally by different countries.

The two BS 7799 parts are:

- BS 7799-1:1999 (Part 1) is a "standard code of practice" and provides guidance on how to secure an Information System (IS).

- BS 7799-2:1999 (Part 2) is a "standard specification" and specifies the management framework, objectives and control requirements for an Information Security Management System (ISMS).

The certification scheme works like ISO 9000. Indeed there are many parallels between ISO 9000 and BS 7799. For example, instead of having a quality policy and a quality management system, there is an information security policy and an ISMS.

3   Security Policy and Functionality

3.1   The Common Criteria Approach

The CC catalogues a wide range of functionality "components" in terms of "families" and "classes". A class is a grouping of components that addresses the solution to a common type of security problem, such as audit or non-repudiation. Classes are made up of "families". A family of components is a grouping of similar components that differ, for example, by their robustness. There are 135 components, 66 families and 11 classes. Components are split into self-contained elements.

The general form of an element is a stylised statement that may contain the following two constructs (the acronyms are explained later): [assignment: *list of things*] and [selection: *choice of things*]. An example is (FRU_RSA.2.1) "**The**

TSF shall enforce maximum quotas of the following resources: [assignment: *controlled resources*] **that [selection:** *individual user, defined group of users, subjects*] **can use [selection:** *simultaneously, over a specified period of time*]". TSF means "TOE Security Function". The TOE is the "Target" (i.e., subject) "of Evaluation". TSF is therefore just a generic name for some module or other part of the TOE. FRU_RSA.2.1 is the formal identifier for this CC component. It shows that it is the first element of the second component in the RSA (Resource Allocation) family of components in the FRU (Resource Utilisation) class. The "F" stands for "Function". If the identifier began with an "A" (e.g. ADV) it would declare the component as an "assurance" component.

3.1.1   Component Operations

There are four types of operation that the CC permits on its functional components. The first two, assignment and selection, instantiate the component.   The assignment operation replaces the words "controlled resources" by the names of the actual resources that are to be controlled. The selection operation selects one or more of the sub-phrases in the phrases *"individual user, defined group of users, subjects"* and *"simultaneously, over a specified period of time"*. An example following the application of both operations would be "The TSF shall enforce maximum quotas of the following resources: mutable persistent memory that subjects can use simultaneously".

Two other operations are possible. The first, called, refinement allows the addition of details.   For example, the word "subject" is a generic term in security terminology for a computer program. In a given situation, a manufacturer may be different names to different types of computer program, for example system programs and applications. If the TSF only operates on applications, then the refinement operator would be used to transform the component into "The TSF shall enforce maximum quotas of the following resources: mutable persistent memory that *applications* can use simultaneously". The other operator allows multiple instances of the same CC component to be generated. Thus a second instance could be "The TSF shall enforce maximum quotas of the following resources: CPU time that *applications* can use *per month*".

3.1.2   Dependencies

The choice of components is not entirely free; some are dependent on others. For example, component FDP_IFF.1 is dependent upon FDP_IFC.1 and FMT_MSA.3. This means that if FDP_IFF.1 is selected, the CC strongly recommends that FDP_IFC.1 and FMT_MSA.3 are selected as well. (Indeed, from a standard's perspective, these dependencies are normative.) If they are not selected, the CC requires that a justification is given instead.

Dependencies need not be to other functional components.   There are some examples where a functional component is dependent on an assurance component.

For example, FMT_MTD.3.1 is dependent on ADV_SPM.1. On the other hand, many functional components are independent.

3.1.3 Component Hierarchies

Some components contain the elements of others. In this case the components are hierarchically related. This is a semantic device that is used to show that one component is in some way superior (e.g. in its ability to withstand an attack) to another.

3.1.4 Inventing New Components

The CC appreciates that its catalogue may be incomplete and that new components may need to be added. There is a formal procedure for achieving this.

3.2 Classes of Function

There are 11 functional classes. Some of them are not mutually exclusive. For example, in order to build a secure communications path between the TOE and some external device, class FCS and class FTP may be used (or perhaps some combination of both).

3.2.1 Class FAU: Security audit

The purpose of auditing is to determine which security relevant activities took place and who is responsible for them. The task involves recognising, recording, storing, and analysing information related to security relevant activities.

3.2.2 Class FCO: Communication

This class is concerned with ensuring that the originator of a message cannot deny having sent the message, nor can the recipient deny having received it.

3.2.3 Class FCS: Cryptographic support

This class is concerned with encryption, decryption, and cryptographic key generation, distribution, access and destruction. It is intended to cover all forms and uses of cryptography, including protection against eavesdropping, digital signatures, identification and authentication, non-repudiation, trusted path, trusted channel and data separation.

3.2.4   Class FDP: User data protection

This class addresses access control. The various components are organised into four groups:

1. Dealing with discretionary and mandatory policy issues. Essentially these components define the access control rules that are to be followed by all other components. It is an important, and interesting topic that is further developed in this paper in §3.3.

2. Dealing with access control itself, the transfer and preservation of integrity of information within the TOE, the re-use of magnetic media and rollback.

3. Dealing with the import and export of information between the TOE and an environment that cannot be trusted.

4. Dealing with the import and export of information between the TOE and an environment that can be trusted.

3.2.5   Class FIA: Identification and authentication

The purpose of this class is to establish and verify a claimed user identity. It is necessary when there exists a requirement to restrict, or hold users accountable for, their actions. The class deals with what happens in the event of failure to authenticate an identity, particularly so that an attacker cannot learn how to defeat the authentication system.

3.2.6   Class FMT: Security management

In many cases a TOE will provide a means for a security administrator to configure the TOE to meet the security policies of a given organisation, and to grant and rescind rights (for example when employees join and leave). The purpose of this class is to facilitate such management activity.

3.2.7   Class FPR: Privacy

This class provides a user protection against discovery and misuse of identity by other users. It allows for anonymity and pseudonymity. (Anonymity ensures that a user may use a resource or service without disclosing the user's identity. Pseudonymity ensures the same but still allows the user to be accountable for that use.) It allows for unlinkability (the ability for a user to make multiple uses of resources or services without others being able to link these uses together). It allows for unobservability (the ability for a user to use a resource or service without others, especially third parties, being able to observe that the resource or service is being used).

3.2.8   Class FPT: Protection of the TOE Security Functions

The purpose of this class is to ensure that security functions cannot be bypassed, deactivated, corrupted or otherwise circumvented.   The class deals with self-testing, integrity checking, resistance to physical, electrical and logical attack, safe failure modes, recovery to a secure state and reliable time stamping.

3.2.9   Class FRU: Resource utilisation

This class addresses fault tolerance, the allocation of resources in favour of the more important or time-critical tasks, and preventing users from monopolising resources.

3.2.10   Class FTA: TOE access

The purpose of this class is to control a user's interaction with the TOE. It deals, for example, with warning banners, what happens if a terminal is unattended for some period of time and how many times a user can be logged on concurrently.

3.2.11   Class FTP: Trusted path/channels

The purpose of this class is to facilitate trusted communication paths between users and the TOE security functions themselves, and between the TOE and other trusted products.

3.3   Mandatory Policies

One of the most interesting functionality components is FDP_IFC. It concerns information flow control policy. It is interesting because it can be used to specify and enforce all sorts of mandatory policies, particularly policies that may be safety relevant.

In information security terms, a policy is "mandatory" if a user can do nothing but follow it (assuming that they do not attempt to break the security of the system). In reasoning about such policies it is usual to associate "security labels" with the active and passive elements of a system, together with a set operations that the active elements may perform on the passive elements, and a set of axioms that define the allowable state transitions. Traditionally the active elements correspond to computer programs that act on behalf of a user. In some sense, therefore, it is the user that is the active element. The passive elements are computer files and information.   The operations are read and write.   The security labels are "clearance" for users and "classification" for files and information. There are two axioms. The first axiom is that a user with clearance Y cannot read information with a classification X where $X>Y$. The second axiom is that information with a classification X cannot be written to a file with classification Y where $X > Y$. This policy represents the simple case of access to classified information. In other words it is intended to prevent someone who is only cleared to see SECRET information from gaining access to TOP SECRET information. In particular the policy prevents someone with a TOP SECRET clearance from copying TOP SECRET information into a SECRET file, so that the person with only a SECRET clearance can read it. If this were allowed then TOP SECRET information would have been allowed to "flow down" to a file with a lower classification. It is this notion of information flow that gives rise to the name of FDP_IFC (information flow control).

Since this policy was first studied by [BEL 76], other workers have been able to model other real-world policies by allowing the security labels to change as a function of past operations. For example [BRE 89] modelled the Chinese wall aspects of the 1986 Financial Services Act in this way. In this case, a user is prevented from accessing information that may result in a conflict of interest. The full set of operations is depicted in Figure 1.

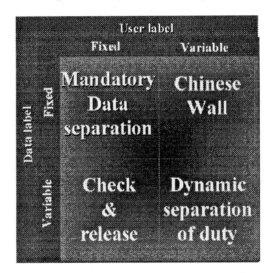

Figure 1: Different forms of mandatory access control policy

In general there are therefore four possibilities, depending on whether the user and data labels are fixed, or are allowed to change. The four cases are:

1. Mandatory Separation. In this case, user and data labels are fixed. It ensures that classified information cannot get mixed up. Indeed, it ensures that information belonging to one customer cannot get mixed up with that of another. This is particularly important in e-Commerce, as the livelihood of the service provider depends on strict separation of data and users. Customers can be competitors, and they will sue if their data falls into the hands of a competitor due to a security failure by the service provider.

2. Chinese Wall. In this case, the data label is fixed, but the user label changes. The data accessible by the computer belonging to different companies is partitioned into conflict of interest classes. Initially, users are free to access any data they choose, but once they have chosen to access the data of any particular company their user labels are changed to prevent them from accessing the data belonging to any company within the same conflict of interest class.

3. Check and Release. This case, often referred to in banking circles as a "check and release" procedure, the user label is fixed (i.e. a user may either be a clerk or a supervisor) but the data label changes (i.e. initially it is "unauthorised" subsequently becoming "authorised").

4. Dynamic Separation of Duty. In this case, both user and data labels are free to vary. It represents the general case within e-Commerce where supervisors are allowed to amend the transactions that they are given to approve, and are therefore not subsequently allowed to authorise them.

In all of these examples the passive element is a file. However, if the various lifecycle states of a system are chosen as the passive element, then FDP_IFC no longer controls information flow. Instead it enforces strict conformance to allowable lifecycle transitions. In this sense it would be able to enforce a policy akin to that of a mechanical interlock.

3.4 Protection Profiles and Security Targets

The security specification for a specific instance of a security product is documented in a "Security Target (ST)". The specification identifies:

- the assets to be protected

- the threats to those assets

- the security objectives that the TOE must meet to defeat, or otherwise reduce the impact of those threats

- the security requirements expressed in terms of the CC functional components

- the assurance requirements expressed in terms of the CC assurance components (see §4.1).

The security specification for a generic class of security products is documented in a "Protection Profile (PP)". The specification is similar in many ways to that of a ST. Examples of PPs can be found on the World Wide Web: [SCI 99] for smart cards, [NIS 99] for firewalls and [NSA 99] for trusted operating systems.

3.5 Dealing with the Environment

The environment of the TOE consists of everything that is relevant to the security of the TOE but is outside the scope of the evaluation. For example, if the TOE is an operating system (e.g. Microsoft NT 4.0) the immediate environment would consist of the computer on which NT is installed, the application software that is subsequently loaded and any network connection. The environment also includes the development, manufacturing and deliver environment. It includes the support environment. It includes the business environment. In other words, the TOE environment includes everything, past, present and future that can affect the security of the TOE.

A number of assurance classes (see §4.2) are devoted to simplifying the treatment of the environment. This, of course, means that certain aspects of the environment are within scope of the evaluation because they are the subjects of various assurance criteria. This represents a paradox. Certain PP authors (see [SCI 99]) feel strongly about this, and are attempting to use the functional component to specify the security aspects of the environment. In this sense, the CC is attempting to grow out from the technical evaluation of security products into a consideration of the security properties of the environment. BS 7799 takes a different approach.

3.6 The BS 7799 Approach

BS 7799-1:1999 presents a catalogue of good practice. It provides advice and guidance using straightforward English text. The content is summarised in the following sections.

3.6.1 Security Policy

The objective is to provide management direction and support for information security. It argues that management should set a clear example of commitment and support through the issue and maintenance of an information security policy for their organisation.

3.6.2 Security Organisation

The objective is to manage security within the organisation. The standard provides advice on how to establish a management framework to initiate and control the prosecution of information security. The standard also addresses the issues of third party access and outsourcing.

3.6.3 Asset Classification and Control

The objective is to maintain an appropriate protection to an organisation's assets. It provides advice on establishing inventory's of assets and a classification scheme.

3.6.4 Personnel Security

This part of the standard addresses a variety of issues including personnel screening, confidentiality agreements and terms and conditions of employment. It addresses training, incident reporting, learning from incidents and disciplinary processes.

3.6.5 Physical and Environmental Security

This part of the standard gives guidance on physical access controls and addresses the threats of environmental hazards and power failure. It addresses the removal and re-use of equipment and off-site working.

3.6.6 Communications and Operations Management

This part of the standard addresses a wide variety of issues concerning the general operation of a computer facility and e-Commerce in particular. The operational issues include change control, incident management, segregation of duties, capacity planning, virus controls, backup and disposal of media.

3.6.7 Access Control

This part of the standard deals with access control rules and the management of user accounts. It deals with network access, remote diagnostics, duress, intrusion detection, clock synchronisation, mobile computing and teleworking.

3.6.8 Systems Development and Maintenance

This part of the standard provides advice and guidance on developing and maintaining a secure information system. It addresses network infrastructure, business applications and user developed applications. It also deals with message authentication and cryptographic controls.

3.6.9 Business Continuity Management

The objective of this part of the standard is advice how to counteract interruptions to business activities and to protect critical business processes from the effects of major failures or disasters.

3.6.10 Compliance

The final part of the standard addresses compliance with legal requirements, including copyright, data protection and admissibility of evidence. It deals with internal reviews and audits.

3.7 Observations and Conclusions

Both standards follow a very similar approach to specifying security functionality, albeit one being more stylised than the other. Together they cover an extremely wide range of functions, many of which are probably relevant to safety critical systems.

4 Assurance and Risk Assessment

4.1 The Common Criteria Approach

The CC catalogues a wide range of assurance "components" in terms of "families" and "classes". A class is a grouping of components that addresses a particular way that confidence can be gained about the correct operation of the security features of the TOE. Classes are made up of "families". A family of components is a grouping of similar components that differ in the level of confidence that they may provide. Families are hierarchical. There are 93 components, 44 families and 10 classes.

Components are split into self-contained elements and grouped according as to whether they are developer or evaluator actions, or instructions to the developer on the content and presentation of evidence. The rationale behind this approach is to instruct:

1. developers on what to do to meet the assurance criterion;

2. developers on how to prepare and present the evidence that demonstrates that they have met the criterion;

3. evaluators on how to check the evidence (or independently establish corroborative evidence) and hence verify that the criterion is met.

The general form of an element is a stylised statement, e.g., (ATE_IND.2.3E) **"The evaluator shall execute a sample of tests in the test documentation to verify the developer test results"**. There are no assignments or selections, and therefore the assignment and selection operations are irrelevant. However, the refinement operator may be used (see §3.1.1). The identifier shows that this is the 3rd evaluator action (by the "E") of the 2nd component in the IND (independent testing) family of assurance class ATE (tests).

4.2 Classes of Assurance

4.2.1 Class ACM: Configuration management

The objective of configuration management (CM) from a security perspective is to help to ensure that the integrity of the TOE is preserved, by requiring discipline and control in the processes of refinement and modification of the TOE and other related information. CM prevents unauthorised modifications, additions, or deletions to the TOE, thus providing assurance that the TOE and documentation used for evaluation are the ones prepared for distribution.

4.2.2 Class ADO: Delivery and operation

This class defines the requirements for the secure delivery, installation, and operational use of the TOE. Its purpose is to ensure that the security protection afforded by the TOE is not compromised during its transfer, installation, start-up, or operation.

4.2.3 Class ADV: Development

This class specifies the nature and form of the design documentation that must be made available for analysis. It covers all aspects of the stepwise refinement of the TSF from a high level specification represented in terms of CC components down to the actual implementation.

4.2.4 Class AGD: Guidance documents

This class addresses information that would be traditionally provided to users and security administrators of the TOE.

4.2.5 Class ALC: Life cycle support

This class specifies the requirements for assurance for all the steps of the TOE life cycle, including "bug" correction procedures, and the measures used to protect the security of the development environment.

4.2.6 Class ATE: Tests

This class addresses the way in which the TOE will be tested. It addresses issues such as functional tests, test coverage and testing independence.

4.2.7   Class AVA: Vulnerability analysis

The purpose of this class is to identify exploitable vulnerabilities introduced in the construction, operation, misuse, or incorrect configuration of the TOE. It addresses covert channel analysis (a specific form of vulnerability analysis that concerns preserving the confidentiality of information). It concerns investigating whether an administrator or user (even with an understanding of the guidance documentation) would reasonably be able to determine if the TOE is configured and operating in a manner that is insecure. It also deals with "strength of function" (an important topic dealt with more fully in §4.3).

4.2.8   Class AMA: Maintenance of assurance

This class is aimed at maintaining the level of assurance that the TOE will continue to meet its security claims even when changes are made to the TOE or its environment.

4.2.9   Class APE: Protection Profile evaluation

The purpose of this class is specify how PPs are to be evaluated, and thus demonstrate that the PP is complete, consistent and provides a technically sound basis from which to develop a ST.

4.2.10   Class ASE: Security Target evaluation

The purpose of this class is specify how STs are to be evaluated, and thus demonstrate that the ST is complete, consistent and provides a technically sound basis from which to evaluate the TOE. It also facilitates demonstration of ST compliance with the PP.

4.3   Strength of Function

Even if a security function cannot be bypassed, deactivated, corrupted or otherwise circumvented, it still might be possible to defeat it by direct attack. Direct attack, in this context, is only possible if the security mechanism involves a "secret". The modus operandi of the attack is to guess the secret. Examples of mechanisms that may be attacked in this way include password and cryptographic systems.

Strength is measured on a three-point scale. The CC definitions are:

> **SOF-basic** — A level of the TOE strength of function where analysis shows that the function provides adequate protection against casual breach of TOE security by attackers possessing a low attack potential.

SOF-medium — *A level of the TOE strength of function where analysis shows that the function provides adequate protection against straightforward or intentional breach of TOE security by attackers possessing a moderate attack potential.*

SOF-high — *A level of the TOE strength of function where analysis shows that the function provides adequate protection against deliberately planned or organised breach of TOE security by attackers possessing a high attack potential.*

4.4   Evaluation Assurance Levels

The CC philosophy asserts that "greater assurance results from the application of greater evaluation effort, and that the goal is to apply the minimum effort required to provide the necessary level of assurance." To assist in this quest, the CC defines 7 packages of assurance components called "Evaluation Assurance Levels (EALs)". They hierarchically arranged so that each higher level includes the assurance components of the lower levels.

The CC enumerates and characterises the 7 levels in terms of the formality of the development process (e.g. formal methods versus conventional programming techniques):

- (EAL1) - functionally tested

- (EAL2) - structurally tested

- (EAL3) - methodically tested and checked

- (EAL4) - methodically designed, tested, and reviewed

- (EAL5) - semiformally designed and tested

- (EAL6) - semiformally verified design and tested

- (EAL7) - formally verified design and tested

4.5   The BS 7799 Approach

The mandatory requirements concern the ISMS. They require:

- the scope of the ISMS, and the information policy to be defined;

- a risk assessment to be performed;

- safeguards to be selected from Part 1: each safeguard must be either be de-selected with justification, or selected. In addition, other safeguards, not included in BS 7799-1:1999 may be selected;

- the safeguards to be implemented and managed appropriately;

- appropriate documentation and configuration management.

Risk management concerns the ability to make timely informed decisions about security. BS 7799-2:1999 provides a weak specification for a system that facilitates this decision-making process, i.e. the ISMS. The specification is weak because it only implies the existence of the feedback loop shown in Figure 2.

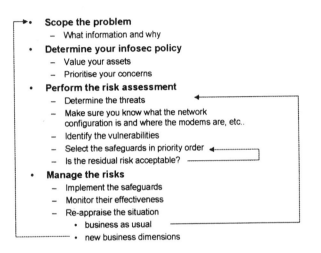

Figure 2: The Risk Management Process

Figure 2 presents the idealised structure for an ISMS. It shows the traditional approach to risk management augmented by the addition of the required feedback loops. In scoping the problem, BS 7799 implies an "information-centric" view of the world, to avoid the trap of failing to take account of less obvious vulnerabilities, such as people, cell phones and laptops. It further implies information policies that clearly identify and explain the business priorities concerning information. In addition, BS 7799 calls for risk assessments that identify what networks really are, not what people think they are! BS 7799 requires management to identify vulnerabilities and select the safeguards with a priority that matches the business priorities specified in the security policy. Reiteration is encouraged, choosing alternate safeguards until management is satisfied with the residual risks and costs involved. Once the chosen safeguards have been implemented, the ideal ISMS monitors their effectiveness. It does not assume that they will work as intended. Management is invited to regularly re-appraise the situation. Even if nothing is supposed to have changed, the risk assessment should be regularly repeated (this is the most important feedback loop). Management should assume, for example, that their networks have changed - most networks do with time! In any case, doubtless someone will have identified new vulnerabilities. Of course, if the business requirements have changed, there will be a need to re-scope the problem and revise the security policy accordingly.

In practice, companies should continually check that the safeguards that they deploy are working as intended. In that sense the ISMS is self-healing. If something does not work, management stands a good chance of finding out before someone else does and can exploit the vulnerability.

4.6 A Method for Assessing Risk

A useful definition of risk, particularly in the IT context is "the combination of three things: a **threat** exploiting some **vulnerability** that could cause harm to some **asset**". Figure 3 illustrates this concept by representing risk as the volume of a cube.

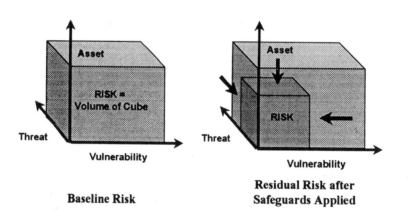

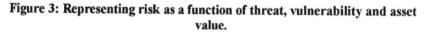

Figure 3: Representing risk as a function of threat, vulnerability and asset value.

Threats can be evaluated in terms of the severity and likelihood of an attack being made. The evaluation would take account of the motivation of the attacker, their capability (in terms of expertise and equipment) and whether the attack is focussed upon particular assets or not. The evaluation would also take account of whether the attacker has physical access to the IT equipment, as would be the case of an attack made by an insider, or electronic access, as would invariably be the case if the attack was made by a hacker. Different parameter values allow a wide range of threats to be modelled including the threat of human error, to the hostile premeditated actions of the organised criminal. Indeed, the standard threat profile includes external and internal risks, premeditated and opportunistic attacks, errors and accidents, malicious intentions and pranks. Companies can vary this profile, for example to reflect the potential increase in internal threat when a take over or merger is announced.

Vulnerabilities can be evaluated in terms of the amount a damage that would be caused were they to be exploited. Vulnerabilities can also be evaluated in terms of the amount of information that is publicly available about them and how old that information is. It is also necessary to know whether the vulnerability can be exploited remotely across a network, or whether the attacker must have physical access to the network.

Assets should ideally be ranked in accordance with the business consequence that would result should an attack on them result in them being made unavailable, lost forever, corrupted, improperly modified or improperly disclosed. The evaluation can take account of the time that an asset is rendered unavailable (e.g., seconds, minutes, days, weeks). It may take account of the degree of corruption or improper modification (e.g. just some or the majority of records in a database). It may also take account of to whom the information is improperly disclosed (e.g. a competitor or an unauthorised but otherwise trustworthy employee).

Safeguards can be modelled the same parameters as used to measure, threats, vulnerabilities and assets. Their effect is to reduce the size of the cube, leading to the concept of residual risk.

4.7 Comparing Risks in Different Systems

The level of acceptable risk is dependent upon the asset value, determined in accordance with the "DTI Scale". This scale maps the DTI's Unified Classification Scheme, augmented by national security markings (SECRET, TOP SECRET etc) on to a logarithmic scale. The Unified Classification Scheme defines three levels:

- *dtiSEC1* represents information which if improperly disclosed, particularly outside an organisation, lost or found fraudulent would be inappropriate and inconvenient.

- *dtiSEC2* represents information which any of these things happen to it would cause significant harm to the interests of the organisation. It includes personnel information and therefore would be the asset value relevant to European Data Protection Legislation.

- *dtiSEC3* represents information which likewise could prove fatal to an organisation.

dtiSEC2 maps directly onto the national security marking termed RESTRICTED (OFFICIAL USE ONLY in the US) and *dtiSEC3* maps directly onto the national security marking termed SECRET. There are higher markings.

The determination of acceptable risk rests upon the assertion that there exists a "dtiSEC0" that represents information that companies do not mind being wrong, given away or lost. The full assertion is that for the risk to protect assets of value dtiSECn (n = 1 or higher) to be acceptable:

Risk with safeguards [*dti*SEC*n*] ≤ Risk without safeguards [*dti*SEC*0*]

Or, in other words, the risk with the assets rated at their true value but with the selected safeguards in place should be (just) less than or equal to the risk that would occur if there were no safeguards but the assets were all valued at *dti*SEC0.

4.8   Observations and Conclusions

The two standards follow quite different but complementary approaches. One is predicated on confidence in the absence of vulnerabilities, the other on managing the risk should vulnerabilities exist and can be exploited. There may be a parallel between risk analysis and hazard analysis.

5   Summary

This paper has reviewed two important security standards and has attempted to highlight areas where there may be synergy between the World of Security and the World of Safety. There may be specific points of interest in these standards to the safety critical engineer. However, the principal offering from the World of Security is a common language (that in its current form may not be too far removed from the needs of the safety critical engineer) with which to describe both functionality and assurance. This paper may also have highlighted some further questions, such as whether there is any true similarity (and indeed should there be) between security risk analysis and safety hazard analysis?

References

[BEL 76]   Bell, D.E., and LaPadula, L.J., Secure Computer Systems: Unified Exposition and Multics Interpretation, Report MTR-2997 Rev.1, MITRE Corporation, Bedford, Mass, 1976

[BRE 89]   Brewer, D.F.C., and Nash, M.J., The Chinese Wall Security policy, Proceedings of the IEEE Symposium on Security and Privacy, pp. 206-214, Oakland, May 1989

[BSI 99]   Information Security Management, Part 1:Code of practice for information security management and Part 2: Specification for information security management systems, BS 7799:1999, British Standards Institute, ISBN 0 580 28271 1

[ISO 99]   Common Criteria for Information Technology Security Evaluation, version 2.0, ISO/IEC 15408, 1999

[NIS 99]   The National Institute of Standards and Technology Interim Registry of Protection Profiles, www.csrc.nist.gov/cc

[NSA 99]   The National Security Agency Registry of Protection Profiles www.radium.ncsc.mil/tpep/library/protection_profiles/index.html

[SCI 99]   The French Registry of Protection Profiles (SCSSI) www.scssi.gouv.fr/present/si/ccsti/pp.html

NEW GROUND

Making Safety Related Networks Work

Mike Ainsworth and David M Jackson

Praxis Critical Systems Limited
20 Manvers Street, Bath BA1 1PX, UK
Tel: +44 1225 466991   Fax: +44 1225 469006
Email: ma,dmj@praxis-cs.co.uk

Abstract

Computer systems are increasingly designed as communicating systems, rather then completely standalone equipment. The use of concurrent communicating systems has the potential to introduce new classes of failure, such as deadlock and livelock, which are not easily handled by existing safety analysis techniques.

This paper is based on the results of a study undertaken by Praxis Critical Systems for HM Nuclear Installations Inspectorate, and provides a survey of the problems that can arise during the development of communicating concurrent systems and the techniques that can be used for demonstrating the safety of such systems.

1 Introduction

Computer systems are increasingly being designed as communicating systems, rather than standalone equipment. Where in the past there might have been a single centralised computer operating simple hardware devices, a modern design may well involve several computers on a shared network, and the hardware devices may themselves have network interfaces and contain a considerable amount of software.

The use of concurrency can be broadly divided into two categories:

1. systems in which concurrency is inherent in the specification, e.g. where a system is required to handle multiple asynchronous tasks; and

2. systems in which concurrency is introduced during the design and implementation, e.g. dividing functionality across multiple processors to improve performance.

The introduction of concurrency can offer considerable advantages — the use of a distributed architecture may offer increased fault tolerance, and re-distributing some of the complexity into the hardware devices can simplify the overall design of the system and offer substantial performance improvements.

However, the problem with such a design in a safety-related system is that while the verification and validation of an individual software program is well understood, understanding the interactions between a number of systems operating concurrently can be extremely difficult.

1.1 Why concurrency is a bad idea

In January 1990 a software error in the switching software of certain AT&T switches caused a widespread communications failure across a large portion of the United States.

The switching software was designed to reconfigure its internal routing tables in response to status messages from other switches, so a failed switch would be noted and traffic re-routed around it. The problem occurred when a switch came back on-line after a failure, sent out a status message to inform the network it was alive, and then immediately started forwarding calls. The other switches started processing the status message, and then received the forwarded calls while they were in the process of resetting their internal tables. This resulted in an error which shut down the receiving switches (and when they subsequently came back on-line they in turn started sending out status messages, resulting in waves of failed switches rippling across the network)

A report [1] on the problems stated:

"The event just repeated itself in every switch over and over again. If the switches hadn't gotten a second message while resetting, there would have been no problem. If the messages had been received farther apart, it would not have triggered the problem."

This is a classic example of a race condition, where the system's behaviour is dependent on events occurring in a specific order. If events occur in an unanticipated order, problems can arise. In this case the race condition gave rise to a livelock, in which each component was busy, but the system was making no useful progress.

1.2 Why concurrency is a good idea

Traditionally, safety-related software has been based on a single-tasking program, since this type of program is the simplest to analyse in a rigorous manner. However, this sometimes resulted in code of the following form:

```
-- Start Task A
initialise_hardware_device;
-- Hardware needs 5ms to initialise, so use the time to start Task B
initialise_task_b;
-- Hardware now initialised, so back to Task A
read_from_hardware_device;
```

Such software effectively interleaves several separate tasks into a single process. Although software of this form may be easier to test and analyse, it can be argued that trying to implement a naturally concurrent design in a single-tasking system adds complexity to the implementation and makes the software architecture far less intuitive.

Over the last few years the tools and techniques needed for designing and analysing concurrent systems have matured considerably, and we believe that it is now possible to design and validate a concurrent system in a way which could be used as the basis of a safety case.

This paper is not intended to represent the cutting-edge of research into concurrency. Our aim is to highlight areas where the use of concurrency introduces particular problems for safety-related systems, and to present mature techniques which can be used to resolve those problems.

2 Failure Modes of Concurrent Systems

Concurrent systems can be extremely unpredictable. A sequential process, given the same inputs, will always behave in the same way. A concurrent system might run quite differently at different times due to subtle time-dependencies or non-determinism in the processes. This unpredictability is not in itself a fault, but it makes testing a concurrent system very difficult. In particular, testing can never possibly cover all the possible behaviours of the system and so we need to rely on more mathematically based techniques to demonstrate that the system will always behave correctly.

Adding concurrency to a design has the potential to introduce new failure modes. That is, in addition to the problems that can occur with any complex piece of software, in a concurrent system there are failure modes that arise specifically from the concurrency. In this section we discuss some of these failure modes, and later will describe how a system's designers might set about demonstrating their absence.

2.1 Deadlock

Deadlock occurs when two or more processes are waiting for each other.

For example, if process A locks a file and then tries to lock the printer, while at the same time process B locks the printer and then tries to lock the same file as process A, the processes will deadlock.

The example also illustrates a major problem with the verification of concurrent systems. Each process will work correctly when tested on its own (so each process meets its individual specification), and the combination of processes will only fail under certain timing conditions. It is extremely difficult to detect such problems during testing.

2.2 Livelock

Livelock is a situation where all the processes are running, but they are not achieving any useful work. It can be thought of as the concurrent equivalent of an infinite loop.

The result of a livelock is that some part of the system stops achieving useful work, as the example in Section 1.1 shows. It may also lead to other processes being unable to proceed because needed resources are being locked or consumed by the livelocked processes.

2.3 Starvation and Unfairness

Starvation is a situation in which some processes cannot proceed because they can never get access to a particular resource. In many systems processes repeatedly choose between a number of equally valid alternatives. If this choice is biased, then some of the alternatives will occur infrequently.

An example of this problem occurred in early networked file servers: if one server failed, other servers which were connected to it had the choice of either dealing with their own requests, or attempting to re-establish contact with the failed server. In some systems the latter was given priority, leading to starvation of the clients attempting to use this second server, which would then appear to those clients as having failed, and the initial failure of one server could thus jeopardise the operation of an entire network.

2.4 Interference

Often resources such as memory or peripherals are shared between processes. If two processes can write to the same resource simultaneously then we have potential for interference — results may be overwritten or garbled.

Interference can be prevented by using mutual exclusion techniques such as semaphores. However, such techniques must operate fairly otherwise starvation can occur.

2.5 Race Conditions

In many systems actions have to occur in a specific order. If these actions are carried out by different processes then the processes must be synchronized in some way to ensure that the correct order is followed. A race condition occurs when the order of the actions is not adequately enforced, and so the system may or may not work depending on which action is executed first.

2.6 Data Consistency & Error Handling

In a sequential system, it is generally easy to identify the location responsible for maintaining an element of the system state. In a concurrent system (and particularly in a physically distributed system), in contrast, data may need to be replicated or shared among several components and maintaining a coherent and consistent system state becomes a major problem.

Related difficulties apply to the process of detecting and handling errors in a concurrent system. Deadlocks and livelocks can occur if a process tries to make use of a failed component, while recovering from an error can be problematic if an erroneous result has already been communicated to other processes.

3 Safety Engineering

The problems described in the previous Section are generally only encountered where some degree of concurrent behaviour is present in a system, and thus may not be familiar to all those involved in development of a safety related system. Specific measures should thus be taken to ensure that such issues are addressed in the specification, design, and implementation of a safety-related network. This Section discusses some current, and possible, approaches.

3.1 Software Safety Standards

The various standards on software safety can be broadly divided into two categories:
- those that say nothing regarding concurrent systems; and
- those that say very little regarding concurrent systems.

Suprisingly, some of the most influential standards are in the former category, including IEC 61508 and DO178B.

The long-standing consensus among many of the safety standards is that any design should be kept as simple as possible, and complex or novel architectures should be avoided where possible.

Some standards explicitly recommend the use of a single-tasking structure, although it can be argued that this is a confusion of requirements and implementation. The requirement is that the system can be demonstrated to be correct. One way of ensuring this may be to use a single-tasking structure, but this clearly not appropriate if concurrency is an inherent part of the design, for example in redundant, fault-tolerant processors.

3.2 Safety Cases for Concurrent Systems

The use of a concurrent design will affect the safety case both by adding new safety requirements which are specific to the use of concurrency, and also by requiring different forms of evidence to be gathered to demonstrate that those requirements have been met.

The additional requirements will involve both the *process* by which the system is designed and built, and also the *product* itself.

3.2.1 Competence

The design and analysis of concurrent systems requires specialist skills. This will mean ensuring that staff involved with the project have the appropriate skills and arranging training where required.

3.2.2 Hazard Analysis

Although a concurrent design does not usually introduce new hazards into the system, it will introduce new failure modes (e.g. deadlock) which arise specifically as a result of the concurrency.

Many traditional safety analysis techniques (such as HAZOPS and fault tree analysis) are based on considering each element of the system in turn. It is difficult to analyse concurrency failures using these techniques because a concurrent failure may involve a large number of elements simultaneously (and the individual elements may all be operating within their specification).

One possible approach is to produce a list of common concurrent failure modes and use these during a HAZOPS-type session to guide a general discussion on whether the failure modes have been considered and suitably analysed. However, in general the complexity of such analysis for even relatively small systems is such that informal manual techniques cannot be relied upon, and systematic analysis of a concurrent system will require mathematical analysis techniques such as model checking.

3.2.3 Design and Development

Using a concurrent architecture will impose specific requirements on the tools and techniques used during design and development. This is considered further in the following sections.

4 Specification

As noted in Section 1, concurrency issues can arise from the requirements placed on a system in two ways: concurrency may be an explicit necessity, or it may be an implicit (but possibly unavoidable) consequence of requirements which do not explicitly constrain architectural decisions.

Examples of more-or-less explicit concurrency requirements include the inherent requirements noted in Section 1, for example, the need to support specific physical interfaces, to conform to particular physical location requirements, or to establish particularly high degrees of physical or temporal independence.

Concurrency may arise as part of the design process as an implicit consequence of functional requirements, but it is more commonly a side-effect of "non-functional" requirements such as demands for higher reliability than can be achieved by single channel hardware (fault-tolerance), or for safety integrity levels which motivate the adoption of diverse implementations.

The above examples show how concurrency may be introduced into a requirements specification; it is equally possible for such as specification to prohibit concurrency and thus place (possibly unintentional) constraints on the developer.

One common form of such (arguably premature) design decisions is to couch requirements statements in terms which can only be interpreted in the context of a single-threaded implementation. Examples include timing requirements which refer to the delay between a change in input conditions and "the corresponding change in software state". In a concurrent system, there may be no single change in software state corresponding to an input. More explicit are constraints, for example on the relative timing of input and output signals which assume a simple loop schedule of the form: read all inputs -- calculate parameters -- generate all outputs. If such requirements are enforced unnecessarily a potentially valuable concurrent solution may be prohibited by the cost of enforcing unnecessary timing constraints between components.

System architecture is a subject far beyond the scope of a paper of this type. We will restrict our attention to factors which effect the ease with which high integrity concurrent systems may be constructed.

Clearly in any safety related system there is a strong argument in favour of employing the simplest appropriate architecture, although we would argue that this does not necessarily imply the choice of a single-thread architecture at any price. Where static timing bounds can be calculated and all components are developed to the same levels of integrity, a simple static schedule may be appropriate, but if some functions have tight latency requirements or if static timing budgets cannot be calculated, then a pre-emptive mechanism is to be preferred.

A compromise is also required in determining the most appropriate levels of diversity and redundancy in a system. As noted above, the use of different implementations of a common function is sometimes recommended as a means of avoiding common-mode failures, but this clearly substantially increases both the development and verification effort required. Unless motivated by unambiguous results from a safety analysis and supported by strong factors to mitigate the risks of common cause failures in the requirements and specification, it may be preferable to use a minimal number of distinct components, subjected to a higher level of verification.

5 System Specification and Design

It is apparent from the preceding discussions that design and development of concurrent systems is a particularly difficult activity, and thus one, we believe, in which we should take advantage of every possible assistance. We thus concentrate on detailed specification and design techniques, which are amenable to rigorous, as well as conventional, verification and validation. We present a brief survey of a number of aspects of such techniques:

- the aspect of the system which is described;
- the notation used for representing it; and
- the verification techniques which can be employed.

There are two main methods of specifying the intended behaviour of a system or component:

- by defining abstract *properties* of the component; or
- by providing a *model* of the intended behaviour.

Taking these classes in turn, property-based descriptions tend to focus on individual features of a system or behaviour which can be combined using logical operations (such as AND, OR, etc). Model based approaches tend to have as their primitive elements items representing complete behaviours, and combining forms which mirror the physical construction of systems (such as sequencing, concurrent execution, and communication).

Turning to the actual notations, a wide variety have been discussed in the literature, although rather fewer have achieved practical acceptance. Among the more mature approches are:

- state-based languages, based on expressing the values of (shared) variables, for example LUSTRE [2];
- process algebras, employing descriptions in terms of patterns of externally observable events. Examples include CCS[3] and CSP[4];
- logic languages, which are property-, rather than model-based. Examples include Temporal Logic [5];
- state transition notations, extend the standard graphical or tabular methods. The StateChart notation [6] perhaps the most popular;
- Petri-nets, a graphical formalism based on non-exclusive occupation of states and execution of transitions [7].

Considering verification techniques, any of the representations here are naturally candidates for conventional V&V activities such as reviews and consistency checks. Techniques using model-based descriptions (and some property-based techniques) are also amenable to animation or execution, and some systems (StateCharts, for example) are supported by sophisticated prototyping environments. Review and animation are inevitably subject to limitations, however, particularly in concurrent systems where behaviour may be both complex and non-deterministic.

Such restictions lead us to consider more formal verification techniques; examples which have yielded at least some industrially useful results include:

- rigorous (manual or machine-assisted) mathematical proof;

- formal proof (generally machine-supported); and

- fully automatic state-exploration ("model checking").

Example systems offering support for these approaches include PVS [8] (a proof tool with some model-checking support for logic languages), SMV [9] (a model checker for verifying logical properties of state-based models), FDR [10] (a refinement-checking tools for comparing CSP models) and StateMate [11] (a system for developing, animating and model-checking StateChart diagrams.

An obvious supplement to being able to represent and check designs is the development of design rules for avoiding specific classes of the potentially hazardous behaviour discussed above. Examples include:

- rules for deadlock freedom in networks [12], based on restrictions to the data-flow patterns within a design or on the communications properties of individual components;

- simple rules for deadlock freedom (such as always claiming resources in a fixed order) which are part of the "folklore" of concurrent programmers (eg [18]);

- rules for avoiding non-determinism in Petri-nets by restricting the interdependencies between potentially conflicting actions [19];

- the substantial body of knowledge on eliminating race-conditions from electrical circuits and similar networks [20[; and

- strategies for establishing livelock freedom by finding some linear order among components which respects conditions on possible communication orders [21].

The maturity of concurrent specification and design methods is much less than that of sequential techniques. Practical applications thus require a combination of concurrency-specific approaches and the use more general techniques to address other aspects of a system's behaviour and structure.

6 Implementation

The design of concurrent systems has many similarities with "conventional" system design, not least because the majority of non-trivial systems exhibit some degree of concurrency even if every effort is made to impose a sequential system -- and thus the problems discussed in Section 2 are familiar hazards of many system engineering activities. Nevertheless, there are particular issues of importance.

At a superficial level, design and implementation documentation must pay particular attention to the problems of a concurrent design: the partitioning of functionality between components, allocation of resources, and the detection and handling of communication errors, for example.

The manner in which concurrency is manifest must also be considered. Concurrent behaviour may be present in the hardware (via the use of multiple processors) or (apparently) in software (via the use of multi-tasking structures). Although a thorough review is beyond the scope of this introduction, we may observe that hardware concurrency is perhaps most likely to be used in applications exhibiting:

- physical distribution or separate interfacing;

- performance requirements beyond the capacity of any suitable single processor;

- high degrees of functional independence between components; or

- high degrees of reliability or safety integrity, which may make redundancy necessary.

Software concurrency is applicable where the following are of concern:

- separation of concerns, eg where inputs and outputs are required at differing frequencies or according to differing synchronisation schemes;

- moderate degrees of functional independence (eg as might be enforced by an operating system with memory protection capabilities);

- a wide range of performance targets, for example where monitoring functions with deadlines of minutes or hours are fitted around a control function with a much tighter deadline; and

- budget or similar constraints motivate the use of pre-existing (and proven) components, and it is desired to add functionality without reworking the infrastructure.

One issue which tends to be considered only in the context of explicit concurrent design, and which is often confused by conflicting use of terms is that of *synchrony*. The words "synchrony" and "asynchrony" are used in (at least) two different senses:

- at an architectural level, in referring to systems where components share a common time reference and advance in lock-step as synchronous; and

- at the level of specific interactions, in referring to interactions which force synchronisation between components (such as the rendezvous in Ada) as synchronous (and thus message passing over buffered communications links might be seen as asynchronous).

By suitable choice of mechanisms, it is quite possible to implement an asynchronous architecture over asynchronous communications mechanisms, and vice-versa. For example, one could implement a system which had no common clock or time-frame, but used the "synchronous" Ada rendezvous as its communication mechanism. It is thus important that a design specifies both the nature and scope of its timing and synchronisation mechanisms clearly and explicitly.

The specification and description techniques outlined in Section 5 differ substantially in the aspects of behaviour which they represent and the structures used to describe these aspects. Similar variations exist in the technologies which may be used to implement a concurrent design (see Section 6.1 below). These variations make the process of proceeding from an abstract design to a concrete implementation particularly difficult. The problems which may arise include:

- significant design features may be left implicit in the design or code, making maintenance risky and expensive;

- excessive effort may be required in implementing a design, if the implementation technology chosen makes different assumptions; and

- excessive effort may be required in verifying an implementation, if features of the implementation technology are difficult to express in the design notation.

It is thus clearly desirable to ensure that the chosen design notations are consistent, as far as is practicable, and that their inconsistencies are clearly understood and documented.

6.1 Programming Languages

It is possible to implement a concurrent system using a wide variety of programming languages and systems, and the basic features of good programming are not generally changed by the introduction of concurrency. Nevertheless, there are substantial differences in the facilities provided as standard features of common languages, and in the degree to which concurrency constructs can be made explicit.

One feature to consider in a choice of language is clearly the facilities provided. The features provided will vary with the application and the design style chosen, but we might expect support for at least some of the following: resource locking, semaphores, global synchronisation conditions, monitors, mailboxes, rendezvous, buffers, blackboard (shared variable) communication, signals and message passing.

The approach taken to providing these facilities varies markedly between languages. Of languages which have reached international standardisation, Ada [13] has perhaps the most explicit set of concurrency features, particularly in the latest language revision. C, however, has no language features for concurrent programming as such, but is supported by standard libraries (such as Posix [14]) and extensions (such as Concurrent C[15]). In some cases, however, the presence of concurrency structures does not necessarily imply that such structures are useful for safety related systems. The standardised Programmable Logic Controller languages in IEC 61131, for example, includes specific communication facilities, but the absence of any detail in the standard regarding the implementation of the languages in general and concurrency in particular has led some authors to propose use of strictly sequential subsets [16,17].

6.2 Timing analysis

One area of particular concern in the design of concurrent systems is that of timing analysis. The execution time of sequential programs can generally be estimated by some form of worst-case or bounds analysis, and their generally deterministic nature means that these analyses can be supported by testing. Neither of these approaches is entirely suitable for concurrent systems. A range of more sophisticated approaches have been suggested, including timed process algebra, stochastic and timed state machine models, queuing theory, and timed Petri nets. It is worth noting, however, that few of these approaches have been demonstrated to scale successfully to industrial problems, and that some concentrate on the prediction of average behaviour, which may be useful for performance prediction but is unsound as an element of a safety argument (unless supported by analysis of variance, for example).

7 Verification and Validation

7.1 General impact

Possible approaches to design verification have already been mentioned in a previous section (5). The more general process of system verification and validation is, however, substantially effected by the presence of concurrency in a design. Those activities which concentrate essentially on static attributes of the system (review, static analysis, and proof, for example) may need to be augmented to handle specific technical difficulties, but are generally unaltered as a process. A much larger issue is the impact of concurrency, and in particular the possibility of nondeterministic behaviour, on dynamic testing.

7.2 Testing

Even if the external behaviour of a system has been designed to be deterministic, so that the results of any two runs on the same input data are identical, the internal sequences of behaviour may vary between runs. This has two important consequences:

- repeated tests cannot be guaranteed to exercise identical execution paths, and consequently:

- if a program is modified to remove an error, subsequent successful executions do not necessarily guarantee that the error has been removed - it may simply mean that the path which exhibited the error has not been exercised since the modification.

A number of approaches can be taken to ameliorate the problems introduced by this issue. One possibility is to make behaviour more deterministic by increasing the detail in which a system can be observed and controlled. We might, for example, attempt to reduce the effect of internal timing variations between processors on our tests by including logic analyser logs of the signals sent between them as part of the observed output of a test, and controlling their clock signals by precision oscillators in order to ensure that the relationship between their speeds was known. The disadvantages of such an approach are obvious -- it increases the complexity (and thus cost, and risk of error) of the testing process dramatically, and also introduces differences between the test system and the final application.

A potentially more promising approach is to reduce the importance of the role which testing plays in the safety case for a system, perhaps by supplementing test results with analytical work aimed specifically at bounding the likelihood of anomalous nondeterminstic behaviour or of the other failure modes discussed in Section 2. Caution must still be exercised in interpretation of those tests which are carried out, however. One approach to the validation of moderate safety requirements (eg for failure probabilities of the order of 10^{-3}) is to use a statistical test programme to bound the probability of undetected errors by showing that a large number of test cases have been executed correctly. A necessary precondition of this approach, however, is that the tests are representative of the operating scenarios. This can be difficult to establish when we must consider not only system inputs and outputs, but also environmental factors which are important in a concurrent system: communications delays and error rates, scheduling decisions, and clock drift, etc, must all be considered as inputs shown to range over typical values.

8 Conclusions

In the course of the work whose results are summarised here, and in our experience of other safety-related development and assessment projects, we have made a number of observations which we consider worthy of note:

- Where concurrency is an inherent requirement it should be clearly acknowledged. Obscuring the concurrency in an artificially sequential architecture can lead to more problems than it solves. A concurrent design may be simpler to understand and implement than a sequential architecture for some systems.

- It is vital to understand what the requirements are, and what evidence will be required to demonstrate meeting them. Making design decisions during the requirements phase can exclude novel, but potentially clearer architectures. On the other hand, failing to understand the level of evidence required can result in an architecture which cannot be certified.

- Concurrency should be used in a way which clarifies the architecture of the system. Each process must have a natural boundary.

- As with any novel technology, it is important to ensure that staff have the necessary training and tools. Use tools and methods which are designed to deal with concurrency and which can deal with industrial-scale problems.

- A concurrent design won't introduce new hazards, but may introduce new failure modes. These failure modes are difficult to analyse using general safety analysis techniques, and techniques specifically designed to handle concurrency should be used.

- The concurrency paradigm used should be consistent throughout the development. Switching between event-based and state-based notations can lead to traceability problems. Any inconsistencies in notations must be clearly understood and documented.

- Remember that in a concurrent system, requirements may be met by a combination of processes. It may not be possible to allocate requirements to a single process. This has implications both for design and for verification and validation.

- Testing concurrent systems is extremely difficult. This means that the use of rigorous analysis techniques will be required during verification and validation.

- Understand what can be demonstrated with current analysis techniques. A safety-related system will usually need to be predictable, which implies that the design should be amenable to rigorous analysis. A design which cannot be analysed is too complex.

In summary, we believe that it is possible to build a concurrent system which is safe, provided that there is a recognition of the fact that concurrent systems can behave in a fundamentally different way to sequential systems, and that this behaviour can only be understood by using specialist techniques.

9 Acknowledgements

The authors would like to thank Bob Jennings, Joe Collins and the HSE TWG for supporting the work described here; Efi Raili, Ian Spalding, Richard Tavendale and Keith Williams at Praxis Critical Systems who took part in the development of these ideas; and particularly Anthony Hall for his work and for many helpful comments on this presentation.

10 References

1. *Cause of AT&T Network Failure,* Telephony, p11, 22nd January 1990 (quoted in comp.risks Volume 9 Issue 62).

2. *Another Look at Real-time Programming*, Special edition of the Proceedings of the IEEE, 79(9), September 1991.

3. R Milner, *Communication and Concurrency* Prentice Hall, 1995.

4. C A R Hoare, *Communicating Sequential Processes* Prentice Hall, 1985.

5. Z Manna and A Pnueli, *Temporal Logic for Reactive Systems,* Springer Verlag, 1991.

6. D Harel and A Naamad, *The Statemate Semantics of Statecharts*, ACM Trans

Software Eng. Method. 5(4), 1996.

7. J L Peterson, *Petri Net Theory and the Modelling of Systems*, Prentice-Hall, NJ, 1981

8. S Owre, J Rushby, and N Shankar, *Integration in PVS: Tables, Types, and Model Checking*, to be presented at the Conference on Tools and Algorithms for the Construction and Analysis of Systems (TACAS '97), Enschede, The Netherlands, April 1997

9. K L McMillan, *Symbolic Model Checking: An Approach to the State Explosion Problem*. PhD thesis, Carnegie Mellon University, 1992.

10. A W Roscoe, P H B Gardiner, M H Goldsmith, J R Hulance, D M Jackson and J B Scattergood, *Hierarchical Compression for Model-Checking CSP or How to Check 10**20 Dining Philosophers for Deadlock*, Proceedings of *TACAS '95*, Springer-Verlag, 1995.

11. I-Logix Inc, www.ilogix.com

12. J M R Martin, *The Design and Contruction of Deadlock-Free Concurrent Systems*, DPhil thesis, University of Buckingham, 1996.

13. *Information Technology -- Programming Languages -- Ada*, ISO/IEC standard 68652:1995.

14. *IEEE Standard 1003.1b POSIX OSE Realtime Extensions* and *1003.1c POSIX OSE Threads*, Institute of Electrical and Electronics Engineers, Inc, 1993 / 1995.

15. N H Gehani, *Message Passing: Synchronous vs Asynchronous* Software – Practice & Experience, 20(6), 1990

16. K Tourlas, *An Assessment of the IEC 1131-3 Standard on Languages for Programmable Controllers*, Proceedings of SAFECOMP '97, Springer-Verlag, 1997.

17. G Egger, A Fett and P Pepper, *Formal Specification of a Safe PLC Language and its Compiler,* Proceedings of SAFECOMP '94, ISA, 1994.

18. PH Welch, *Emulating Digital Logic Using Transputer Networks,* Parallel Architectures and Languages Europe, LNCS 258, Springer-Verlag 1987.

19. W Reisig, *Petri Nets*, EATCS Monographs on Theoretical Computer Science, Vol. 4, pages 1-161. Springer-Verlag, 1985.

20. S Hauck, *Asynchronous Design Methodologies: An Overview,* Proceedings of the IEEE, Vol 83, No 1, pp 69-93, January, 1995.

21. A W Roscoe, *The Theory and Practice of Concurrency,* Prentice-Hall, 1998.

Managing and Supporting the Use of COTS

Steven K. Dawkins,
British Aerospace Dependable Computing Systems Centre (DCSC),
Department of Computer Science,
University of York, YORK, UK

Steve Riddle,
British Aerospace Dependable Computing Systems
Centre (DCSC), Centre for Software Reliability,
University of Newcastle upon Tyne, NEWCASTLE, UK

Abstract

The use of Commercial Off The Shelf (COTS) systems is becoming a practical reality for many systems development teams. The most compelling argument for this is the economic one: COTS systems are cheaper than bespoke ones because they enjoy economies of scale that are rare for development projects conducted "in house". Other advantages are the level of support provided by the COTS supplier and the potential to share in the COTS supplier's research and development. Whilst these advantages are well understood, the disadvantages of COTS use in the development of high integrity, dependable systems are less clear. The potential for "discontinuities" in design intent, traceability and maintenance are of particular concern as they may lead to systematic errors in the final product, increasing the potential for hazardous situations or accidents to occur.

This paper considers these problems as an information management issue. Without structures to record, reference, and reconcile the information regarding a given COTS component, it is difficult to perceive where problems or weaknesses lie - let alone express concerns about them to the COTS supplier. The challenge is to apply the information available about the COTS component to argue that system integrity has not been reduced.

We also show that certification of a COTS component is not possible without an understanding of the application context: arguing safe use of a COTS component is only one part of system level certification.

1. Introduction

Why is there a move towards using COTS components? A good example comes from the military industry. The market for military specification ("mil-spec") Integrated Circuits (IC's) is reducing as a proportion of the total worldwide IC market, as shown in Table 1. The military market is not expected to disappear, but is becoming less significant to the major IC suppliers.

The increasing commercial market allows a high rate of technological progress and research that a smaller market (such as Military Aerospace) could not sustain. To embrace the enabling technologies required to meet customer requirements in future will require the use of COTS components. Those developers that limit themselves to the smaller military specification market run the risk of becoming "technology followers".

	Total WW	Military/Aero.
1985	$20B	$1.9B (9.5%)
1995	$300B	$1.2B (0.4%)
	(and increasing)	(and reducing)

Table 1: Market perspective on IC's (Source: Texas Instruments Future Directions [Kroeger 1997])

The need to meet increasing customer requirements and adopt new technology drives the use of COTS components. As a result, the use of COTS components is becoming a recognised part of the design approach. The design team must have a good understanding of the possible "discontinuities" between the design and the COTS component. For example, a military system may require that a rugged "mil spec" component is used in a particular case because of the heat and vibration it must withstand. These requirements make the use of a more advanced or innovative COTS component in place of the "mil spec" component inappropriate unless the system design is revised to provide extra cooling and protection.

The primary intent of this paper is to describe a method for managing discontinuities and the risks they represent, allowing an argument to be made that the use of a COTS component does not introduce additional unacceptable risks into the system. A secondary intent is to show that it is not possible to certify a COTS component without an understanding of the particular context or application for which the COTS component is to be used.

In the following section we explain the concept of discontinuities, the practical concerns that they introduce for COTS use, and information structuring techniques to manage these discontinuities. Section 3 characterises the relationships between target system and COTS component in terms of the functionality that each requires and provides. Sections 4, 5 and 6 introduce the techniques and notations used to structure information about the target system and to record evidence (and hence build an argument) about safe use of COTS components, using a running example of a computer-controlled syringe. Section 7 relates arguments about safe use of COTS components to a system-level safety analysis. In Section 8 we summarise and draw some conclusions about the maturity of the approach.

2. Managing Discontinuities

2.1 Discontinuities

The principal danger posed by the use of COTS components in dependable systems lies in the *discontinuity* it creates in the understanding of the system as a whole. Design information available with commercial components is typically limited.

They are often provided as 'black boxes' - where, for example, visibility of software source code is prohibited. Also, there is usually little revelation of the rationale underlying the product design - the assumptions, justifications and underlying principles. This deficiency of information increases the possibility of introducing design errors when integrating the component into the target system. Other practical concerns of COTS use are:

- Unused functionality [Kohl 1998] which may be of low integrity.

- Lack of evidence, if the COTS developer holds the Intellectual Property Rights (IPR).

Each of these (negative) points are only one side of the relationship. The positive side of COTS is that by addressing the needs of a wider market, the cost per unit decreases and the research of new technology and techniques can be sustained. It is therefore a practical reality that these discontinuities will exist because the benefits stem directly from them. If these discontinuities did not exist, many of the benefits of COTS would also disappear.

Many bespoke designs also contain discontinuities, which are recognised as part of the design and tracked in a controlled manner to ensure they do not represent a challenge to design integrity. For example, cost savings can be achieved if a computer system can be designed for use in several different models of aircraft.

A balance must be achieved between using flexible components and preventing design errors in specific applications of such components. There is a need to explicitly reconcile these two aspects of modular design to reach an acceptable balance.

There are four main issues to allow reconciliation to take place:

1. Information about the COTS component is necessary for us to be able to trace between the component and its intended use in a target system. We can identify the following information types:

   Services: The component will provide services to the system. What are the implications (good and bad) of these services? Could they contribute to top-level hazards? What failure modes do they have? Do they represent a single point of failure? In addition the component will require services from the target system in which it is placed. This "dual relationship" is described in detail in Section 3.

   Operational Data: One of the benefits of a COTS component is the amount of operational data generated from use in several different systems across many markets.

The remaining three points help to support the management and use of this information.

2. The operational data will only be useful to us as information if it can be managed - we need a structure to record and interpret it.

3. Depending on the relationship with the supplier, there may be limited information available - but operational data may still be captured during

testing and demonstration projects. Capturing and structuring information in this way will provide a stronger foundation for arguing the safe use of COTS components and improve the relationship with the supplier.

4. To interpret structured information we need to be able to analyse it, to see how it relates to the product design and safety argument. Analysis should bring to light discontinuities between the design and the COTS component.

2.2 Information Structures

Information structures are required to address the issues above and record design intent and assumptions behind the target system and the COTS component. We use two structuring techniques:

1. Target System: Traceability structures [Pearson 1998] are used to provide the information structure for the target system. The structures are flexible enough to capture any environment that may require COTS technology [Riddle 1998]. Three types of structure are described in this paper: Artifact Synthesis, Plan Synthesis and Argumentation structures.

2. COTS component: Goal Structuring Notation (GSN) is used to record the different characteristics and associated evidence related to the COTS component. GSN is particularly suited to this role as it is designed to show how specific claims can be supported. [Dawkins 1997]

We use two different techniques because the scope of information available regarding the two artifacts is different. The target system must be modeled in its entirety and refined towards an implementation (i.e. "top down"), whereas information about the COTS component will focus on particular claims or details of implementation which must be reconciled to the target system (i.e. "bottom up"). The purpose of this reconciliation is to assess how well the COTS component fits into a wider context and highlight any discontinuities. A process for performing this is shown in Table 2, together with the techniques used at each stage.

Stage	Technique
1. Define Requirements	Artifact Synthesis Structure
2. Plan to meet requirement	Plan Synthesis Structure
3. Gather Evidence	Goal Structure Notation
4. Argue safe use	Argumentation Structure

Table 2: Process for reconciliation

The particular techniques applied in practice will depend on several factors, for example, preferred work practices, experience of particular techniques etc. The exact techniques used are less important than the fact that some process is in place to record and reconcile information concerning the relationship between systems and the components used. This paper illustrates how this process is executed through the use of a worked example.

3. System Component Relationship

For dependable systems, it is essential that the relationship between the target system and the COTS component be correctly and appropriately matched. This relationship is a complex one, made up of different elements as shown in Figure 1 below [Dawkins 1997].

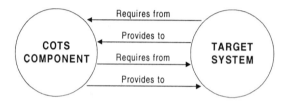

Figure 1: Model of the System-Component Relationship

Figure 1 shows that the relationship consists of two main components, emphasising that there is a dual relationship between the target system and the COTS component.

3.1 Requires from: (or "what does A want from B?")

For systems S_1, S_2 we use $RF(S_1, S_2)$ to denote the set of services (functionality) required from S_2 by S_1.

- The target system requires from the COTS component some useful service or functionality, this is represented by $RF(T,C)$.

- In order to provide this functionality, the COTS system requires from the target system some operational environment. This is represented by $RF(C,T)$.

3.2 Provides to: (or "what does B give to A?")

For systems S_1, S_2 we use $PT(S_1, S_2)$ to denote the set of services (functionality) provided to S_2 by S_1.

- The target system provides an environment containing services required by the COTS component, this is represented by $PT(T,C)$

- The COTS component provides the functionality or service required by the target system, this is represented by $PT(C,T)$

These two relationships need to reflect one another if the COTS component and target systems are to work without discontinuities that may represent risks. This requires two conditions:

1. Firstly, the functionality *required from* the COTS component by the target system is a subset of that *provided to* the target system by the COTS component:

$$RF(T,C) \subseteq PT(C,T) \qquad \text{(Equation A)}$$

This is a subset because it is possible that the COTS component provides extra functionality not used by the target system. (This is an example of a discontinuity. The risk associated with any faults in unused functions would need to be assessed, as discussed in Section 2)

2. Secondly, the environment *required from* the target system by the COTS component is a subset of those *provided to* it by the target system

$$RF(C,T) \subseteq PT(T,C) \qquad \text{(Equation B)}$$

The "requires from" and "provides to" relationships both have a top down and a bottom up component as shown in Table 3.

	Top Down	Bottom Up
Requires From	RF (T,C)	RF (C,T)
Provides To	PT (T,C)	PT (C,T)

Table 3: Top down and Bottom Up portions of the system-component relationship

The equations A and B above show how the top down part of the "requires from" relation must reconcile to the bottom up part of the "provides to" relation.

In the next three sections we describe the use of information structuring techniques to manage the system-component relationship.

4. Requirements Definition and Planning

In this section we describe the use of traceability structures to structure the information about the proposed target system and plans for implementation. To illustrate the process, we use a small example based on a computer-controlled syringe designed to control the injection of a set quantity of medicine into a patient over a set duration.

The traceability structures are adapted from Klein's Design Rationale Capture System (DRCS) [Klein 1993]. These are a set of self-contained information structures, which are used to record and trace the rationale for design decisions. Information entities such as Modules and Attributes are linked together by pre-defined relationship types. Figure 2 shows a simple traceability structure (called an *artifact synthesis structure*) which gives an architectural decomposition of the computer-controlled syringe. This type of structure emphasises a top-down approach; as such it is a useful tool for tracing design rationale and decisions. It also illustrates the discontinuities that are favourable or intended. For example, different capacities and flow rates are shown for different types of syringe.

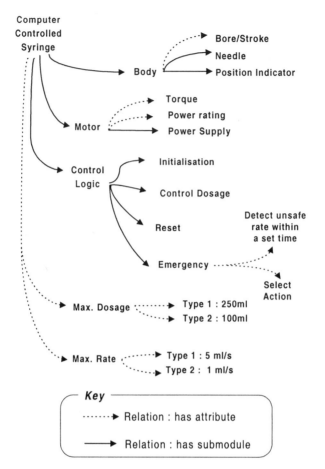

Figure 2: Artifact Synthesis Structure for the Computer Controlled Syringe
Example

4.1 Requirements Definition

The structure allows us to derive the properties required by the syringe from the "Control Logic" submodule. These properties are the top down part of the "Requires from" and "Provides to" relations of the system-component relationship. For example, the relations for the "emergency" function are shown in Box 1.

Equality (1) in Box 1 shows that the target system (the syringe) requires a "timely safe action" from the control logic in response to an emergency condition. Equality (2) describes the inputs that *may* be provided to the controller by the syringe to perform the emergency function.

These two equalities can be derived from the Artifact synthesis structure in Figure 2, and are shown in bold to indicate that they relate to "top down" design information.

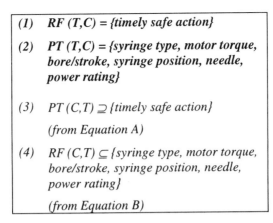

> (1) $RF(T,C) = \{timely\ safe\ action\}$
>
> (2) $PT(T,C) = \{syringe\ type,\ motor\ torque,\ bore/stroke,\ syringe\ position,\ needle,\ power\ rating\}$
>
> (3) $PT(C,T) \supseteq \{timely\ safe\ action\}$
>
> (from Equation A)
>
> (4) $RF(C,T) \subseteq \{syringe\ type,\ motor\ torque,\ bore/stroke,\ syringe\ position,\ needle,\ power\ rating\}$
>
> (from Equation B)

Box 1: System component relationship for syringe (*T*) and control logic (*C*) after top down analysis for the "emergency " function.

The third line shows the *minimum* specification that the control logic must meet to remain consistent and maintain a safe relationship between the control logic and the syringe as a whole. Whether or not the control logic, when implemented, fulfils this minimum requirement will be determined by complimentary "bottom up" analysis later in the process. Line 4 shows all possible inputs that the target system can provide to the control logic. Again, complementary bottom up analysis will identify if these inputs are sufficient and/or necessary to allow the control logic to perform its function of timely, safe action.

4.2 Planning

Having determined the requirements for the syringe control logic, the next concern is how to implement or acquire this component. The plan synthesis structure shown in Figure 3 records the rationale behind the decision to use COTS technology. The COTS solution is chosen on the basis of two main criteria, (i) adequate performance and (ii) cost. Of the two other options, a bespoke development is seen as too expensive and a reduction in functionality would prevent the syringe meeting performance objectives. Notice that COTS use is conditional on the ability to ensure the "Provides to" and "Requires from" relations are consistent.

Implications of COTS use:

The relationships RF and PT in Box 1 show that the emergency function requires several inputs to produce a timely, safe action. The quality of those inputs and the way they are communicated could affect the integrity of the results from the emergency function. For example,

- Communication: Is the motor and syringe data communicated or stored in a way that is accessible to the COTS emergency function?

- Timing: Can the COTS emergency function operate quickly enough for the worst case?

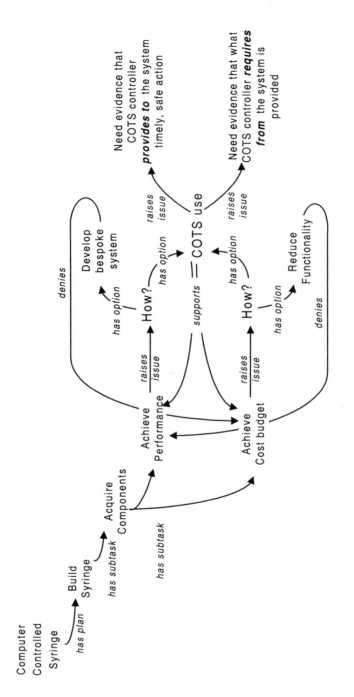

Figure 3: A plan synthesis structure recording rationale for the use of a COTS component

- Context: Does the COTS emergency function appreciate that some injections are critical only when stopped? (For example, Anaesthetic)

These issues cannot be resolved with the traceability structures alone and prompt the need for detailed information about the COTS component itself. (The traceability structure is better at exploring the design space rather than constraining it). It must be possible to check not only if the COTS component meets its minimum specification, but also to identify any constraints that its use will impose on the target system. For example, the COTS component may need additional inputs from the target system to fulfil the minimum specification. This requires a structured set of information associated with the COTS component itself and its capabilities.

5. A Foundation for Evidence

This evidence will provide the bottom up component of the "Requires from" and "Provides to" relationships. This achieves two things:

- Identifies any inconsistencies in the system-component relationship.
- Increases the utility of evidence that is available by placing it in the system context.

The attributes of Goal Structuring Notation (GSN) [Wilson 1995] that make it an appropriate technique for recording evidence about COTS components are:

- **Claim based**: A series of claims are made about each component. These claims are augmented by:
- **Contextual information**: Resolves any ambiguities associated with each claim (E.g. what is meant by "Fault", "Safe" etc.)
- **Underlying Assumptions**: That may have an influence on the design principles and intent.
- **Solutions**: Appeals to operational data, COTS documentation, commercial standards etc.

The GSN has been developed to support the description of safety arguments. Using GSN it is possible to present claims concerning a component and to show clearly on what basis those claims are made (by explicitly including notions such as context and assumption).

Figure 4 shows an example claim based on the syringe controller. It shows a claim associated with the COTS control logic expressed using GSN. Goals (Claims) in the goal structure are shown as rectangles. The round-ended rectangles represent additional context information. The ellipses denote assumptions. Circles represent solutions (references to evidence).

The fragment of goal structure shown in Figure 4 expresses the claim, "Emergency stop provides timely and safe action for 10^4 operational hours". It is shown that the validity of this claim relies on assumptions regarding the power supply used and the independence of the data inputs. The definitions of 'safe', 'timely' and 'fault' underlying the claim are also given. The structure communicates that operational data is available to back up the claim, but makes clear that this data is based upon having exercised the component for 5000 hours of laboratory use. In this way, the goal structure has added depth and value to the initial claim.

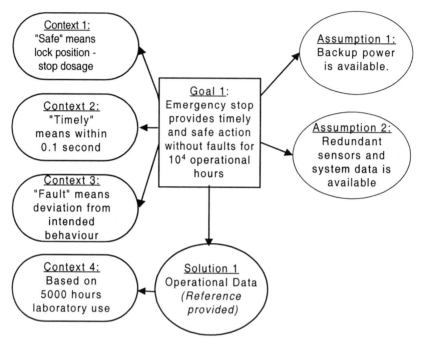

Figure 4: Part of the evidence structure for the emergency stop routine

It is now possible to use the information given in Figure 4 to refine the information about the system-component relationship by extending it to include backup power and redundant sensors required by the COTS controller, as shown in Box 2.

> (1') $RF(T,C) = \{timely\ safe\ action\ \}$
>
> (2') $PT(T,C) = \{syringe\ type,\ motor\ torque,$
> $bore/stroke,\ syringe\ position,\ needle,$
> $power\ rating,\ \textbf{back\ up\ power,\ redundant}$
> $\textbf{sensors}\ \}$
>
> (3') $PT(C,T) = \{timely\ safe\ action\}$ **Equation B**
>
> (4') $RF(C,T) = \{syringe\ type,\ motor\ torque,$
> $bore/stroke,\ syringe\ position,\ needle,$
> $power\ rating,\ \textbf{back\ up\ power,\ redundant}$
> $\textbf{sensors}\ \}$

Box 2: System component relationship after top down and bottom up analysis

In Box 2, the bold part of equality 4' shows the new information added as a result of bottom up analysis using the evidence in the GSN fragment about the COTS component. To maintain the symmetry of the relationship, equality 2' must also include the new elements - as required by equation B.

These two new requirements are extra facilities that the syringe design must provide to this COTS controller if the reliability claim in Figure 4 is to be part of the safety argument for the syringe.

To summarise, the syringe design requires the emergency function within the COTS control logic to discharge a reliability claim. To uphold this claim, the COTS developers made several assumptions that have implications for the syringe design proposed by the traceability structure shown earlier.

The "Requires from" and "Provides to" relations are merely a model of the system component relationship. The simple act of equating the different relations in this model does not presume that safety requirements have been discharged. However, some key issues have been identified which have implications for the syringe designers:

5.1 Implications for the Syringe Design:

1. Back up power should be available
    Inclusion of a rechargeable battery in the syringe product structure?

2. Redundant Sensors must be employed
    Does the syringe design provide for this?

3. Potential Safety Hazards
    Fail safe is always provided by stopping the syringe (Possible hazard in some situations).
    Assumes the syringe cannot do anything hazardous within 0.1 second. (This requires further analysis of Motor and Syringe Cylinder to verify).

4. Validity of Operational Data
    "Laboratory use" may be a different context - is 5000 hours illustrative for this type of component?

Having described the main concerns associated with the use of the COTS controller it is possible to prioritise these concerns. The potential safety hazards would be dealt with first, but the other points could also reveal potentially hazardous discontinuities.

5.2 Lack of Evidence

We have described a systematic approach to assessing the evidence that *does* exist for a given COTS component and using that evidence to identify derived safety requirements for the system design. In many situations, very little evidence may exist about the COTS component, apparently reducing the utility of the approach. We would argue that the lack of evidence increases the need for a structured and systematic investigation driven by system design and safety issues. In particular:

- The approach allows us to <u>focus</u> on the evidence we require about the COTS component by making explicit what the system requires from and provides to it. This allows key safety claims to be derived and used to structure and motivate further investigation of the COTS component.

- This approach highlights the need for <u>consistency</u>. Each piece of new evidence can be interpreted from a system perspective and the impact assessed at a system level. Increasing the utility of evidence that is available.

- The approach is <u>intuitive</u>, reflecting and formalising design principles. The structures can form the basis of a "what if?" style of analysis to highlight needs for further evidence. The completeness of the structures (in particular the evidence structures) directly reflect the completeness of a COTS investigation.

- Finally, if no evidence of any sort is available for a COTS component it would be unwise to use it. The approach highlights key omissions in evidence and relates those omissions to the system design. The designers must then make a decision based on the context. (In the syringe example, the lack of timing information for the emergency function may have caused the syringe designers concern.)

The next section considers the last point in more detail by describing how an argument may be formulated to show safe use of a COTS component.

6. Arguing Safe Use of COTS

Having defined the system-component relationship using the "Requires From" and "Provides to" model, we can now use it as the basis of an argument for safe use of the COTS component. Figure 5 shows the argumentation structure for the computer-controlled syringe. The left-hand side of the diagram is copied from the earlier plan synthesis structure in Figure 3. The argumentation structure shows how the two issues for safe COTS use are elaborated in the context of the information provided about the COTS control logic unit. The structure terminates with several questions that must be resolved before the argument for safe use of the COTS control logic becomes complete. Two issues are evident from this analysis.

6.1 Can all the queries shown be resolved?

If not, then the query becomes a discontinuity adding to the residual risk associated with COTS use. The designers may either accept that risk or reject it by either appealing for more evidence, looking for a different component, or identifying derived safety requirements on the target system to remove the discontinuity altogether.

6.2 Are there any important queries omitted?

If queries are omitted, then discontinuities (and hence, risks) may be overlooked. The systematic approach of deriving requirements on a COTS component from the design of the target system is intended to ensure the completeness of the argumentation structure. However, if the structures used to record COTS evidence are incomplete, the argumentation structure may also contain omissions.

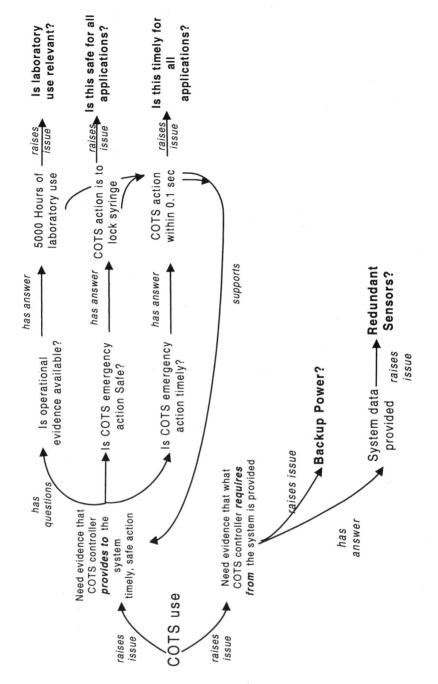

Figure 5: Argumentation Structure for the safe use of the COTS component-
potential risks are shown in **Bold** Type

This last point relates to the maturity of this approach and the ability to construct useful evidence structures for COTS components based around key safety claims. A useful structure for COTS evidence will prompt questions and highlight concerns about the key areas that affect the safe use of a component.

To help develop these structures, it would be helpful to:

- Stipulate a set of GSN patterns for the purpose of assessing COTS components [Kelly 97].

- Provide a set of guidelines documenting the different types of evidence required for different types of COTS component. For example, can we document the key risks associated with syringe controllers?

The reconciliation between target system and COTS component should provide a "profile" of the potential risks of using a particular component within a given system. If there were a lack of information on a specific component then this would lead to a high-risk profile. Valid responses to this may be to source a different unit, perform tests on the component, or contact the supplier.

7. Towards Certification of COTS-based Systems

Note that the argumentation structure shown in Figure 5 shows the risks associated with *safe use* of a specific component. It provides no justification that the target system itself can be shown to be safe, only that use of a COTS component does not add unacceptable additional risks if the issues raised can be resolved.

It is not uncommon to hear claims such as "this real time operating system has been cleared to Safety Integrity Level (SIL) 4"[1]. It is difficult to see on what basis such claims about certification can be made without reference to a specific application context, and a set of hazards. Figure 6 illustrates the contribution of COTS "safe use" arguments to wider certification of an entire system.

This diagram shows that arguing safe use of COTS is only a small part of certifying the target system that uses that COTS component. Through (possibly iterated) systematic assessment of the "requires from" and "provides to" relations as described, it is possible to show that a portion of the system safety argument is sound. However, the certification of the target system is a broader problem.

8. Conclusions

The use of COTS is inevitable because of economic and technical advantages, however this does present a challenge to the traditional "top-down" approach to developing systems and the associated safety arguments.

This paper has described the nature of the relationship between the COTS component and the target system. A model of this relationship has been used to show one approach to managing and assessing the risk of discontinuities that emerge as a result of COTS solutions.

---

[1] "Safety Integrity Levels" are described in some UK defence standards, for example, see [Def-Stan 1997].

The main points to consider are:

Dual Relationship: The relationship between COTS component and target system involves both top down refinement and bottom-up reconciliation to maintain the symmetry (and integrity) of the relationship.

Managing Discontinuities: It is inevitable discontinuities will exist, we must learn to track and manage them to allow us to assess the risks they represent.

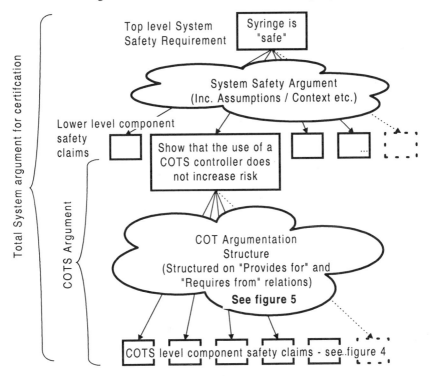

Figure 6: Contribution of COTS "Safe Use" argument to overall system certification

Structure Information: Design rationale is recorded by the traceability structure that provides the underlying framework of the high level argument for a safety case. Structured (and complete) information and context about the claims made for a COTS component is required to support these arguments.

Reconciliation: The two kinds of *structures* are systematically checked for unintended *discontinuities*. The approach taken in this paper was to reason about the *dual relationship* between the target system and the COTS component that could highlight these discontinuities.

As COTS use becomes more widespread, experience of supporting techniques must be developed and refined. This is the only way to improve maturity and prevent omissions in the analysis. Possible approaches may be to specify generic GSN patterns for structuring evidence about COTS claims, or provide checklists for particular types of COTS components.

Whilst the approach outlined does not guarantee to identify all discontinuities that have potential to emerge through COTS use, it does provide a systematic framework for reasoning about them. However, COTS components cannot be certified in isolation, without a specific application context. The framework supports system level safety certification by providing an argument that no unacceptable additional risks are added by use of the COTS component.

References

[Dawkins 1997] Dawkins S, Kelly T, "Supporting the use of COTS in Safety Critical Systems", in *COTS and Safety Critical Systems*, Colloquium Digest No 91/013, Institute of Electrical Engineers (IEE), 28th January 1997

[Def-Stan 1997] Defence Standard 00-55, Requirements for Safety Related Software in Defence Equipment, UK Ministry of Defence, August 1997

[Kelly 1997] Kelly, T.P. "Safety Case Construction and Reuse Using Patterns", in Proceedings of 16th International Conference on Computer Safety, Reliability and Security, York, 7-10th September 1997.

[Klein 1993] Klein, M., "Capturing Design Rationale in Concurrent Engineering Teams". IEEE Computer January 1993.

[Kohl 1998] Kohl, R.J., "When Requirements Are Not Isomorphic To COTS Functionality: 'Dormant Code' Within A COTS Product", in Proceedings INCOSE 98, Vancouver, Canada. July 1998

[Kroeger 1997] Kroeger B., "Texas Instruments Future Directions", Boeing Commercial Aeroplane Group Electronic Component Management Program Users Forum II, March 5, 1997,
http://www.ti.com/sc/docs/military/cotspem/cots_pem.htm

[Pearson 1998] Pearson, S., Riddle, S., Saeed, A., "Traceability for the Development and Assessment of Safe Avionic Systems", in Proceedings INCOSE 98, Vancouver, Canada. July 1998

[Riddle 1998] Riddle S., Saeed A., "Tracing Support for Variants and Evolutionary Development", British Aerospace Dependable Computing Systems Centre (DCSC), Report TR/98/1, University of Newcastle, 1998

[Wilson 1995] Wilson S. P., Kelly T. P., McDermid J. A., "Safety Case Development: Current Practice, Future Prospects" *in Proceedings of 12th Annual CSR Workshop, Bruges, Belgium 1995 (Springer-Verlag)*

Acknowledgements

The authors would like to thank the following for their help and support: British Aerospace (BAe) for the funding of the Dependable Computing System Centre (DCSC); Mr Mike Burke, BAe DCSC Research Manager; Dr Tim Kelly from the University of York, and Dr Amer Saeed from the University of Newcastle upon Tyne.

AUTHOR INDEX